KNOWING BEYOND KNOWLEDGE

This book builds on contemporary discussion of 'mysticism' and religious experience by examining the process and content of 'religious knowing' in classical and modern Advaita. Drawing from the work of William Alston and Alvin Plantinga, Thomas Forsthoefel examines key streams of Advaita with special reference to the conditions, contexts, and scope of epistemic merit in religious experience. Forsthoefel uniquely employs specific analytical categories of contemporary Western epistemologies as heuristics to examine the cognitive dimension of religious experience in Indian Vedānta.

Showing the developing nuances in the analysis of religious experience in the thought of Shankara and his immediate disciples (Sureśvara and Padmapāda) as well as in the teaching of Ramana Maharshi, an understudied but important South Indian saint of the twentieth century, this book offers a substantial contribution to studies of Indian philosophy as well as to contemporary philosophy of religion. Using the tools of exegesis and comparative philosophy, Forsthoefel argues for a careful justification of claims following religious experience, even if such claims involve, as they do in the Advaita, a paradoxical 'knowing beyond knowledge'.

Ashgate World Philosophies Series

The Ashgate World Philosophies Series responds to the remarkable growth of interest among English-language readers in recent years in philosophical traditions outside those of 'the West'. The traditions of Indian, Chinese, and Japanese thought, as well as those of the Islamic world, Latin America, Africa, and of Aboriginal Australian, Pacific and American Indian peoples, are all attracting lively attention from professional philosophers and students alike, and this new Ashgate series provides introductions to these traditions as well as in-depth research into central issues and themes within those traditions. The series is particularly designed for readers whose interests are not adequately addressed by general surveys of 'World Philosophy', and it includes accessible, yet research-led, texts for wider readership and upper-level student use, as well as research monographs. The series embraces a wide variety of titles ranging from introductions on particular world philosophies and informed surveys of the philosophical contributions of geographical regions, to in-depth discussion of a theme, topic, problem or movement and critical appraisals of individual thinkers or schools of thinkers.

Series Editors:
David E. Cooper, University of Durham, UK
Robert C. Solomon, University of Texas, Austin, USA
Kathleen M. Higgins, University of Texas, Austin, USA
Purushottama Bilimoria, Deakin University, Australia

Other titles in the series:
An Introduction to Yoga Philosophy
An annotated translation of the Yoga Sutras
Ashok Kumar Malhotra

Knowing Beyond Knowledge

Epistemologies of religious experience in classical and modern Advaita

THOMAS A. FORSTHOEFEL
Mercyhurst College, USA

Routledge
Taylor & Francis Group
LONDON AND NEW YORK

First published 2002 by Ashgate Publishing

Reissued 2018 by Routledge
2 Park Square, Milton Park, Abingdon, Oxon OX14 4RN
711 Third Avenue, New York, NY 10017, USA

Routledge is an imprint of the Taylor & Francis Group, an informa business

Typeset by Bournemouth Colour Press, Parkstone.

A Library of Congress record exists under LC control number: 2002024890

ISBN 13: 978-1-138-72150-0 (hbk)
ISBN 13: 978-1-138-72149-4 (pbk)
ISBN 13: 978-1-315-19440-0 (ebk)

For Therese, Andrew, Caitlin and Luke

Contents

Acknowledgements ix
Abbreviations xi

1 A brief history of experience 1
Prolegomena 1
Religious experience: historical context 10
Religious experience: contemporary philosophical context 15
Epistemology of religious experience 23
Epistemologies of religious experience in classical and modern Vedānta 32

2 The epistemology of religious experience in Śaṅkara 35
Introduction 35
Internalism and externalism in Śaṅkara 39
Knowledge and the means of knowledge in Advaita 42
The culture of liberation in Śaṅkara 56

3 Later Advaita on religious experience 73
Sureśvara, Padmapāda, the *Vivekacūḍāmaṇi* 73
Sureśvara 76
Padmapāda 98
The *Vivekacūḍāmaṇi* 108

4 The sage of pure experience: the Advaita of Ramaṇa Maharṣi 123
Introduction 123
Ramaṇa Maharṣi: life and works 129
Ramaṇa's philosophy 133
Revalorizing the culture of liberation 138

5 The cognitive and social implications of the epistemology of religious experience 156
Cognitive implications 156
Social implications 161
How and what we know in Rāmānuja's soteriology 167
Conclusions 176

Bibliography 183
Index 196

Acknowledgements

There are so many persons to thank, beginning with my parents, Mark and Joan Forsthoefel, and my parents-in-law, Vincent and Mary Theisen, for their support in completing this project, which has undergone numerous incarnations since I formally began studying Indian religion and philosophy in graduate school. I especially want to thank my mentors at the University of Chicago during this project's earlier 'lifetimes', especially Paul Griffiths, Wendy Doniger and Francis Clooney, all of whom have helped and have inspired me in ways too numerous to name.

At Mercyhurst, I wish to express gratitude to Dr William Garvey, President of the College, for the course reduction which has allowed me to finish this project expeditiously and with a modicum of sanity. In this regard, I also thank my colleague and friend David J. Livingston PhD, who was the driving force behind the college's new course reduction programme. I also wish to express my heartfelt gratitude to Mary Hembrow Snyder PhD, for her unfailing generosity and support in this project and in so many others. Many thanks, also, to all my colleagues at Mercyhurst, especially Dorothy Stoner, OSB, Gerry Tobin, Rhonda Clark, Alice Edwards and Ralph Perrico. Let me also extend grateful thanks for every kind of support to dear friends here and elsewhere: in Erie, the Dunsmores, Grants, Snyders, Mimi O'Connor and Vlado Benden, Bruce and Sheila Baldwin, Brian Pardini and Patty Baldwin, Sandy Merrifield, Dinesh Khera, Michelle Tobin, Joan Livingston and Jamie Borowicz; in Chicago, the Murphys, Jaroscaks, Daskovskys, Prucnals, Taylors, Soules, Walters, Fureys, Ingrid Dorer-Fitzpatrick, Richard Dolezal, Gene Lockwood, Kathleen Weber, Robert King and Joan Lourie; in India, T. Sampatkumar, Meena and Venket Narayanan, the Bavinck family, David and Philomena Morris and especially Mahesuari; other dear friends from other places include Greg Corrigan, Gene Geinzer, Paul Mueller, Terry Charlton, Susan Ackerman, Todd and Ann McCormack, Patty and Bill Higgins, Jason DeParle, Margaret Egler, Deepak Sarma, Joseph Gower, Jim Fleming, Mary Ellen and Paul Keyes. I also wish to name several of my students here at Mercyhurst – Religious Studies majors – whose own wonder and love for India is not only a joy to behold but also a true inspiration: Billy Byrnes, Lisa Tredway, Jennifer Cheripka, Nate Wallace, Natalie Zofko, Jennifer Smolinski, Kelly Froelich and Chantell Haughwout.

I wish to make special mention of three great mentors and friends, Paul Cioffi SJ, Paulinas Forsthoefel SJ and Mudumby Narasimhachari PhD, each of whom has modelled in outstanding ways for me lives committed to faith and scholarship, to 'knowing' in all its rich and unfathomable dimensions.

Finally, I wish to thank my children – Andrew, Caitlin, and Luke – for their remarkable kindness and patience during this arduous effort. Their gentle smiles, genuine interest and words of encouragement have so often helped and have led me to marvel at their goodness. Above all, I wish to thank my wife Therese for the innumerable ways that she has helped me bring this project to fruition. Being hyper-focused, at least in the last stages of finishing a book, is certainly useful and perhaps necessary, but it also taxes everyone's physical and emotional reserves. I am grateful for the example of her own penetrating focus and profound commitment, replete, as it is, with great strength, honesty and love.

Abbreviations

AU	Aitareya Upaniṣad
BGB	*Bhagavad-Gītā Bhāṣya*
BSB	*Brahma Sūtra Bhāṣya*
BU	Bṛhadāraṇyaka Upaniṣad
BUB	*Bṛhadāraṇyaka Upaniṣad Bhāṣya*
BUBV	*Bṛhadāraṇyakopaniṣadbhāṣyavārtika*
CU	Chāndogya Upaniṣad
CUB	*Chāndogya Upaniṣad Bhāṣya*
KeU	Kena Upaniṣad
KU	Kaṭha Upaniṣad
IU	Īśa Upaniṣad
MU	Māṇḍūkya Upaniṣad
MuU	Muṇḍaka Upaniṣad
NS	*Naiṣkarmyasiddhi*
PU	Praśna Upaniṣad
ŚB	*Śrībhāṣya*
SK	*Sāṅkhya Kārikā*
SV	*Saṁbandhavārtika*
TU	Taittirīya Upaniṣad
TUB	*Taittirīya Upaniṣad Bhāṣya*
TUBV	*Taittirīyopaniṣadbhāsyavārtika*
TVM	*Tiruvāymoḻi*
Up.	*Upadeśasāhasrī*
UPB	Upaniṣadbhāṣyam
VC	*Vivekacūḍāmaṇi*
YS	Yoga Sūtra

CHAPTER 1

A brief history of experience

Prolegomena

This study is motivated by a central question that can be phrased in numerous ways with admittedly different nuances. The central question is: does religious experience, whatever *that* is, provide warrant for claims about God and the universe? In other words, do claims about God, deities, or an impersonal Absolute, following upon certain mental or physical events, contain valid cognitive content, or are they merely psychological projections, wish-fulfilling fancies or expressions of ethical standards or compelling emotion? In short, do these claims enjoy 'epistemic significance'? This question not only asks whether they enjoy a healthy (cognitive) self-esteem but intends to probe the extent, if any, of the stake these claims have on knowledge. If knowledge is a 'diploma' word (Hick, 1966: 206), conferred on judgements and propositions about certain states of affairs, can we know anything from religious experience? More specifically, can we know anything about God through religious experience? Indeed, can we know God at all? Although this study will consider in detail the obvious epistemological issues involved here, it also recognizes important related issues in linguistic theory, especially in the relationship between language and experience. For it seems difficult at best, and perhaps impossible, to extricate the one from the other. Language consists of symbols of our conceptual baggage (much of whose content is experience), but that baggage is preceded by language, thus raising the question whether or not 'reality' is constructed by language.[1]

Bracketing, for the moment, the relationship between language and experience, questions concerning the cognitive content of religious claims are slightly different to the purely philosophical inquiry, 'Just what is out there?' or, as someone once asked, 'Are there any medium-sized pieces of dry goods in the universe?' These ontological forays are, of course, usually followed by the related epistemological concern – if so, how do we know it? – although, in the Western context since Kant, the systematic study of what-is-out-there has been more often than not eschewed in favour of strict analyses of knowledge. The reasons for this are well known and need no discussion here. Suffice it to say that Kant raised significant challenges to traditional methods of philosophical theology; in his view, arguments for the existence of God were doomed to fail as illegitimate extensions beyond what we can

---

[1] Grace Jantzen (1995a) raises the question of the relationship between language and 'reality'; her deconstructive approach is demonstrated in an extended analysis of Christian mysticism (Jantzen, 1995b).

validly know within the limits of space and time and the categories of judgement. According to Kant, the philosopher of religion ought not to argue for or against religious beliefs, but instead map their structure and limits and offer an account of their origin in practical reason. However, while we cannot technically 'know' God according to this view, the idea of God remains a necessary postulate for the moral life. The 'essence' of religion, for Kant, is morality.[2] Contemporary philosophers of religion, such as C.B. Braithwaite and D.Z. Phillips, accept and adapt the Kantian (and Wittgensteinian) limits of religious language and consider narratives, myths, dogmas and doctrines as evocative of ethical standards (Braithwaite) or simple emotions (Phillips). They thus reject the cognitive content of religious expressions; this conclusion may validly follow from their premises but, of course, it dismisses outright the usual understanding of religious expressions held by so many adepts, thinkers, devotees and storytellers of numerous religious traditions.

But the rejection of metaphysics by contemporary philosophers, no less than Enlightenment thinkers, often assumes what is to be proved – namely, the rejection of entities which our senses seem poorly equipped to perceive. We shall determine whether our sensory equipment is truly incapable of receiving data on 'spiritual' realities as is usually assumed. However, what is often forgotten in the summary rejection of spiritual realities, whether by Enlightenment thinkers or twentieth-century positivists, is that such positions also involve heavy doses of metaphysics which are often assumed and unestablished, except by rhetoric or assertion. F.R. Tennant reminds us that:

> As the futility of metaphysics could only be demonstrated by metaphysical arguments – the success of positive methods being in itself no proof of the necessary failure of others – it must be assumed that at least so much of metaphysics must be admitted into philosophy as is essential to prove the barrenness of all the rest. (Tennant, 1913: 33f.)

Metaphysics invariably pervades our theoretical and practical commitments, and it seems the better part of intellectual virtue to make explicit the metaphysical assumptions underlying our academic agendas. This does not mean that it is necessary to engage in an intellectual confession at the outset of every academic project. But it serves to remind us that the uncritical rejection of (usually theistic) metaphysics frequently involves metaphysical commitments that are unstated or unproved.

In the West, while it may be proper to say that, since Kant, epistemology has taken precedence over metaphysical inquiry, it is also proper to admit that the two disciplines are mutually necessary and presume each other. Metaphysics, however that discipline may be construed – the study of 'being', 'first principles' or 'reals' – cannot rest independent of epistemology. And the justification of the cognitive

---

2 See especially part four of Kant (1960).

claims of metaphysics is one of the principal roles of epistemology. How one construes the universe cannot be established philosophically by mere feeling or intuition, but by rigorous scrutiny of what and how we know, and that is the work of epistemology. Similarly, what and how we know often involves metaphysical assumptions. In the Indian context, this is most evident in Advaita Vedānta, which liberally draws upon its metaphysical theories in order to explain certain problems of perception. As D.M. Datta has pointed out, this may strike some students as dogmatic, 'its epistemological conclusions being vitiated by gratuitous metaphysical assumptions' (Datta, 1972: 32). Yet, Datta adds:

> … if we closely examine the modern epistemological theories of perception, it will not be difficult to find that in spite of their loud protests against metaphysics, epistemologists have tacitly assumed without criticism certain theories of reality, on the truth of which alone their epistemological conclusions can stand. (Ibid.: 33)

Thus, in the Indian context, metaphysical questions were often self-consciously accompanied by epistemological analyses, and properly so. The answer to the question 'What is out there?' needed careful authentication of the mechanisms which produce knowledge, the *pramāṇas*. Among the various philosophical schools lively debate occurred over the relative merits of the various *pramāṇas* such as scripture, perception, inferential reasoning, comparison and testimony. All this was included under the rubric of *pramāṇa vicāra*, the investigation into the means of knowledge. Accompanying this was the more metaphysical search, *prameya vicāra*, the investigation of knowables, which included axiological studies (*kāma*, *artha*, *dharma*, *mokṣa śāstra*) as well as philosophico-theological studies on the world, self and God (Balasubramanian, 1990: 15).

I wish to underscore the necessary partnership of metaphysics and epistemology in answering the related questions 'What is out there?' and 'How do we know it?' Doing so affirms the sensible strategy in Indian philosophy of *pramāṇa* and *prameya vicāra*. The stakes, in any context, it seems, are high and the implications many. Questions concerning the structure and scope of what we can know lead reasonably to the question of whether there is a divine being, or divine beings, or some supramundane impersonal reality and whether we can know it. How one answers these questions invariably affects a variety of theoretical and practical commitments, although no doubt a gap between theory and practice often occurs (and perhaps is the norm) in human experience. Still, the stakes are high. Life, after all, is short, and if the claims of a certain religion or tradition include claims concerning the truth of reality in its most comprehensive context, then it would seem to be among the intellectual virtues to pay close attention to these claims, resisting the temptation to dismiss them out of hand under the force of one's cultural and philosophical conditioning. This seems all the more important when we study those religio-philosophical traditions which index thinking to soteriological consequences. For example, Śaṅkara is quite clear about his reasons for undertaking an interpretation of the Brahma Sūtra: 'In order to destroy (wrong notion), the cause of evil, and to prove the unity of the Self, the study of the entire Vedānta is begun.'[3] In this, and in virtually every Indian tradition, wrong notion, *abhimāna*, or ignorance, *avidyā*, is indexed to a downward spiral of egotism and selfishness, which inexorably produces suffering. Conversely, knowledge or right view (*vidyā* or *samyag dṛṣṭi*) is indexed to freedom, here taken to mean freedom from all suffering, whether mental, physical or celestial. The ubiquitous existential reality of suffering is the starting point for the search for saving knowledge in all Indian traditions, not a Western-style peripatetic search for abstract truth. Illustrative of this is Śaṅkara's comment, above, and the sixth-century *kārikā* of the Sāṅkhya school: 'Owing to the affliction of the threefold suffering, the inquiry into the means of its cessation (begins)' (Sastri, 1948: 1).[4]

Now, a question appropriately arises when one recognizes the indexing of knowledge to salvation: what exactly is meant here by knowledge? Does the instrumental role of knowledge in the economy of salvation in India vitiate any *prima facie* parallels to Western concepts of knowledge? Does it create an insuperable barrier to constructive philosophical comparison between Indian and 'Western' epistemologies? The question concerning the Indian concept of knowledge will be considered in detail in Chapter 2. However, concerning the doubts over the possibility of constructive epistemological comparison on account of the putative soteriological value of knowledge in Indian materials, I offer the following response: recognizing that there is no univocal agreement in Indian intellectual history over the nature and function of the mind and the soul, the size and degree of pervasion of each, and the extent of potential suffering attributed to the soul, the indexing of knowledge to salvation in the Indian *darśanas* is both important and unimportant in a comparative epistemological study such as this. It is important, obviously, because it represents the highest value possible for the soul, which is implicated in a psycho-physical matrix and in some relevant sense is dependent on cognitive processes for release. It indicates just how high the stakes are for understanding the proper functioning of those cognitive processes. We will see how important 'proper function' is both to medieval Indian thinkers and to some contemporary anglophone epistemologists.

On the other hand, the indexing of knowledge to salvation should not deter comparative philosophers, since this gesture seems unimportant in relevant senses as well. For example, Indian thinkers as a matter of course affirmed the basic *āstika* axiom of the authority of the Veda as the source of their doctrines, but then occasionally spun theories that appeared to have little to do with the Vedic world-view. Śaṅkara's Advaita is an example of such gymnastics: although he is constrained by cultural assumptions to accept the Veda, his metaphysic forces him

3 ... *anarthahetoḥ prahāṇāya ātmaikatvavidyāpratitpattaye sarve vedāntā ārabhyante.*

4 ... *duḥkhatrayābhigātāt jijñāsa tat abhighātake hetau.*

in the end to accept at best the provisional value of the Veda. Some versions of atheistic Mīmāṃsā and Sāṅkhya also engage in their own versions of *āstika* gymnastics. Much in the same way Indian philosophers also appear to swear fidelity to the assumption that knowledge is paramount for salvation, but then get on with their work at hand, the familiar grunt work of arguments and counterarguments that constitute the substance of philosophy. For example, Nyāya Sūtra 1.1. holds that 'attainment of final beatitude (*niḥśreyasādhigamaḥ*) follows from the knowledge of the nature of the sixteen categories (*tattvajñānāt*)' (Vidyābhuṣana, 1975: 1). Having stated such, the real business of the Nyāya system gets under way: logic and epistemology. The Western scholar can recognize this gesture in the Nyāya, or similar gestures in the other schools, without needing to forswear fruitful examination of Indian categories because of the soteriological value of knowledge in Indian philosophical discourse. Inevitably, substantive epistemologies and metaphysics follow the soteriological assumption, and it is here that the Western philosopher of religion will find a locus for a constructive programme in comparative philosophy.

Such a programme argues that it is not only theoretically possible for persons of one tradition to add to their conceptual framework the categories of another tradition, but that it is necessary for the philosopher of religion to do so. 'Necessary' is a strong term, but if much of the agenda of philosophy of religion consists in careful examination of the claims of faith, then an appropriate responsibility of the discipline logically extends this programme and considers the claims, content and conditions for saving knowledge in non-Western traditions. Indeed, doing so in a careful, self-conscious manner may in fact constitute the most creative role for the philosopher of religion, for the fruit of such study may contribute to our understanding of human 'nature' in its most complete context. What does it mean to be human? How far does our environment extend? Is there a divine reality and, if so, how do we know it? These are some of the questions that classical and contemporary philosophy of religion have addressed. By paying careful attention to the answers which other traditions have proposed to these questions and others, we may add to our self-understanding and to our understanding of our environment in its broadest scope. Thus cross-cultural efforts in philosophy of religion, intimately reviewing the mechanics and outcomes of 'religious knowing', clearly impact philosophical anthropology and metaphysics.

That it is possible to engage in such constructive 'thinking across cultures' is a matter of historical and contemporary witness: early Christians appropriated Greek concepts of the all-pervading logos, Sufi mystics roaming the Gangetic plain in the fifteenth century adopted elements of Vedāntic thought, and contemporary New Age gurus sometimes borrow wholesale philosophies of the 'East'. This last example perhaps amounts to the best argument why philosophers of religion need to learn the languages and conceptual systems of Indian thought: many of the popular advocates of 'Eastern' wisdom – Indian immigrant-gurus no less than American apologists – are often rather unclear about the various historical and philosophical contexts of

Indian philosophy.[5] In fact, the philosopher of religion provides an important service by accurately representing the various streams of thought and practice that have developed in India's many traditions of philosophical and theological reflection. And yet, mere representation does not suffice. Many of the philosophical issues that provoked inquiring minds in India are issues that hardly have their sole province on the subcontinent. Problems of causality, substance, the identity of the soul and the processes of knowing are live issues in any philosophical tradition. Philosophers of one tradition can only gain by investigating the analyses of their fellow philosophers of another time and era. Such investigation provides an opportunity to see things afresh and stimulate constructive insight. That, at least, is the hope and goal of this project. In one of the early works of his career, Karl Potter lamented the mere cataloguing of Indian doctrines and the absence of an engaged, philosophically astute, critical inquiry of Indian philosophy. He addressed the need for philosophers who were willing 'to push to the limit the presuppositions of Indian thought, to work along original lines either to refute or to justify them, but at any rate to address them as living ideas and not as dead ones' (Potter, 1991: 258). Doing so in fact honours best the great tradition of Indian thought.

Potter, Paul Griffiths, Francis Clooney, Eliot Deutsch and the late Wilhelm Halbfass all represent this tradition, naturally with different nuances in approach and goals. All are philosophically and theologically trained in Western and Indian philosophy and take seriously and critically engage with Indian philosophical and religious texts for constructive purposes. This approach differs considerably from the one that William James advocates in his classic study, *The Varieties of Religious Experience*. For James, philosophy is relegated to something of a surgical role, merely debriding dead historical constructions of the divine and deleting absurd dogmas (James, 1990: 408). In addition to this deconstructive role, for him, philosophy has a conciliatory task, especially in identifying the common elements among religions in order to promote greater harmony. This role has been well represented at James's Harvard. It was the philosophical role of choice of the late Wilfred Cantwell Smith and the Harvard Center for the Study of World Religions.

Such an approach has significant value, but philosophical differences tend to be persistent, and those who take them seriously tend not to allow those differences to be glossed over, even under the consoling goal of 'harmony'. This was evident at the centennial session of the Parliament of the World's Religions, held in Chicago in 1993. In choosing the legitimate goals of inclusivity, harmony and tolerance, the

---

5 This position admits that these advocates know what they are *doing* when they use 'Eastern wisdom', often, with good intentions or ill, using these materials to support a therapy, movement, lineage, or even spiritual industry, sometimes at high personal or economic costs. Agehānanda Bharati is rather critical of dilettantism. In one example, he reminds the reader that the classical commentators on the *cakra* system do not take it to be a literal physiology, but an imaginary construct (*kalpanātmikā*) which serves meditation (Bharati, 1976: 164–66). This distinction is absent in many contemporary, popular representations of the system. See also Hammer (2001) for a brilliant review and analysis of New Age epistemologies.

Parliament risked alienating groups that could not, in good conscience, abide serious doctrinal differences with other religious groups. Indeed, this actually occurred when certain Orthodox Jews and Greek Christians abandoned the conference on finding themselves sitting under a theological umbrella with polytheists and pagans. Certain Buddhist groups also quietly protested the dominant use of monotheistic language in various public prayers and plenary sessions. And these observations do not include various political tensions that were evident among certain national religious groups, such as Indian Sikhs and Hindus.

There are two morals to this story. One is that the legitimate goals of harmony and tolerance can be subverted all too easily by glossing over significant doctrinal differences. The other is that overlooking these differences may be proper in some circumstances and for some people, but not for philosophers and theologians. If one wishes to avoid what Thomas Merton called 'a facile syncretism, a mishmash of semireligious verbiage and pieties, a devotionalism that admits everything and therefore takes nothing with full seriousness' (Merton, 1975: 316), then accepting the mantle of critical thought is necessary. With regard to the goal of harmony in the scholarship on religion, R.C. Zaehner writes as follows:

> Nor do I think that it can be a legitimate function of a university professor to attempt to induce harmony among elements as disparate as the great religions of mankind appear to be, if, as seems inevitable, the resultant harmony is only to be apparent, verbal, and therefore fictitious. Such a procedure may well be commendable in a statesman. In a profession that concerns itself with the pursuit of truth it is damnable. (Zaehner, 1970: 6–7)

Indeed, John Carman, who took over Cantwell Smith's legacy at Harvard, recently called into question his own hesitation in challenging Indian colleagues at the Center for the Study of World Religions, out of deference to their religious world-view. In a convocation address at the Harvard Divinity School, he said, 'I should seek, not only to listen sympathetically to others' views, but also to "speak the truth in love", to express my viewpoint on reality' (Carman, 1993).

It is my intention here to 'seek the truth' concerning religious experience, and then speak it. James and others, however, are often relentless in their insistence that, if there is such a thing (a dubious proposition to many), we are not equipped to discover it. For example, James asserts in his *Varieties* that 'the attempt to demonstrate by purely intellectual processes the truths of deliverances of direct religious experience is absolutely hopeless' (James, 1990: 408). This, of course, is true, depending on the particular epistemology one employs, but, for the moment, I hesitate to make such a categorical dismissal. In the meantime, I plan to read closely and expect to learn from Indian thinkers. As Carman noted later in his speech, a creative opportunity exists in thinking across cultures; there is no *prima facie* reason why members of one culture cannot enhance their own conceptual categories by close readings of another religious or philosophical system. Indeed, some missionary efforts demanded creative interchange with novel conceptual systems.[6] Klaus Klostermaier also believes that a creative opportunity exists in cross-cultural dialogue, arguing that 'we cannot consider cultures and races as eternally immovable barriers – nor can we ignore them. We can penetrate them and enter into exchange' (Klostermaier, 1989: 6). Adding a rhetorical flourish, he quotes Louis Dumont: 'Cultures not only *can* be made to communicate, they *must*' (Dumont, 1970: 161). The argument, made all the more compelling in the terrible wake of 11 September 2001, involves the rhetoric of global interpenetration. This is fine as long as one proceeds, as Halbfass urged, with 'much critical reflection and hermeneutic awareness' (Halbfass, 1990: 433).

I shall use a programme of comparative philosophy to explore the truths delivered of religious experience. But what exactly is comparative philosophy? While there has been ample debate in the West as to what exactly philosophy is, one kind of construal of that term seems straightforward and unobjectionable: reasoned discourse, systematic reflection or, simply, thinking clearly. And, of course, these patterns of thought have their object, so that reasoned discourse on knowledge becomes epistemology, on thought it becomes logic, on values it becomes axiology and so on. While this is not the place to enter into a history of Western philosophy, this study takes as its starting point certain themes and debates in the West over the cognitive value of religious experience. The setting of these debates is important and is considered below. Yet, at the same time, this project holds, from the outset, the value of the systematic reflection of non-Westerners on this and related questions. Considered negatively, it seeks to avoid an intellectual imperialism which steamrolls as (philosophically) meaningless the considered reflection of non-Western traditions. In the words of the Sanskrit apothegm, it seeks to avoid the problem of '*kupamaṇḍūkanyāya*', the frog in the well. Instead, it expects, unlike the isolated frog, to gain insight into persistent and vexing issues in philosophy and theology by virtue of extending one's conceptual horizons. At the same time, it rejects pure programmes of deconstruction which reduce philosophy to the role of the ideological strong-arm of competing polities.

That political issues abound in the putative 'clear thinking' of philosophers and other writers is important and interesting: there will always be a place for the 'hermeneutics of suspicion' to reveal political and social agendas of authors and texts. But to argue that analysis of philosophical discourse has no value other than revealing social and political agenda is tendentious. While it is interesting, useful and necessary to consider how social and political realities contribute directly or

6 Another example of cross-cultural programmes of transmission, far removed from twentieth-century discourse on the 'global village', would be the massive translation projects – with state support, no less – of Buddhist texts into Chinese and Japanese. A principal axiom operating here is that there is no sacrosanct language; texts are translatable. Buddhism has a universalist metaphysic, and Buddhist teachers have always thought that persons of other cultures could – and should – understand it. It seems evident that much doctrine and practice are context-specific, but more abstract discourse may be extricated from one culture and transmitted to another culture, where, of course, it becomes implicated in various cultural forms.

indirectly to the discourse of philosophers, it is imperialistic, not to mention self-referentially incoherent, to dismiss such sustained reflection as mere ideology, as if the only things worth talking about in Indian philosophy are the material and political conditions of its possibility, and not the substantive ideas which these thinkers took seriously. It is also thus disrespectful of these thinkers, especially when these scholars and the communities of their followers (in the East and in the West) stake their lives on the entailments that follow from their reasoned consideration.

Positively, this project assumes a sympathetic approach to philosophical questions considered beyond the contexts of European and American intellectual history. Its openness to other traditions of reflection contains the assumption that, as humans, we come equipped to experience and consider thoughtfully certain universal and inevitable events, principal among which are suffering and death. Such experiences lead a thoughtful person of any culture to consider the value of existence, the cultural values of a given society, the origin and destiny of a 'person' (however that technically loaded term is construed). It is not germane to this project to enter into the anthropological debate over varying 'rationalities'; while that question may be useful in analysing mythologies of non-literate communities, it is irrelevant to the non-Western texts I will examine – Indian scholia on scripture and metaphysics. And anyone who has read even a little Indian philosophy knows that it often contains just as much difficult material as any Western philosophy. Such seems to overthrow the postmodern contempt for universals; obtuse thought appears to be a universal occupational hazard of philosophers!

Some have raised the objection that what they do in India is not philosophy, riddled as it is with unfounded speculation and dependent on revelation. This, of course, contains another imperialistic judgement: 'Their method is not exactly like ours; therefore, they are at fault.' True, Indian traditions of thought count revelation as foundational to their conceptual systems, a starting point with important implications and parallels for some Western epistemologies. But as suggested above, some Indian scholiasts, in an effort to stay within the 'orthodox' Vedic fold, took pains to reinterpret revelation according to their metaphysical or ritualistic schema. Indeed, while this project enters into comparative philosophy, an interesting future project may be comparative revelation, a programme to understand better the event and transmission of what cultures consider to be divine disclosure. Still, within the framework of revelatory disclosure, Indian intellectuals employed rigorous patterns of thinking and argument, equal to or surpassing those of any in the history of Western philosophy. Moreover, some thinkers, while recognizing the debt to revelation, virtually ignore or downplay it in their treatises. This is evident in some versions of Advaita; Śaṅkara certainly is 'revelation-dependent' as he attempts to construct a coherent non-dual metaphysic within the framework of a transmitted Veda, but his agenda demands that he 'transcend' the Veda. Other Advaitins, on the other hand, developed treatises less dependent on revelation and more strictly involved in negative dialectics. This is particularly evident in Maṇḍana, Citsukha and Śrīharṣa.[7]

Comparative philosophy thus optimistically explores fundamental and compelling questions that benefit by extending into other intellectual horizons. One of these questions concerns the epistemic significance of religious experience. Although systematic analysis of religious experience in the manner of recent anglophone philosophy is understandably absent in classical Indian texts (owing to different historical conditions), one can use, as I do in this study, a Western epistemological heuristic as a lens to examine Indian concepts of religious experience – to illumine certain aspects of the Indian thought and return afresh to our fundamental question, having perhaps won constructive insight for our endeavours. However, as contemporary philosophers of religion take seriously the issues involved in metaphysical and epistemological discourse, examining those issues through the lens of experience presents special problems. It will be the burden of the rest of this introductory chapter to examine these particular problems.

Religious experience: historical context

The consideration of religious experience as a category for philosophical and historical inquiry is a relatively recent phenomenon, and here I particularly mean as it applies to the West. Indeed, as mentioned above, the term 'religious experience' is certainly absent in Indian texts if, in using that term, we hope to discover a formal operating category which has been used in the same manner as the Western discussions of religious experience since the Enlightenment. That there is discussion of 'religious experience' (*anubhava*, *anubhūti*, *sakṣātkāra*) in Sanskrit and vernacular texts in India is clear; indeed, the Veda has been represented by some Indian thinkers as a record of the experiences of ancient seers. Still, what is meant by the Sanskrit terms in their various contexts is often less clear. And if the meanings of the Sanskrit terms are hardly obvious, the meanings of the English terms are no more so. As Vergilius Ferm once wrote, 'If "experience" and "religion" suffer as weasel words, by a simple arithmetical process "religious experience" is a double weasel expression' (Ferm, 1971: 27).

In any case, what is clear in the Indian situation is the freedom, up until this century, from the pressure found in Europe after the Enlightenment which demanded a systematic analysis of 'religious experience' for theoretical or polemical purposes. This pressure, however, did develop in the Indian academy in the late nineteenth and twentieth centuries, partly out of reaction to early Orientalist dismissals of

7 'Śaṅkara's use of argument is apologetic, though forceful; Maṇḍana, on the other hand, appears to revel in it' (Potter, 1991: 165). A systematic epistemology is presented in Dharmarāja Adhvarindra's *Vedānta Paribhāṣa* (seventeenth century). For a masterful comparative study of reason and revelation, see Clooney (2001).

'Hinduism' as 'low, foolish, and immoral' (Inden, 1990: 91). James Mill's commentary on Hindu cosmology typifies early negative evaluations of Indian mythologies where 'no coherence, wisdom, or beauty, ever appears: all is disorder, caprice, passion, contest, portents, prodigies, violence, and deformity' (ibid.). Reacting to a history of slights such as these, Indian scholars of the twentieth century began to use the expression 'religious experience' in Indian thought and practice in ways that the original authors could not have foreseen or intended – as apologetic devices used to exalt the pre-eminence of Indian religion and philosophy over Western rationalism. Hinduism presents an 'intimate inseparability of theory and practice' in which 'every doctrine has been turned into passionate conviction, stirring the heart of man and quickening his breath, and completely transforming his personal nature' (Radhakrishnan, 1957: xxiv). Indian philosophy now was construed as 'intuitive' and leading to 'direct awareness' of religious truths, in contrast to the rationalist, linear and discursive thought of Western philosophy. The following quote from Sarvepalli Radhakrishnan is symptomatic of the tendency among some twentieth-century Indian scholars to put a premium on 'intuitive apprehension' of truth over and against the 'objectifying' spirit of Western analytical philosophy:

> Indian philosophy makes unquestioned and extensive use of reason, but intuition is accepted as the only method through which the ultimate can be known. Reason, intellectual knowledge, is not enough. Reason is not useless or fallacious, but it is insufficient. To know reality one must have an actual experience of it. One does not merely *know* the truth in Indian philosophy; one *realizes* it. (Radhakrishnan, 1957: xxv)

This apologetic strategy is evident among contemporary Indian scholars as well. For example, the coverleaf of Sharma's *The Experiential Dimension of Advaita Vedanta* explains that his study 'provides a clear, concise, and precise introduction to Advaita Vedanta on the basis of something more powerful than argument, namely, experience' (Sharma, 1993a). And Sharma himself writes:

> For the natural consequence of an experiential presentation of Advaita Vedanta is to disengage it from its cultural contingencies and to unencumber it from its religious baggage. What is then left is something which we as human beings may appropriate or choose not to, depending on our judgment about it. (Sharma, 1993a: 101)

Let us examine briefly the historical development of the Western analysis of religious experience, for even Indian apologists, such as Radhakrishnan and Sharma, often uncritically adopt the Western analysis of religious experience and buy into some of its assumptions.[8] For example, not only does Sharma's conclusion

---

[8] Wilhelm Halbfass (1990) superbly demonstrates this, as does Anantanand Rambachand (1991), who surveys and cites neo-Hindu appropriations of Western categories such as 'religious experience'.

cited above suggest a neo-Hindu (or at least neo-Advaita Vedānta) theme in his programme, but it also reflects unargued Enlightenment assumptions of the possibility of a universal, immediate 'religious' experience which is uninflected by cultural trappings – a highly controverted position to say the least. Thus, the second part of this section examines the contemporary anglophone discussion of religious experience and attempts to make some sense out of these troublesome 'weasel words'.

It is important to contextualize the discussion of religious experience in the West, and to see it as part of a wider discourse in which it was conceived.[9] William James's seminal work, *The Varieties of Religious Experience*, is perhaps the best known of early attempts to offer a systematic philosophical analysis of religious experience in the West; however, even this justifiably celebrated study is not without significant conceptual antecedents in the seventeenth through nineteenth centuries. In the seventeenth century John Locke developed a sensory epistemology based on his readings of Newton's *Optics*. Newton provided a scientific basis for epistemology: how we know anything about the external world was demonstrated neurophysiologically on the basis of sight and the so-called corpuscular theory of light; in this case, the retina apparently is agitated by minute 'stuff' which produces images for our mind. Locke extended this theory. Sense was feeling-based, and affective stimuli the basis of knowledge. Following upon the sensory psychology of Locke, *feeling* – experiential sensation – became a primary category that disclosed the spiritual state of the individual. The eighteenth-century Scottish economist and philosopher Adam Smith, for example, assumed that there existed an innate capacity to know through feeling. For him, the basis of all morals was 'sympathy'; only on the basis of feeling can appropriate moral response be generated. Feeling was the basis of knowledge, and morals revealed religiosity. This position was also held by Smith's contemporary in America, the Puritan theologian Jonathan Edwards: fits of emotion and extraordinary events such as glossalalia demonstrated the particular status of the elect.

Such a position has long endured in American religious history, where varieties of Pentecostals and charismatic Christians, from urban Catholics to rural snake handlers, cite as proof of divine presence the manifestation of the 'gifts of the spirit'. This attitude, however, is not exclusive to the West, either in its medieval or contemporary form. The *bhakti* movement in India, in any of its permutations, put a premium on the value of personal experience in religious practice and, like some Enlightenment theologians, downplayed ritualism in favour of religious experience as essential to 'true' religion.[10]

For Edwards, however, religious experience was pre-cultural, pre-linguistic and

---

9 This paragraph owes to Gary Ebersole.

10 See Hawley (1988: 6). Note Kabir's anti-clericalism and anti-ritualism, 50–61. See also A.K. Ramanujan (1973), especially his discussion of the Viraśaiva search for direct, unmediated Experience (Ramanujan uses the upper case), *anubhava*.

immediate, in accord with the Enlightenment assumption of a universal, shared, fundamental religious experience behind all cultural differences. Most expressive of this view in Europe was Schleiermacher, who, in writing to his Romantic friends, argued that the essence of the experience evoked by artists was the same essence of religious experience. Religion is a sense, taste, a matter of feeling and intuition. It is original, unmediated, irreducible, unitary. But Schleiermacher's search for the essence of religion had, of course, an apologetic agenda. If piety is a matter of feeling, then, according to Schleiermacher, it is unscathed by Kant's contention that our experience is structured by the categories and thoughts we bring to it. As a sense that precedes and is independent of all thought, religion should not be confused with doctrine or practice and, conveniently, can never be in conflict with the findings of modern science. Religion is an autonomous moment in human experience, and in principle invulnerable to rational and moral criticism. By locating 'piety' in feeling, not in the intellect, and insisting on the tenuous position that it is immediate and unshaped by thought, Schleiermacher and others assumed they had transcended petty and divisive argument over doctrine and dogma (Proudfoot, 1985: 1–15).

James and Otto are heirs of this legacy. Each agrees that feeling is the deeper source of religion, not to be identified with belief or practice. Although they differ in their methods – James is the pragmatist, Otto the Kantian phenomenologist – and in whether they construe the universal religious experience to be singular (Otto) or many (James), they agree that intellectual operations over doctrine presuppose religious experience as their subject matter. These operations are consequent upon feeling, not independent of it; feeling, the 'better part of religion', is direct, unmediated by concepts and known only by acquaintance. For Otto, the sacred was a primary datum of psychic life; human beings are innately endowed with an *a priori* faculty that recognizes the divine: we can know God in a pre-cultural, pre-linguistic feeling-based knowledge. This feeling response is a form of knowing, however unschematized and unconceptualized. Otto joins Schleiermacher in employing something of a missionary strategy; both use the language of evocation to arouse those hidden religious sentiments in their readers.[11]

Otto, in any case, had an additional agenda, which included constructing an analysis out of which Christianity emerges as the superior manifestation of God's presence on earth.[12] This particular tendency to hierarchize religious expressions

---

11 The Holy 'cannot strictly speaking, be taught, it can only be evoked, awakened in the mind ... ' (Otto, 1923: 7). Such a strategy has been used before, memorably by the author of the fourteenth-century English mystical treatise, *The Cloud of Unknowing and Other Works*, a text not intended 'for the merely curious'. See the prologue to *The Cloud of Unknowing and Other Works* (Wolters, trans., 1983: 51–52). According to Frederick Streng (1976), the evocative function of mystical language 'serves as a catalyst for release from conventional thought, perception and desire' (quoted in King, 1978: 449).

12 For example, Christianity 'stands out in complete superiority over all its sister religions' (Otto, 1923: 146). Despite such strategies, one should recall that Otto was also an important early leader in ecumenism. As an alternative approach to non-Christian religions, see Fredericks (1995) and Clooney (1995), among other Christian theologians; their method, comparative theology, has close affinities with

according to the metaphysical pivot of the scholar recurs often in the history of religions and is hardly limited to scholars committed to a theistic metaphysic.[13] Few, however, are as bold as Zaehner, who rather baldly revealed the motivation of his scholarship in his Gifford lectures, 'In all my writing on comparative religion my aim has been to show that there is a coherent pattern in religious history. For me, the centre of coherence is Christ' (Zaehner, 1970: 31).

That metaphysics leaks into the scholarship on religion is not necessarily improper and in fact is probably unavoidable. Papers, books and theories obviously involve argued points of view, and these spring from (and reinforce) the intellectual commitments of the scholar. These, of course, include metaphysical commitments, whether theistic or materialistic. Wayne Proudfoot's *Religious Experience*, for example, is an important contribution to the contemporary analysis of religious experience. Proudfoot argues that no experience or interpretation is void of conceptual content; no 'immediate' experiences are available to us. So his is a 'constructivist' or 'conceptualist' position whose intellectual roots go back many years and which has a powerful voice in the academy today. However, the subtext of his thesis reveals an argument for a normative way of doing philosophy: 'We must explain why the subject was confronted with this particular set of alternative ways of understanding his experience and why he employed the one he did. In general, what we want is a historical and cultural explanation' (Proudfoot, 1985: 223).

So, we are back at the position that the only interesting thing philosophy can do is 'explicate the concept' – the historical, political, linguistic or aesthetic conditions in which religious experience occurs. God, in principle, is ruled out, and the question of the veridicality of the experience is either sidestepped or assumed to have a negative answer. But an exclusively 'naturalist' approach to religious experience does not adequately 'penetrate' the religious experience to determine whether or not the experience is veridical; indeed, it merely juxtaposes the explanation of the naturalist scholar with the explanation of the supernaturalist mystic.[14] As Michael Peterson and others have correctly observed:

> To assert that 'what we want is a historical or cultural explanation' begs the question which belief system provides the appropriate framework for explaining events, for why should one assume that a historical or cultural

---

my own comparative approach here; Clooney has ambitiously epitomized the project of comparative theology as having as its ultimate horizon 'nothing less than knowledge of the divine, the transcendent' (Clooney, 1995: 521).

13 For example, the nineteenth-century British anthropologists and twentieth-century thinkers, such as Durkheim and Freud, among others.

14 Bagger (1999) tends toward this position, arguing that 'human epistemic flourishing' of the postmodern era vitiates the epistemic merit of supernaturalist explanations. While rich with insights, Bagger's position seems, in the end, to vitiate the very contextualism that he seeks to affirm. See Forsthoefel (2001a).

explanation is more to the point than a supernatural or theistic one? (Peterson *et al.*, 1991: 22)

One way of 'penetrating' religious experience – apart from having a religious experience oneself – is to examine the mechanisms of knowing and the method of justification; this extension of epistemology into religious experience has been advanced in important ways by William Alston and Alvin Plantinga, and it is their work that I will use as heuristics to review 'religious experience' in Advaita Vedānta. However, before I discuss their work, some prelimary issues concerning the contemporary philosophical context of religious experience must first be addressed.

Religious experience: contemporary philosophical context

In the contemporary philosophical discussion of religious experience, three difficulties seem especially important, for intertwined among them is the question of what we can know from religious experience. These difficulties are the problems of identification, constructivism and epistemology. I am most concerned with the third issue, and the latter half of this section lays out the theoretical issues involved. The problems of the identification of religious experience and constructivism are either implicit or have been suggested above. For instance, I have been using the term 'religious experience' as if the meaning of the term is self-evident. Forgetting for the moment the endless disputes over what exactly religion is before one asks what religious experience is, one should ask: what, indeed, is *experience*?

Let me suggest that experience is any mental event that has sensory, affective or volitional dimensions. Admittedly this is a broad definition, but it is necessarily so. When we add the qualifier, *religious* experience, we understand that that locution picks out some particular kind of event. But we are faced with the dilemma of what precisely counts as religious experience. Does a wedding of unchurched Catholics count as religious experience? Tears of joy at born-again revival? Buddhist meditation with phenomenal properties? With no phenomenal properties? This last example presents another difficulty, since the normal use of term 'experience' involves the kind of intentionality explicated by Franz Brentano. 'Experience' tends toward an object; a subject experiences an object which can be physical (nature, body, sport, sex), emotional (love, anger, other feelings), or supernatural (God, gods, ghosts and so on). The last category might be comprehended in the expression 'religious experience', although more precision and clarification would be necessary. More importantly, while this account of religious experience may be fine for the vast majority of the world population which assumes a realistic dualism of subject and object, for the minority of non-dualists in the world using the term 'religious experience' is philosophically careless (it is redundant) and heavy-handed (when it presumes dualism). For these persons, there is *only* experience. Advaita

Vedāntins belong in this camp. The question in this case becomes how to talk meaningfully about experience as such, which in turn necessitates philosophical and phenomenological inquiry. Chapter 2 examines this issue. The more general question here is this: how do we isolate a useful set of things? In other words, what strategy should we employ to arrive at relevant criteria which pick out religious experience?

One strategy might be to employ self-identification: an experience is religious because a person says it is. This is too broad, however, and not sufficiently narrow for useful classificatory analysis. Another strategy may be to develop an *a priori* formal definition of religion – a stipulative definition. In other words, one decides first what religion is and then uses that definition to pick out what is religious. This returns to the problem of what exactly religion is, and here the minefields are many. One of them is the unseemly arbitrariness of the definition; another is the temptation to contort one's data to square them with one's *a priori* formula. Walter Stace (1961), Evelyn Underhill (1963), and R.C. Zaehner (1961) used this method, and its weakness is perhaps most apparent in Zaehner's *Mysticism Sacred and Profane*. His cross-cultural typology is 'phenomenologically suspect' according to Steven Katz, for it forces data into improper interpretative categories 'which lose sight of the fundamentally important difference between the data studied' (Katz, 1978: 25).[15] Worse, according to Hans Penner (1983), Zaehner's programme is misguided not just because he thinks he can compare different mystical systems, but because he believes he can judge which systems are valid, genuine or true.[16]

Although recent scholarship on 'mysticism' has become much more philosophically refined and historically alert, comments on Katz and Penner are in order. These scholars, and many others, have reacted to earlier studies of mysticism which assumed or argued for a single essence or core of mysticism that is universal but inflected in a variety of cultural contexts. This is the so-called 'perennial philosophy' that was popularized by Aldous Huxley (1946), Frithjof Schuon (1975), and Huston Smith (1958, 1987). However, philosophical analysis of perennialism shows it to be problematic at the very least and perhaps even incoherent.[17] Also, the

---

15 Criticisms of Stace's work have abounded in many recent studies of mysticism, the hue and cry over which indicates its importance, however flawed it may be. Although most criticisms are of a philosophical nature, none is more devastating than the methodological criticisms of J.M. Masson and T.C. Masson (1976: 109–25).

16 Penner's criticism involves the issue of commensurability. I earlier suggested that languages, concepts and doctrines can be translated across cultures (an empirical issue) and ought to be for greater conceptual understanding. Negatively, radical incommensurability implies no normative evaluation of doctrines or ideas, an irresponsible position in the face of deadly religious communities such as Aum Shinrikyo, Jonestown, Heaven's Gate, the violent Christian (anti-abortion, Identity) groups and the Islamic fringe.

17 Paul J. Griffiths (1991: 45–59) argues that this position (what he calls esotericist perspectivalism) and a similar version of it (universalist perspectivalist) are, in the first case, inaccurate, and, in the second case, incoherent.

search for the 'common essence' tends to create an elitist understanding of religious phenomena, in effect establishing a meta-religion – a radically revisioned, ahistorical entity. This is particularly evident in Schuon's *The Transcendent Unity of Religion*. However, Smith himself understood the problem of such an approach, calling it 'cut-flower esotericism'; it is devoid of roots (that is, context), thus soon to wither and die. Moreover, the destabilizing tendencies of contemporary discourse analysis hardly admit that there is such a thing as a common human nature, let alone common mystical experiences. The net result of these criticisms has shifted scholarly attention to the social, political and historical context of these putative 'mystical' experiences.

The fruit of these criticisms has enriched scholarship about religions and religious experiences. Too often, the *a priori* pattern of the researcher was rather forcefully squeezed on to religious and cultural events. Philosophically, scholars have accepted Katz's 'plea for the recognition of differences', paying much closer attention to the social and historical context of those events and properly admitting the interplay between politics and power formations in their construction. So, on the one hand, reifications such as 'core mystical experience' were eliminated. No longer was one experience admitted, but many: a Buddhist experience, a Jewish experience, a Christian experience, a Hindu experience (and numerous versions thereof), and so on. Failure to admit the obvious pluralities has the potential to steamroll a culture's self-understanding: recall the Buddhist leafleteers protesting monotheistic terminology at the 1993 Parliament of the World's Religions.

Katz also criticized scholars such as Zaehner for using typologies, yet finds himself hard pressed to avoid using them himself, indulging in the use of labels such as 'absorptive' and 'non-absorptive' forms of mysticism (Katz, 1978: 41). The fact that even Katz's nominalist tendencies were overcome by the temptation to use categorial devices highlights the persistent attractiveness of typologies. In fact, these are useful instruments to help make sense of vast amounts of data and should not be eschewed as a matter of course. Typologies are not 'cast in stone' or inscribed in the fabric of the universe; they are the intellectual artifacts of their authors. Nor are typologies context-neutral; rather, they are indexed to the purposes and goals of their authors and can be judged by whether they fulfil or achieve them. In short, typologies are necessary heuristics; with no level of abstraction, mysticism is reduced to case-by-case scenarios. While the plea for the recognition of differences has been an important corrective in the study of mysticism, if there are *only* differences, then we are reduced to merely picking out cases of mysticism but saying nothing about them. Huston Smith argues against this conclusion in his rebuttal to Katz; he suggests that, despite humanity's diverse cultural backgrounds, we can rise to a level of abstraction in the discussion of 'mysticism' to meet specific purposes or goals, just as, for example, 'the diverse cultural experience of delegates to the World Health Organization [hardly] prevents them from getting past Irish potatoes and Peking duck to talk about carbohydrates, nutrition, and (quite simply) food' (Smith, 1987: 556). The late Ninian Smart made this point as well, also using a vivid illustration; recognizing both uniqueness and typology in objects of study, he wrote:

> It is like our own case; my nose is like others' noses, but it is also unique in its configuration and history (even identical twins have tiny differences, as well as divergences of location and experience). We would expect, then, some typological likenesses in other traditions than our own. (Smart, 1985: 82–83).

However, recognizing the pitfalls of the *a priori* method of picking out religious experience one may instead choose an *a posteriori* analysis as a descriptive account of those events most often considered religious. On this strategy there seem to be four kinds of religious experience which appear to exhaust possible candidates:

1 supernaturalist intentional experiences
2 non-intentional experiences
3 non-experiences
4 insight experiences.

The first category uses 'intentional' in Franz Brentano's sense of distinguishing consciousness. Among the properties which constitute the mental event – call these the phenomenal properties – is the property of being intentional – that is, being directed to something other than itself. As mentioned above, this assumes a duality – a subject experiencing an object. The term 'supernaturalist' suggests that the event is not amenable to naturalistic explanation; the event even defies the possibility of naturalistic explanation. These experiences contain phenomenal properties which can include visual and auditory properties, perhaps less frequently the senses of touch and smell. But they can also include affective stimuli without sensory inputs.

The second category of experiences are those that are not directed towards anything; no subject–object duality emerges. These are non-intentional. This category naturally refers to the time of the event being experienced, and not to the judgements or interpretations following the event. Examples of this category might be intense physical pain; for a moment perhaps, one is completely identified with that pain – one *is* that pain. Then, only afterwards, one records the interpretation, '*I* was in pain', thereby re-establishing subject–object duality. The penultimate stage of yogic meditation, *asamprajñāta samādhi*, is an example of this radical identification as well. This category is necessary because adepts and scholastics of some traditions say that God or the Supreme is not an object, a proposition that we shall explore further in Chapter 2.

'Non-experiences' suggest those events which do not appear to be anything at all: sleep, coma or swoons might be examples here. This category is important because some traditions valorize some non-experiences as salvifically good. Hindu thinkers, for example, paid much attention to levels of consciousness, including dream states and dreamless sleep, as a teaching instrument concerning the supreme self. Indeed, the psychological exposition of the states of consciousness occurs in one of the oldest extant upaniṣads, the Māṇḍūkya.[18] What is at stake in these accounts is determining the presence or power of a form of consciousness which is not indexed to mental apparatuses, the so-called conceptualizing faculty, the *buddhi* or the sensory intake faculty, the *manas*.

The fourth category, insight experiences, suggests those particular moments in which something is learned whose scope goes far beyond the moment at which it occurs and is not limited to it. Conversion experiences may be examples of this, also flashes of understanding as exemplified by the Buddha's awakening or the *satori* of Zen masters.

Constructivism

The second problem in the contemporary discussion of religious experience is constructivism, although constructivism itself has a long intellectual history. Nevertheless, it seems reasonable to hold that human experiences could not occur unless the subject were in possession of certain culturally acquired habits and knowledge. All experience is culturally constructed, at least in part. In other words, culturally specific skills are among the necessary conditions for the possibility of the religious experience.

But are *all* religious experiences mediated by culture or are some not mediated? Earlier scholars thought there was some identifiable, isolatable, unique core experience, *sui generis*, and independent of culture or conditioning. This position was implicit in the work of early historians of religion, philosophers of religion and phenomenologists, and was popularized in the work of Huxley, Schuon, Smith and others. Katz, however, argues that conceptual and cultural conditioning is a causal factor in one's experience. This makes sense, but, at times, Katz makes a stronger claim, suggesting that such conditioning is *determinative* of the experience, in which case the experience seems wholly to be a product of intellectual, institutional and historical events.

Katz is making a transcendental claim about the nature of experience and sets out the necessary conditions for the possibility of an experience. However, arguing for strong causal connections between the experience and the antecedent cultural habits and training is one thing, and arguing that the very phenomenal properties of the experience are themselves always informed by local variables is another thing. It is for this reason that Katz's position has been viewed as 'hyper-Kantianism' by J. William Forgie (1985). Not only are the traditional (and universal) Kantian categories of judgement and the forms of sensuous intuition the conditioning factors

18 The continued appeal of the psychology of the Māṇḍūkya is evident in Sharma (1993a) and Indich (1995).

in knowing, but, according to Katz, (non-universal) concepts and beliefs of a particular religious tradition are as well. These 'category analogues', as Forgie calls them, operate causally and determine the phenomenological content of experience. Recognizing causal processes is important, especially in evaluating their contribution to justification or warrant. But there is a significant difference in saying that cultural habits are among necessary conditions for the experience and saying that these habits inform that experience at a given time. One may have a vision of Mary who may appear to me in ways that I have learned; but this training may not necessarily inform the experience when I have it. So, at least two forms of constructivism are possible. One is the transcendental position marked out by philosophers such as Steven Katz, which hold that cultural habits are among the necessary, and apparently sufficient, conditions for the possibility of the experience. The other position suggests a relationship of varying strength between cultural training and the particular experience. In this case, mediation is admitted to be necessary but need not be part of the phenomenal content of the experience.

Epistemology

The third problem is epistemological. When is it reasonable to say that religious experience is productive of knowledge? This, of course, is the heart of this book, but the answer to the question depends on how one responds to the problems of the identification of religious experience and its construction. But perhaps an even more basic question than the relationship between religious experience and knowledge is this: what exactly is knowledge after all? The answer to this question involves a complicated history, but several short notes should be sufficient to plot the trajectory of this study. Classical Greek concepts of knowledge included two themes, the second of which was later developed by modern epistemologists. The first theme suggests that knowledge involved direct, infallible acquaintance with reality, the participation in the ideal forms (Hick, 1966: 200). The second theme, found in the *Meno*, suggested that knowledge involved true beliefs. It is this second formulation that has been the source of much analysis in modern theories of knowledge. But since to say 'I know' registers the highest possible cognitive claim, the expression 'true belief' is an insufficient formulation of knowledge. To report that X knows P entails that P is true; however, to say X believes P does not entail that P is true (Hick, 1966: 201). P obviously could be false or P could even be true by the grace of good guesswork; and while P being false is obviously not an instance of knowledge, we are intuitively hard pressed to grant the 'diploma' of knowledge to beliefs that are true by chance or luck. So, contemporary formulations of what constitutes knowledge usually involve grounds or reasons for holding the belief to be true. But, as we will see in the next section, even this formulation is problematic. Nevertheless, the emphasis in Western epistemology has been on propositional knowledge – knowledge *that* something is the case. As John Hick suggests, 'to know', in this view, 'is to be confronted with fact or truth, and to be aware that one is confronted by it' (Hick, 1966: 201).

In India what counts as knowledge depends on the epistemological framework of the *pramāṇas*, the mechanisms which produce knowledge. This foundational premise is shared among the six *darśanas*. Cognitive outputs are properly called valid knowledge (*pramā*) when produced by properly functioning perceptual and reasoning equipment. For example: 'Right knowledge is accompanied by the mechanism of right knowledge' (Cowell and Gough, 1989: 228);[19] also, 'That which is the cause of valid knowledge is termed *pramāṇa*' (Revathy, 1994: 26).[20] In fact, the Nyāya Sūtra does not even offer a definition of knowledge, but instead first enumerates the mechanisms of right knowledge, in this case perception, inference, and testimony (1.3); this strategy appears to follow the maxim 'to know the thing to be measured, you must first know the measure' (Cowell and Gough, 1989: 228).[21] And both the Yoga Sūtra (1.7) and the *Sāṅkhya Kārikā* (1.4) also emphasize the mechanisms which produce knowledge: 'for the establishment of what is to be known depends on the means of right knowledge' (Sastri, 1948: 9).[22] In Chapter 2, I will expand this short discussion by an analysis of Vedāntic conceptions of knowledge which has its own sets of peculiarities.

Two related epistemological concerns include self-guaranteeing experiences and ineffability. Veridicality always relates to the external object. Are there experiences that guarantee veridicality? Is the supposed object in fact the way it appears? Many experiences involve powerful feelings of certainty, but certainty has to do with strong psychological conviction and not veridicality. One cannot read off veridicality simply by virtue of having had the experience. Veridicality is not given merely from the way it seems.

The other problem is ineffability, where the experience is inaccessible to language. This sentiment is neatly captured by a variety of upaniṣadic maxims such as is found in the *Brahmānanda valli* in the Taittirīya Upaniṣad, 'whence words return, along with the mind, failing to have grasped it (Brahman) ...'.[23] The Kaṭha Upaniṣad also speaks to the failure of language to express the Supreme, 'not indeed by speech, nor by the mind, nor by sight can it be attained'.[24] Yet, ineffability can be understood on two levels of varying strength. Strong ineffability is incoherent. If a person claims that the experience is inaccessible to language, then that person has said at least one thing about that experience and thus it is not technically ineffable. A weaker form of ineffability, however, seems to be a matter of common sense. Language never fully captures *any* experience, let alone religious experience. As Keith Yandell rather bluntly puts it, 'Your ordinary orange or toenail or window pane has a history whose details escape us ... but it does not follow that an orange

19 *pramāvyāptaṁ pramāṇam*

20 *pramāyāḥ karaṇaṁ yat tat pramāṇam iti gīyate*

21 *mānādhīnā meyasiddhiḥ iti nyāyena*

22 *prameyasiddhiḥ pramāṇāt*

23 ... *yato vāco nivartante, aprāpya manasā saha* (TU 2.4.1).

24 ... *naiva vācā na manasā prāptum śakyo na cakṣuṣā* (KU 2.3.12).

or toenail or window pane is ineffable' (Yandell, 1993: 68). The point is clear. Any object or event exists in a complex set of relations to whose complete content we have limited access. As someone once said, 'menus, after all, are not meals', and Indian teachers themselves are often fond of saying that one must actually taste sugar, not describe it. Nevertheless, words can make conceptual inroads to the object or experience, perhaps asymptotically approaching it. Indeed, Yandell reminds us that 'partial describability rules out ineffability' (Yandell, 1993: 68).

But Yandell makes a more important point – namely, that what is ineffable is equally distant from all concepts. If this is the case, then all descriptions are equally good or bad regarding the putative ineffable event or object. Considering religious experience, then, any description will do, since on this view language has no purchase whatsoever on the experience. The unfortunate conclusion is that any description will do on account of the insuperable gap between the object and its description. We may describe the experiences differently, 'perhaps as experiences of making cotton candy, or being tortured by a real expert or eating a bran muffin or going to the dentist …' (Yandell, 1993: 68). The point, finally, is that a strictly ineffable experience can have no religious significance. An experience becomes 'religious' when it links up with various content and actions: the experience is implicated in a variety of practices, doctrines and institutional settings. But an ineffable experience is 'unmoored', as it were, removed from such implications and thus removed of content or significance.

This point seems to have been overlooked by Steven Katz in a more recent edition in his series on mysticism, who accepts 'that all mystics claim ineffability', a position which is disputable on historical grounds (Jantzen, 1995a: 134). Moreover, Grace Jantzen's study of Christian mysticism calls into question the post-Enlightenment assumption (which Katz appears to accept) that mysticism always concerns intense, private, subjective experience and not, say, the mystical meaning of scripture, sacraments or the development of a mystical theology, which, in Christianity, concerns the mystery of God, not the subjective experience of believers (Janzen, 1995a: 134–35).[25] In addition to the philosophical criticisms of the ineffability thesis above, these criticisms indicate the need to examine, on historical grounds, claims about ineffability.

Even upaniṣadic intimations of ineffability, such as in the Taittirīya and Kaṭha Upaniṣad above, are balanced by suggestions of the importance of the mind as well as by two strategies for defining Brahman. So, in Kaṭha Upaniṣad 2.1.11 we see 'by mind alone is this to be obtained';[26] and in the Taittirīya we read the famous essential and accidental definitions of Brahman: Brahman is the real, the conscious, the infinite, and that which is the cause of the evolution and dissolution of the universe.[27] What should be clear from these comments is that putative claims to

25 Katz (2000) has since pressed his researches into the mystical significance of scriptural traditions.

26 *manasaiva idam āptavyam*

27 … *svarupalakṣaṇa; taṭasthalakṣaṇa: satyam, jñānam, anantam* (see TU 2.6, 2.7).

ineffability may often be better read as less literal cognitive judgements about the experience and more as value judgements: *there is something about this experience that is exceedingly special.* But even value judgements contain cognitive implicates, for such statements are not free-form and 'disembodied', as it were, but are instead 'enveloped' by intention, will and affect, all of which have cognitive associations. Moreover, despite the difficulty of capturing the experience in language, there is often an irresistible tendency among the subjects of varied experiences to communicate, convey and impart *something* of that event or experience. Few make the Buddha's or the *muni*'s choice of silence on these matters, but even silence speaks loudly about the experience: something extraordinary occurs in enlightenment events. However, for most of us, verbal communication seems normal and appropriate, for humans are not isolated units but persons implicated in settings where the sharing of ideas, feelings and experiences is the usual (and compelling) course of things. And this does not even take into consideration that, often, a stake is involved in communicating as clearly and effectively as possible the content of one's ideas or experiences.

In summary, then, the following questions continue to feature in any discussion about religious experience:

1 Exactly what is religious experience and what are the criteria used to pick it out? What counts as a religious experience?
2 What kind of constructivism is in place, causal or deterministic?
3 When is it reasonable to say that religious experience is productive of knowledge?

This book is most concerned with this final question, and so the remainder of this chapter will further unpack the scope of the problem.

Epistemology of religious experience

There are two main positions staked out here, cognitivism and non-cognitivism. Non-cognitivists, such as Katz, hold that there is no epistemic significance to religious experience. Non-cognitivism has varied nuances in this century and has roots in logical positivism and in the language game theory of Wittgenstein's later work. Bertrand Russell, for example, considered 'mysticism' to be merely emotional attitudes towards truths discovered by science and logic. Since emotions are subjective in the sense that they supply no objective truths about the extramental world, then mysticism is subjective and supplies no objective truths about the extramental world (Stace, 1961: 14). According to Russell, 'mysticism is in essence little more than a certain intensity and depth of feeling in regard to what is believed about the universe' (Russell, 1921: 3). Ignoring, for the moment, a rebuttal which argues for a significant cognitive dimension in human emotions, Russell's position nevertheless is a good example of one version of non-cognitivism.

Wittgenstein's later work replaced his own early version of positivism with language-game theory – namely, that words derive their meanings within given contexts or sets of language rules. In this case, the proper approach to religious language eschews the attempt to determine its meaning but instead determines its use. Meanings are no longer seen as labels, what the word 'pictures', as it were, but are now understood in terms of the function of the word. Words and sentences in themselves are not meaningful or meaningless, but make sense only in terms of doing something with them. Extending this to religious belief, Wittgenstein holds that the purpose of religious language is not to state empirical facts or to use language in the same manner as scientific standards and empirical verification. When theologians attempt to do this, religion amounts to 'bad science'. Instead, religious belief involves using a picture, and allowing it to regulate one's life. With regard to religious language, 'We don't talk about hypothesis, or high probability. Nor about knowing' (Wittgenstein, nd: 57). Bracketing, for the moment, certain criticisms of Wittgenstein's programme – such as his static concept of language[28] – this position reflects another important stream of non-cognitivism, one which emphasizes the performative use of language rather than the emotional content of religious terms. The most pressing problem with this philosophical project is not so much with the positive injunction to examine how religious language is actually used, but with rejecting the rational justification of religious language (Watts and Williams, 1988: 46). Fraser Watts and Mark Williams have argued that, if pushed to its limit, this position reaches a point of absurdity where it would prohibit all rational discussion of religious claims (ibid.). Moreover, 'neither Wittgenstein nor his followers have produced compelling arguments as to why religious beliefs *should* not be taken as involving rationally justifiable factual claims. At best, it has been shown that they *need* not be taken in this way' (ibid.).

The other camp wishes to affirm the cognitive content of religious claims, and one strategy used to achieve this goal pays close attention to the claims that follow religious experience. According to this approach, religious experience stands up to scrutiny and yields, according to certain scholars, positive epistemic results. Two prominent members of this group are William Alston and Alvin Plantinga. The work of these two scholars represents an important development in contemporary epistemology, for their theories of how we know anything at all decisively breach the forbidden Kantian territory of knowledge of God; perhaps more precisely, their work examines the epistemic nature of a person and the epistemic status of belief in God and concludes favourably for theism.[29] Indeed, Plantinga's work appears to be motivated by the inspiration of Anselm's creed, 'I believe in order to understand (*credo ut intelligam*)', and quite consciously indexes epistemological theory to a

28 And John W. Cook (1988) has called into question the entire language-game theory.

29 Richard Swinburne (1991) engages this project in his own way as well, mounting a massive cumulative case argument, complete with stultifying statistical analysis, by which he concludes that God's existence is more probable than not. This conclusion would hardly serve to warm the cockles of a *bhakta*'s heart, but it is an outcome of an original approach to philosophical theism.

theistic metaphysic. While I have sympathies with this approach, I do not think Plantinga's indexing of knowledge to theism is either necessary or advisable. His externalist account of knowledge is powerful as it stands; requiring theism to support it seems to be an extraordinary stretch, especially when non-theistic epistemologies, such as those of medieval Buddhist thinkers, are every bit as compelling.

Internalism and externalism

In any case, while Plantinga and Alston may be motivated by their faith commitments, their projects function within a broader epistemological conversation, one which responds to fundamental questions that have troubled thinkers in every generation: how is it that we know anything at all, and how do we know that we know? In contemporary Anglo-American philosophy, responses to these questions are captured by two theories of knowledge, 'internalism' and 'externalism'. Although many philosophers do not use these terms in a univocal sense, useful general characterizations can be made if we keep in mind our earlier disclaimer about typologies: these categories are not inscribed in the universe but are intended to sort through varied theoretical data and generate insights about how we come to know. Moreover, while the categories 'internalism' and 'externalism' are useful heuristics, we should not think that an 'iron curtain' separates the two; indeed, the 'bleeding of the boundaries' of externalism and internalism has already been recognized by some scholars (Fumerton, 1988; Alston, 1989; Swain, 1988). Furthermore, one conclusion of this study is that such synthetic projects should be advanced: a creative synthesis of the two epistemologies promises to resolve some of the theoretical and practical difficulties of each and may extend the boundaries of human knowledge, including knowledge of our environment in its broadest scope. But that is a later matter; first, let us consider the two categories which I will use to interpret certain medieval and modern Vedāntic soteriologies.

Internalism and externalism attempt to answer how we know and how we know that we know. Although these two questions constitute the two principal axes of epistemology, the internalism–externalism distinction has largely been applied to theories of epistemic justification – that is, how we know that we know. For my purposes, I will be using the terms as they apply to both questions, although I will take care to distinguish when I am addressing the mechanisms which produce knowledge and when I am addressing the justification of beliefs. Concerning the latter, internalism holds that the method for arriving at 'justified true belief' is, in a relevant sense, internal to the subject. The 'introspective turn' which often characterizes Enlightenment thought suggests that 'internalism' may find its intellectual roots in seventeenth- and eighteenth-century thought. In fact, Plantinga has argued that internalism has been the dominant epistemological tradition since the Enlightenment, although, according to his interpretation of the history of epistemology, one that interrupts the externalism of Aquinas and Aristotle

(Plantinga, 1993b: v). Externalism, on the other hand, is sometimes defined in opposition to internalism; for example, according to Kevin Meeker, the relevant distinction between the two terms is that 'Internalism, roughly speaking, is simply the thesis that the justifiedness of a belief is always a function of states internal (i.e., introspectively available) to the subject. As the name might suggest, externalism is the denial of this thesis' (Meeker, 1994: 107). In other words, externalism is the theory that at least some of the mechanisms that confer justification are not limited to internal states or inward processes of the subject; instead, some of these processes may be external to the believer's cognitive perspective. A more precise explanation follows, but let us first make sure that the framework of this discussion is properly circumscribed.

We must keep in mind that, in discussing theories of knowledge, we invariably focus on beliefs, the discursive verbal formulations of a subject. But, as we noted earlier, beliefs do not attain the status of knowledge without the assistance of other conditions; the belief must be true and the 'true belief' must, in some sense, be justified or warranted. Happenstance or luck cannot be the conferring authority to knowledge, but some other quality or property must be 'added' to the true belief in order for the belief to have 'positive epistemic status'.[30] Such a status suggests both evaluation and commitment; the belief has grounds, good reasons; it may be strongly warranted, and consequently we vigorously assent to it. Examples of such beliefs might be 'The sun will rise tomorrow', 'The sky is blue' and 'Two plus two equals four'. Beliefs that have negative epistemic status are weakly warranted; one grants assent, though dubiously. Here I may assent to the belief, but I do not feel entirely secure in my conviction. It may be that I do not understand the subject matter itself and instead must rely on the testimony of others. Examples of such beliefs might be 'The universe is infinitely large' or 'Betacarotene minimizes the impact of free radicals in the body'. I may know very little about either astrophysics or micronutrients, but I am willing to assent to these propositions based on the testimony of those who do know about them. All this suggests that the epistemic status of beliefs comes in varying degrees of justification or warrant. But this, in turn, raises fundamental questions, the answers to which distinguish our two epistemological theories. What criteria are used to decide when a belief has positive or non-positive epistemic status? In other words, what criteria are to be used to determine whether or not the belief is warranted? It is precisely the relationship to the warrant-producing quality that serves to distinguish internalism and externalism.

Internalism involves justification; in other words, a belief is justified by a rational process internal to the subject, and, according to some versions of

[30] Many epistemologists have attempted, with little unqualified success, to add a 'fourth condition' to mollify the famous examples. Edmund Gettier strikingly illustrated the limitations of the traditional definition of knowledge as justified true belief (1963: 121–23). Plantinga thinks the whole business is wrong-headed and indicates the need to rethink epistemology in terms of externalism.

internalism, when justified, *ought* to be granted assent. Plantinga expends considerable energy demonstrating the seamless garment of internalism, justification and deontology (Plantinga, 1993b: ch. 1). It is for this reason that he uses the term 'warrant', thereby hoping to escape the negative associations with deontology. An externalist account of knowing holds that at least some of the relevant warrant-conferring processes are external to the subject. According to some deontological accounts, however, rational persons, in fact, *must* assent to beliefs that have been justified; otherwise they fail in their epistemic duties. In reply, theorists of externalism argue that one cannot be held responsible for a duty that is, in principle, impossible to execute. It is unreasonable, for example, to expect one to track down the warrant of some propositions accepted through testimony – for example, 'The universe is infinitely large'. To do so would entail learning highly complicated mathematics and reviewing the relevant research in astrophysics, a project clearly beyond the abilities of most people. Besides, according to Plantinga, the vast majority of beliefs are not under our control at all; one cannot have a duty with regard to beliefs that are not voluntary. Discussion over epistemic duties suggests that we know how we got the belief. But we frequently form beliefs without being able to reproduce the causal chain of knowledge. Only a small set of beliefs is voluntary – Plantinga suggests 1 per cent – and these are the interesting ones for epistemology.

Although Plantinga's interpretation of classical epistemology is persuasive, I see no necessary link between internalism and deontology, and for this reason I use the terms justification and warrant interchangeably. Nevertheless, much of the debate surrounding internalism concerns justification. According to some versions of this epistemological tradition, what gives 'positive epistemic status' is the mechanism of introspection; through the process of introspection, the knower has some sort of privileged access to a standard or state which in turn confers justification. Although he does not use the term 'internalism', John Hick has aptly characterized this theory as follows:

> There can therefore be no question of a criterion of knowledge external to the act of knowing; knowing is a self-contained process. The claim to know requires no endorsement from outside; knowledge shines in its own light with a sufficient and self-certifying authority. (Hick, 1966: 202)

This passage captures well the claim and spirit of internalism, and we shall have occasion to recall it when we come to important parallels in Indian materials. For now, the epistemological method of internalism should be clear; in this scenario, the subject introspects and examines beliefs to determine whether they are self-evident or incorrigible. Descartes is the classic example of subjectivist introspection. His strategy of methodic doubt demanded a scrutiny to determine one thing certain and indubitable – 'I am a thing that thinks' – from which one eventually arrives at clear and distinct ideas as touchstones of truth.

Owing to this process of determining touchstones of truth – foundations of knowledge – internalism is sometimes associated with another subset of epistemology, foundationalism. According to this theory, certain beliefs are self-justifying – that is, they require no further justification – and form the basis of other, more complicated beliefs. These 'epistemologically basic beliefs' constitute the foundation on which a superstructure of other beliefs is constructed. While foundationalism has been associated with classical modern internalist epistemologies, some theorists of externalism, including Alston and Plantinga, appeal to it as well. Plantinga, for example, argues that belief in God might be considered 'properly basic' while Alston, as we will see, argues that beliefs based on mystical perception require no further justification other than the perception itself, much in the same way as beliefs that follow sense perception. What is important to note about foundationalism, for our purposes, is the immediacy of the internal state implied in the basic beliefs and the ability of the subject to somehow access it. This, we will see, has direct application to Indian theories of saving experience, for 'religious experience' (*anubhava*) is sometimes represented as an experience of 'direct perception' or 'immediate awareness', both self-justifying and self-authenticating. In sum, internalism involves, above all, individual and subjective introspection, a privileged access to inner standards or states, and, sometimes, foundationalist accounts of justification and epistemic 'duties' to believe.

Externalism, as suggested above, involves warrant-conferring mechanisms which are external to the agent. In this case, the subject has no privileged access to standards by which to judge data, and this seems to be the relevant distinguishing characteristic among the various forms of externalism. An important version of externalism is reliabilism; in this case, the subject is engaged in (external) belief-forming processes that should be evaluated in terms of their reliability in producing true beliefs; justification of the belief is largely a result of an 'appropriate causal ancestry' of the belief and its relationship to reliable belief-forming mechanisms (Swain, 1988: 461). Laurence BonJour (1992: 133) considers reliabilism to be the most prominent version of externalism; and, indeed, Plantinga himself admits that it is an approximation of epistemological truth, perhaps even 'a zeroeth approximation to the truth of the matter' (1993b: 212). The main requirement for justification in this version of externalism is roughly 'that the belief be produced in a way or via a process that makes it objectively likely that the belief is true' (BonJour, 1992: 133). What distinguishes this view from internalism is the relationship to justification. According to some versions of internalism, the subject introspects and, through this inward process, is aware of the justifying grounds of belief (a strong version) or at least is capable of becoming aware of them (a weak version). According to some versions of reliabilism, the subject is not required to have a reason for thinking that the belief is true, but is nonetheless epistemically justified in accepting it on account of the (external) (reliable) process. One can see that such a view does indeed mark a break from classical modern epistemology, especially that of Descartes, which 'identifies epistemic justification with having a reason, perhaps even a conclusive reason for thinking that the belief is true' (ibid.).

But Plantinga faults versions of reliabilism for failing to include a crucial component of warrant, namely 'proper function'. His epistemology is thus 'naturalized'; humans are equipped with a cognitive 'design plan': we are endowed – by God or evolution or both – with cognitive faculties to be utilized in an environment properly suited to them. When these faculties function properly, and in an appropriate cognitive environment, the outputs of such processes have warrant. Examples of such mechanisms which produce knowledge are perception, testimony and memory. These mechanisms, of course, have been long debated in Indian epistemology. However, I wish to extend them as far as possible into the *paramārthika*, asymptotically approaching a cognitive realm beyond concepts, a 'knowing beyond knowledge'. To do this I wish to consider the epistemic efficacy of 'spiritual' perception, the testimony of the saints and sacred memory, the fountainheads for divine knowledge. These all presume socially established 'doxastic practices' which, under specific conditions, confer at least *prima facie* justification on religious beliefs. A very useful entrée into doxastic practice theory, especially that of 'spiritual' or mystical perception, is the important work by William Alston, and it is to his version of externalism that I now turn.

Alston's externalism: perceiving God

William Alston's strategy is to show that direct experiential awareness of God – what he calls mystical perception – enjoys *prima facie* justification much in the same way that we take it for granted in sensory perception. Alston argues that there is a generic identity of structure between mystical perception and sensory perception. In both cases, Alston argues, *something* is presented to the perceiver. Here he rejects the usual construal of 'mystical experiences' as purely subjective events with no objective reference; in this case, the subject of experience is often forced to generate reasons for supposing a transcendent cause for the experience. Instead, according to Alston's perceptual model of religious experience, perceiving God is direct and does not require further justification, much in the same way that perceiving the tree outside my window is direct and requires no further justification. In both cases, something is presented to consciousness. Given his perceptual model of mystical experience, 'we will at least have to take seriously the view that a claim to be perceiving God is *prima facie* acceptable just on its own merits, pending any sufficient reason to the contrary' (Alston, 1991: 67).

Alston recognizes that the perceptual model of religious experience has been argued in various forms before. A variety of Catholic mystical theologians have taken mystical experience to be a form of perception. Thomas Aquinas, for example, described knowledge by 'connaturality', which he saw as the basis of the contemplative knowledge of God. The union of the lover and the beloved involved a 'knowledge by acquaintance', but such knowledge also implies an enrichment of understanding; thus Aquinas's epistemological framework makes room for the possibility of direct religious knowing. Contemporary writers have also defended treating experiential awareness of God as a mode of perception, including John Hick, William Wainwright, and Watts and Williams, although these last writers approach perception more from the perspective of cognitive psychology. Nevertheless, Watts and Williams, with Alston, argue that 'there are essential similarities between religious knowing and other everyday forms of knowing' (Watts and Williams, 1988: 38). In this programme, religious knowing is 'cognitive in the sense that it is reached by cognitive processes that are somewhat similar to those by which other forms of human knowledge are reached' (ibid.: 5). Walter Stace has also argued the same point in *Mysticism and Philosophy*; reacting, as does Alston, to the criticism that mystical states are purely subjective while sense perceptions alone have objective reference on account of their supposed external stimuli, Stace writes:

> The existence of the external stimuli in the case of sense perception is not known independently of the sense experience. Their existence is itself an interpretation of that experience. Hence in this respect sense experience and mystical experience are on the same footing. In both cases the existence of anything objective to which they refer is an interpretation of the experience and nothing more. If the fact that we cannot perceive material objects without eyes, ears, and brains does not prevent us from interpreting sense experiences as having objective reference, neither need the fact that we cannot have mystical experiences without its appropriate physiological machinery cause us to conclude that it can be nothing but subjective illusion. (Stace, 1961: 28–29)

Alston argues there is no non-circular way of justifying perceptual beliefs, and Stace comes to much the same conclusion: 'Indeed, the very existence of a world independent of consciousness is an interpretation of sense experience which is not capable of being logically demonstrated.' And Joachim Wach argues, with John Baillie, that knowledge of the reality of God is not the result of an inference of any kind, 'whether explicit or implicit, whether laboriously excogitated or swiftly intuited' (Wach, 1966: 51). Indeed, Wach notes with approval an observation that 'one does not want merely inferred friends, so how could one possibly be satisfied with an inferred God?' (ibid.). These passages all suggest that the perceptual beliefs which are the outcome of mental and perceptual faculties are at least *prima facie* justified. However, while there are important similarities in the reflections of these authors and in Alston's position, there is one important difference. Alston admits that normal adult sense perception is heavily conceptualized; it is 'shot through with "interpretation"' (Alston, 1991: 27). Still, he insists, against Katz, Proudfoot and others, that something is *given* or directly presented to consciousness which is distinguishable from any elements of conceptualization. Criticizing Proudfoot and other subjectivists who insist, following Kant, that there is no uninterpreted *given* (a view, according to Alston, which has 'attained the status of dogma' in philosophy),

Alston enters the narrow gate of the psychology of perception and argues for the 'essentially nonconceptual, nonjudgmental character of *appearance* or *presentation*' in both sensory and mystical perception. 'From the fact that we use concepts to identify something as of a certain type (How else?!), it does *not* follow that *what* we are identifying "involves" concepts and judgments' (ibid.: 41). This is the most important point of continuity among the structures of mystical perception and sensory perception. Establishing the shared generic structure is central to his argument: just as sensory perceptual beliefs, produced of established practices and free of the witness of 'overriders', are granted *prima facie* justification, so mystical perceptual beliefs, produced of socially established practices and free of the witness of overriders, are granted *prima facie* justification.

Alston, it should be pointed out, speaks in terms of epistemic justification of perceptual beliefs, rather than in terms of knowledge, because of the complicated issues surrounding knowledge adverted to in the previous section. For example, 'I can't know that God is loving unless it is true that God is loving, and the latter in turn implies that God exists, something I will not be arguing for in this book ...' (ibid.: 2). This is a decidedly more cautious approach, but still worthwhile, for it probes the possibility and scope of the cognitive dimension of religious experience.

The troubling concern, however, and one that Alston recognizes but pays insufficient attention to, is how to reconcile the variety of mystical beliefs. On the model of sensory perception Alston introduces a variety of checks and balances for producing and evaluating beliefs – what he calls socially established doxastic practices. Alston argues that it is rational to engage in any socially established doxastic practice provided that we do not have sufficient reasons for regarding it as unreliable. The questions here, of course, are what counts as reliable and who establishes such standards? Nevertheless, Alston extends this framework to religious experience; mystical perception, like sensory perception, is considered a socially established doxastic practice. However, the difficulty is clear: the plurality of mystical, doxastic practices, many of them with mutually contradictory output or background belief systems, confuses matters. He concludes that, although this is 'not epistemically the best of all possible worlds, it is rational in this situation for one to continue to participate in the (undefeated) practice in which s/he is involved, hoping that the inter-practice contradictions will be sorted out in time' (ibid.:7). This is a weak conclusion, although it is an honest admission of the challenges facing the philosopher of religion.

Thomas Merton made a similar appeal to monks and theologians just prior to his untimely death in Bangkok; with regard to those moments when philosophical differences among religions seem utterly intractable, he urged his fellow contemplatives, Buddhist and Christian, to 'let them be left intact until a moment of greater understanding' (Merton 1975: 316). I will suggest in Chapter 5, however, that the implications of *prima facie* justification are profound, for they challenge philosophers of religion to examine 'inter-practice contradictions' in a careful, systematic way, allowing, minimally, for the potential of increased self-understanding and understanding of the broadest scope of our environment. Such outcomes reveal once again the intimate relationship that obtains between epistemology, anthropology and metaphysics.

While Alston has been criticized for establishing 'mere' *prima facie* justification and the 'reasonableness' of a religious universe characterized by mutually contradictory doxastic practices, his is a major contribution to the study of religious experience which also has important implications in interfaith dialogue. What I wish to bear in mind from Alston's epistemology of religious experience are two elements: the continuities between sensory and mystical perception and the importance of external means for producing religious beliefs. Both these ideas will be important factors in our analysis of certain Indian accounts of worship and meditation.

Epistemologies of religious experience in classical and modern Vedānta

Building on the previous section, I will use the distinction between internalist and externalist epistemologies as an interpretative tool in an important stream of Indian thought, Vedānta. Vedānta is one of the six *darśanas* of Indian philosophy and has been the object of much study and fascination among Western scholars. This is due in part to the early Romantic projections on to Vedānta as well as to its use among neo-Hindu apologists, such as Vivekānanda. But Vedānta, while operating out of a set of peculiar intellectual presuppositions and goals that are unique among the *darśanas*, is by no means homogeneous. The usual representation of Vedānta considers this field of inquiry to proceed from the knowledge portion of the Veda (*jñāna kāṇḍa*). The term 'Vedānta' means 'end of the Vedas', and apologists for this *darśana* often construe this expression to include both literal import and axiological value. Thus, Vedānta has, for its central texts, the end or the last texts of the Vedic canon, the upaniṣads, and Vedānta itself is the 'last word' on Vedic reflection. An attempt at a coherent expatiation of the central teaching of the upaniṣads took shape in a lengthy series of aphorisms, often unintelligible without commentary, called the Brahma Sūtra, ascribed to Bādarāyaṇa (*c.* 100 BCE). This foundational text of Vedānta includes redactions from numerous editors over the span of several centuries and received its final form by the middle of the fifth century of the common era (Mayeda, 1992: 12). Later, the Vedānta school represented itself as that body of thought founded on the threefold foundation (*prasthānatraya*): the upaniṣads, the Brahma Sūtra and the *Bhagavad-Gītā*.

Classical Vedānta is usually inflected in three main schools, all founded or organized in India between the eighth and thirteenth centuries of the common era. These are the Advaita of Śaṅkara (*c.* eighth century CE), the Viśiṣṭādvaita of Rāmānuja (*c.* eleventh century CE), and the Dvaita of Madhva (*c.* thirteenth century). All of these schools of Vedānta share similar rhetorical strategies and metaphysical presuppositions: soteriological problems of ignorance and action implicate the embodied soul (*jīva*) in the round of birth, death and rebirth; the Supreme Brahman is, in some relevant sense, both transcendent with respect to the universe and immanent within it (*antaryāmin*); the Brahma Sūtra is the authoritative epitome of upaniṣadic doctrine (although the founding *ācāryas* felt impelled to interpret the sūtras according to their metaphysical predilections).

Despite these and other shared values, there are considerable differences among these schools, the most important being the way in which the relationship between the Supreme Brahman and the individual Self, the *ātman*, is understood: Advaita presents a radically non-dualistic metaphysic; Viśiṣṭādvaita argues for a non-dual real which is nonetheless qualified by sentient and insentient reals (*cidacidīśvara*); and Dvaita propounds a straightforward dualism that perhaps formally comes closest to the traditional philosophical theism of Christianity.

I will be most concerned with Advaita in two historical permutations, the classical Advaita of Śaṅkara and his immediate disciples and the Advaita of a modern proponent of non-dualism, Ramaṇa Maharṣi. Additionally, I will refer to Rāmānuja, the *darśana pravartaka* of Viśiṣṭādvaita, whose reflections, including those on religious experience, are often in stark contrast to those of Śaṅkara. With special regard to Vedāntic soteriology, I will use the categories of internalism and externalism to examine the processes of knowing religiously and the epistemic status of beliefs that follow from those processes. Using the background of the contemporary debate on the epistemic significance of religious experience outlined in the previous section, I will demonstrate that, while both structures of internalism and externalism are evident in these representations of Advaita, internalism is dominant, ambiguously in the case of our classical subjects, and unambiguously in the case of Ramaṇa Maharṣi. Although Advaita is my primary focus, for contrast I will argue, in Chapter 5, that Viśiṣṭādvaita operates decisively from externalism with concomitant social and epistemic implications.

Our classical Advaitin subjects, while ostensibly internalist, nevertheless place high value – despite theoretical disclaimers – on external mechanisms, especially *śruti*, *adhikāra*, *varṇāśrama* and karma; these create a culture of liberation. The extent to which these external, socially established mechanisms are among the necessary conditions for saving knowledge determines whether the tradition is universalist or locked in its local context. A tension between the poles of internalism and externalism is seen in classical Advaita, but the Advaita of Ramaṇa Maharṣi operates decisively from internalism. This modern version of Advaita, revealing a greater congruence between its metaphysic and epistemology of religious experience, liberates Advaita from its local context and is properly universalist.

Chapter 5 addresses these social observations and returns to the epistemological questions that serve as the inspiration for this project: what do we know in religious experience, and how do we know it? Based on our analyses of Advaitin epistemologies of religious experience, I argue that there is a knowing beyond knowledge or, perhaps more precisely, that the claim 'there is a knowing beyond knowledge' is *prima facie* justified. Such a conclusion might be considered minimalist in terms of epistemic merit, but it should also be considered maximalist in terms of opportunity. While *prima facie* justification here does not demonstrate apodictically the truth of non-dualism, it offers a critical and constructive opportunity for philosophers: by examining the range and conditions of such justification, we approach, asymptotically and conceptually, the knowing beyond knowledge that is at the heart of Advaitin religious experience, which, according to Advaita, is the very heart of reality itself.

CHAPTER 2

The epistemology of religious experience in Śaṅkara

Introduction

This section examines Śaṅkara's work and concludes that, in the main, his dominant epistemology of religious experience is internalism. Perhaps in the best of philosophical worlds, cleanly contoured boundaries in which all things neatly fall into place might be considered a desideratum. But this hardly ever happens in life or in philosophy. Things are always a bit more complicated, a bit muddy. This is why I argue that Śaṅkara's epistemology of religious experience is *in the main* internalistic or in its *most important sense* internalistic, a controverted position, even with its qualification. Recent work by Anantand Rambachand (1991) and Francis Clooney (1993), for example, tends to emphasize the external structures for producing saving knowledge in the thought of Śaṅkara. But the scope of internalism and externalism includes theories of justification or warrant in addition to reflections on processes which generate knowledge. This chapter will examine Śaṅkara's epistemology of religious experience and argue that, while an important creative dialectic between externalism and internalism is evident in his reflections, internalism best accounts for his method of gaining saving knowledge, and, more importantly, justifies the sacred experience (*anubhava*) itself.

Before launching into our study, a word justifying yet another examination of Śaṅkara is in order. While it is true that Śaṅkara's work has appealed to Western scholars since at least the eighteenth century, there is good reason for this, even apart from intellectual predilections on the part of those scholars. Śaṅkara's work is compelling, challenging, radical and, moreover, sufficiently ambiguous to warrant repeated inquiries. A comparison to ongoing reappraisals in Western philosophy may be the perennial studies of Aristotle, Kant or Hume.

Moreover, it is precisely because of the enduring scholarly – and popular – appeal of Śaṅkara that a fresh study is warranted. Considerable discussion of *anubhava* in Śaṅkara has already emerged in the academy, although it is my view that this discussion has not been exhausted. I wish to join that conversation and add to it, especially by using the interpretative epistemological categories of internalism and externalism as heuristic devices to generate insight into the prospect and possibility for a knowing beyond knowledge.

These categories allow us to examine the statements of Śaṅkara on the method and means of 'producing' religious experience and its consequent justification. This in turn allows us to re-examine not just the scholarly, but the popular, appeal of Śaṅkara and determine its range of coherence. If the primary engine for awareness is internalism, a cross-cultural, universal programme of salvation seems reasonable, for it makes certain assumptions about the nature of the human person and his or her powers of accessing saving knowledge. If the primary engine for awareness rests fundamentally on an externalist methodology and proposes a self-contained circle of justification, a more culturally restrictive agenda for liberation emerges. This in turn may make some universalist programmes of propagation and conversion incoherent – a dilemma which subverts various neo-Vedāntic versions of inclusivism as a response to the problem of religious pluralism. However, if the dominant theory of saving knowledge and its justification is largely internalist, then Advaita succeeds as a universalist movement. And, while epistemologies of religious experience cannot exhaustively account for a tradition's universality – other dynamics, both intrinsic and extrinsic to the tradition, must be factored as well – an internalist methodology in Advaita contributes in no small measure to its successful migration to the West.

Two other reasons for returning to Śaṅkara can be advanced. First, Śaṅkara is the great systematizer and institutional founder of Advaita; it would behove virtually any analysis of Advaita to return to its organizing source. Versions of Vedānta have, of course, existed in India since before the common era. One Vedāntin philosopher, Bādarāyaṇa, attempted a coherent interpretation of the upaniṣads in the Brahma Sūtra, although we have little hard evidence of any monastic or other institutional programme which he supported beyond the Brahmin ideology of *varṇāśramadharma*. Moreover, although Śaṅkara interprets the Brahma Sūtra according to Advaita, some contemporary scholars tend to think that a version of Viśiṣṭādvaita more accurately represents Bādarāyaṇa's thought.[1]

Gauḍapāda is another candidate to begin a study of foundational Vedānta, although his work is perhaps even more controverted than that of Śaṅkara.[2] I will refer to Gauḍapāda's thought where appropriate, especially since Śaṅkara's radical Advaita is no more so than Gauḍapāda's. Advaita tradition, of course, considers Gauḍapāda to be the *paramaguru* of Śaṅkara. Śaṅkara's work, however, involves a broader scope, more texts and perhaps more nuances. It has been the foundation on which rests the thought of his immediate and later disciples. In addition to the literary and philosophical reasons for beginning this study with Śaṅkara, another reason is that Śaṅkara is also reputed to have organized monastic institutions, *maṭhas*, for Advaitin renunciants – an important and telling development since it represents the creation of a particular

[1] A.B. Keith, for example, cites the work of Thibault, Suktankar and Jacobi and agrees with them that 'the real view taken by Bādarāyaṇa was more akin to, though not identical with, that taken by the commentary of Rāmānuja ...' (Keith, 1989: 508). Radhakrishnan, one of the principal apologists for Advaita in this century, concurs (1989: 669).

[2] For example, just who Gauḍapāda was and to what extent his *kārikā* is Buddhist remain live issues. See Karmarkar (1973: introduction), Fox (1993: 3–40), and King (1995).

culture which conduces to liberation; such institutionalization has important externalist implications in Advaita epistemology of religious experience.

Additionally, a study of Śaṅkara yields benefits also due to the later challenges of Rāmānuja, the formidable exponent of Viśiṣṭādvaita. There are considerable differences between these two thinkers; for our purposes, we will consider Rāmānuja's challenges to Śaṅkara's epistemology of religious experience. While a delicate balancing act between externalism and internalism can be seen in Śaṅkara, Rāmānuja's epistemology of religious experience is decidedly externalist. Moreover, he holds out for a clear cognitive output of religious experience, a conclusion that obviously accords well with traditional Christian thought, not to mention the contemporary work of Alston and Plantinga. By carefully marking out the boundaries of internalism in our Advaitin thinkers, we will see the stark contrast of Rāmānuja's externalism. The study of these two traditions in Vedānta has the added benefit of showing that the dilemmas of religious experience, including the tension between cognitivism and non-cognitivism, were live issues in classical India far earlier than they developed after the Enlightenment in Europe.

Finally, a word is necessary on the selection of texts and the method I have chosen to select them. There have been many approaches to the study of Śaṅkara over the years, with philological, philosophical, historical approaches perhaps taking the lead. Each of these approaches has contributed to our understanding of Śaṅkara's thought, but each comes with its own set of assumptions and a particular framework that may be reductive or procrustean. Much recent work has criticized the philosophical approach for excising Śaṅkara's 'philosophy' (itself a Western term packed with Western assumptions) from its exegetical and ritual contexts. Francis Clooney, for example, has argued that Vedānta is properly understood 'only when we understand it as a conscious intersection between the philosophical and the commentarial projects, and not as one or the other alone' (Clooney, 1992: 48). His own model, the first plank in a broader programme of comparative theology, retrieves the Advaita 'Text' by closely following the inter- and intratextual developments in the commentarial programme of Advaita (Clooney, 1993). Resituating Advaita philosophy in the context of commentary is an important corrective in the study of Vedānta, for it protects against overly abstract and decontextualized interpretations, perhaps best exemplified by the nineteenth-century German Romantics.

While contemporary scholars of Vedānta have recently redirected their attention to commentary and exegesis, in 1959 the French Indologist Madeleine Biardeau also sounded an early warning note concerning too philosophical an approach to Vedānta; in an article analysing Śaṅkara's use of apophatic speech, she cautioned, 'There is, perhaps, a danger in wishing to over-systematize the thought of an author and to perceive relationships between different aspects of his work which appear as being independent because they respond to different problems.'[3] This 'danger' again

---

[3] Il y a peut-être un danger à vouloir trop systématiser la pensée d'un auteur et à percevoir des

speaks to the problem of excessively tidy evaluations of a particular thinker. Biardeau's caution suggests the need to recognize an appropriate 'localism', not just of a thinker's body of work situated in a particular historical and philosophical context, but also of the specific problems which the thinker addresses in that body of work. But, as Jonathan Bader has observed, Biardeau herself nonetheless presses on with her own analysis of Śaṅkara's use of language 'on the assumption that in a coherent philosophy the basic postulates are implicit throughout' (Bader, 1990: 21). This is my assumption as well. There are subtleties, nuances, ambiguities and apparent contradictions in Śaṅkara's work, many of which have been carefully examined by contemporary scholars. Nevertheless, there is a rather clear metaphysic operating in Śaṅkara's texts, which often serves as the principal focus of exegesis or discussion in many of his comments on the Brahma Sūtra, the *Gītā*, and the oldest upaniṣads; and much of this discussion is reviewed and re-presented in the *Upadeśasāhasrī*, the one *prakaraṇa* text which most scholars hold to be properly ascribed to Śaṅkara. While Śaṅkara's understanding of the nature of reality is the primary focus of his comment and exegesis, it also serves as the inchoate backdrop for discussion of all other issues as well, from painstaking word-for-word comment on upaniṣadic texts to important matters of social intercourse and spiritual methodology.

Moreover, the broadest context of Śaṅkara's works is the problem of suffering and the hope of liberation, so his metaphysic is decisively indexed to soteriology. Since these intimately related areas constitute two of his main theoretical and practical concerns, I shall focus on texts that directly engage them. Certainly, Śaṅkara himself was concerned with the problem of religious experience, although he was hardly burdened with the same kinds of question that I bring to it. More specifically, his work concerns the nature of experience *per se* and the appropriate methods to access it. Although obviously the context, goals and methods of Śaṅkara's interpretation of the *prasthānatraya* are different from those of my study of Śaṅkara's thought, there is a common ground between them – namely, an interest in experience and, more specifically, saving experience. Indeed, discovering the common ground in classical and modern philosophical inquiry may be the first step in gaining fresh insight into particularly persistent questions. By bringing contemporary Western discussion of religious experience to bear on relevant metaphysical and soteriological discussion in Śaṅkara's work, I hope to gain insight into what we can know in religious experience and what we can say about it. For Śaṅkara and non-dual *jīvanmuktas*, such insight perhaps matters little and, by definition, is impossible. Still, it matters much to many thinkers and may have deep implications for those who not only think about spirituality but practise it.

A final word about the dates and texts of Śaṅkara. Although the issue is fraught with much controversy, most contemporary scholars of Advaita now hold that

---

relations entre différents aspects de son oeuvre qui se présentent comme indépendants parce qu'ils répondent à des problèmes différents' (Biardeau, 1959: 87), quoted in Bader (1990: 21).

Śaṅkara lived sometime between 700 and 750 CE.[4] And, while traditional followers of Advaita often attribute hundreds of texts to Śaṅkara, careful historical and literary analysis by Paul Hacker, Hajime Nakamura, Sengaku Mayeda and others have reduced the 'authentic' corpus of Śaṅkara to the following texts: *Brahma Sūtra Bhāṣya* (BSB), the *Bhagavad Gītā Bhāṣya* (BGB), the *Upadeśasāhasrī* (Up.) and the commentaries on the so-called principal upaniṣads: Bṛhadāraṃyaka (BU), Chāndogya (CU), Aitareya (AU), Taittirīya (TU), Kena (KeU), Īśa (IU), Kaṭha (KU), Muṇḍaka (MuU), Praśna (PU), and Māṇḍūkya (MU).[5] I will comment on relevant passages in these texts which address 'religious' experience (*anubhava*) as the process and terminus of authentic saving experience. But it should be noted once more that Śaṅkara's own method situates him in an exegetical tradition which weaves philosophical and social analysis into the interpretation of the fundamental formative texts of the tradition. These texts and the process of commentary are crucial doxastic mechanisms, and thus a critical externalist constraint on knowledge becomes apparent from the outset. To explain, let me now turn to the internalist and externalist processes in Śaṅkara's thought.

Internalism and externalism in Śaṅkara

Although there are very strong internalist tendencies in Śaṅkara's programme – which I will highlight – his work nevertheless engages a culturally powerful programme of Brahmin ideology among whose most persistent concerns is the authority of the Veda and its proper transmission. This fact alone necessitates the recognition of a significant element of externalism in Śaṅkara's thought, for the objective, impersonal Veda (however one interprets its contents) is the premier pattern and guide for all Vedāntins, Advaitin or not. Just how this guide is used or viewed is another question. With this concern in mind, I will examine the externalist dimension in Śaṅkara's Vedānta in 'The Culture of Liberation in Śaṅkara'. Here, let me engage a 'first take' on the tension between internalism and externalism in Śaṅkara.

While the mechanisms of externalism begin or generate the programme for

---

4 'Setting the date of Śaṅkara's birth is probably one of the most controversial problems in the history of Indian philosophy, not only because he is one of the greatest Indian philosophers but also because a solution is inseparable from the correct understanding of one of the most important and critical periods of the history of Indian thought' (Mayeda, 1992: 3). Mayeda briefly reviews the literature on Śaṅkara's dates and agrees with Nakamura, Renou and Ingalls.

5 When referring to Śaṅkara's commentary on a particular upaniṣad, I append the abbreviation 'B'. The editions of Śaṅkara's texts which I will use are the following; *Upaniṣadbhāṣyam: With Commentaries by Ānandagiri and Others*, 3 vols, ed. S. Subrahmanyaśāstri (nd); *Śrīmad Bhagavad Gītā Bhāṣya of Śri Saṁkarācārya*, ed. and trans. A.G. Krishna Warrier (1993); *Brahmasūtra with Śaṅkarabhāṣya* (1990); *Upadeśasāhasrī with the Commentary of Ānandagiri*, ed. S. Subrahmanyaśāstri (nd).

liberation, in the end it must surrender its authority to a profoundly internalistic mechanism for producing saving knowledge. In this there may be a parallel with the early Buddhist assessment of desire or craving (*tṛṣṇa*). Desire, in this view, is the fatal flaw which creates attachment, which in turn produces inevitable suffering. The Noble Eightfold Path is the means by which desire or craving is subdued and which thereby eliminates suffering. But obviously some sort of desire is needed to begin the Buddhist path of salvation. This Buddhists admit, but claim that after 'jump-starting' the soteriological programme, desire, even for salvation, falls away and dissolves as a substantive contradiction.

Similarly, externalism 'jump-starts' the programme of salvation in Śaṅkara's Advaita, but eventually yields to a profoundly internalistic dynamic. Thus the Veda reveals the non-dual real, but even the Veda, as an external mechanism of revelation and instruction, must eventually fall away owing to its concern with multiple empirical distinctions; recall the instruction of BU 4.3.22: *atra vedāvedāḥ*, which Śaṅkara glosses as that state beyond ignorance, desire, and action.[6] *Gītā* 2.45 echoes this sentiment as well: 'The Vedas have as their content the three constituents; be free of these, Arjuna!'[7] What is it that the Vedas illustrate, according to Śaṅkara? The scope of transmigratory existence: *traiguṇyaṁ samsāraḥ viṣayaḥ prakāśayitavyaḥ* (BGB 67).

Still, the Veda is often understood as the oral accounts of the religious experience of ancient seers. 'Seeing' (*darśan*) is particularly important on many levels in Indian thought and practice, and has been the subject of numerous studies, most notably those by Diana Eck (1985) and Lawrence Babb (1981). Our concern later will be the apparently cognitivist thought of Rāmānuja, which at face value recalls the perception of the ancient sages – what Gonda calls 'mystical supernormal beholding' or 'visionary experiencing' (Gonda, 1963: 28); in several remarkable passages Rāmānuja addresses a heightened state of meditative absorption in which a form of spiritual beholding is possible, desirable and indicative of the most sublime states of *bhakti*. Such considerations of spiritual beholding or mystical perception will reflect back on our earlier discussion of William Alston's epistemology of religious experience. For now, the importance of the Veda as a record of experience cannot be underestimated. For the Advaitin, however, the Veda is 'represented as the objective guide which anticipates and guides all legitimate religious experience but which ultimately negates itself in non-dual realization' (Halbfass, 1990: 391).

For Śaṅkara the external aids – testimony, perception and scripture – have relative value on account of their location in time and space (*vyavahārika*), although he labours methodically to ensure the superiority of the Veda as the pre-eminent revelation of the transpersonal, transworldly real. Nevertheless, the primary assumption in his metaphysic, the non-dual real, implies a turn to the subject to

6 ... *avidyākāmakarmavinirmuktam eva tadrupam* (BUB 332).

7 ... *traiguṇyaviṣayā vedā nistraiguṇyo bhavārjuna.*

determine the truth of that assumption; 'on account of being the Self of all, the truth of Brahman is established'.[8] The fact of the Self is self-evident for Śaṅkara – 'for everyone is conscious of the Self and no one thinks, "I am not"'.[9] But the precise nature of the Self is uncertain, and the bulk of his analysis of the Brahma Sūtra and the upaniṣads argues for its non-dual nature. However, while scripture and argument are necessary for establishing this, in the end one needs to go 'within' to determine the truth of supreme consciousness which ultimately is self-established (*svataḥ siddhaḥ*) and self-validating (*svataḥ prāmāṇyatva*), and here crucial internalist mechanisms are operating, especially concerning the justification of the experience. Alain Danielou may overstate the Indian case by arguing that outward perception is in fact inferior to the inward (yogic) perception governed by the identification of subject with an object, 'the only true form of experience, the only absolute method of knowing' (Danielou, 1955: 5). Still, a crucial internal mechanism of assimilating religious experience is fundamental to some forms of Indian practice, and this includes Śaṅkara's.

What, following Halbfass, I do not hold is that Śaṅkara argues his position from 'personal experience'. Nowhere does Śaṅkara establish universal claims based on any experience of realization; however, as John Taber has suggested, it seems reasonable to assume that Śaṅkara at least implicitly drew upon his experience as he reflected on the purport of the upaniṣads (Taber, 1991: 232). Nevertheless, while he does not offer his own experience as a normative example, he does impute a significant role to experience (***anubhava***) in the plan of salvation. Later Advaitins follow his lead and emphasize this role; indeed, a verse circulating among Advaitin teachers affirms this: 'This manifold universe is mere illusion. I am Brahman, the non-dual Real. The proofs of this are the upaniṣads, (realized) teachers, and (one's) experience.'[10] Still, Śaṅkara himself never marshals either his own experiences or the experiences of great sages as part of his argument for the truth of non-duality. Late in the Brahma Sūtra, however, he raises, but does not expand upon, an intriguing question rather suggestive of the self-guaranteeing, authoritative nature of lived experience: 'How is it possible to deny to someone, still embodied, realization of Brahman when his own heart confirms it?'[11] This notion of self-confirmation is manifest in the case of Ramaṇa.

To continue with Halbfass's analysis of 'religious experience' in ancient India, he adds, with his usual precision, that the Vedas themselves are not even records of personal experiences, but an 'eternal, impersonal structure of soteriologically meaningful discourse' (Halbfass, 1990: 388). In this view the Vedas are not a

---

8 … *sarvasyātmatvāc ca brahmāstitvaprasiddhiḥ* (BSB 1.1.6, 6).

9 … *sarvo hy ātmāstitvaṁ pratyeti na nāham asmīti* (BSB 1.1.6, 6).

10 *Ayam prapañco mithyaiva satyaṁ brahmāham advayam / atra pramāṇaṁ vedāntā guravo' nubhavas tathā* (Alston, 1987: 62).

11 *Kathaṁ hy ekasya svahṛdayapratyayaṁ brahmavedanaṁ dehadhāraṇaṁ cāpareṇa pratikṣeptuṁ śakyate* (BSB 4.1.15, 475).

documentation of subjective experiences, but an 'objective structure which guides, controls, and gives room to legitimate experience' (ibid.: 388). Here the Vedas shape and define experience, and create the space in which reason, meditation and personal experience all have value. Truth, then, is founded not on a particular individual's 'personal experience' but on the timeless, impersonal Veda. Indeed, ignoring the Veda and relying on the experience of another ushers in the slippery slope of heterodoxy, best exemplified, according to Brahmin ideology, by Buddhists and Jains. And, although the importance of 'personal experience' in Buddhism is sometimes represented as a reaction to Vedic formalism and upaniṣadic speculation,[12] little room is given to experience as some sort of independent psychological research apart from right teaching and right practice. Indeed, the experience of the Buddha replaces the Veda as an objective norm and supreme model for monks of the *saṅgha* to imitate and internalize. In this view 'Be ye a lamp to yourselves' hardly suggests an independent programme of experimentation; rather, this testimony of the Buddha is an exhortation to his disciples to work diligently and confirm by their meditation the truth of the primordial experience of the Buddha. For Śaṅkara the external norm is the Veda; thus a significant externalist element is inevitable in his programme, and perhaps in all religions. In the end, however, the most important epistemological mode is internalism, and this is necessarily the case on account of the axioms of Advaita.

Instead of using his own personal experience as guide, Śaṅkara reflects on the nature of self-awareness and immediacy; he develops what Debabrata Sinha has called a 'metaphysic of experience' (Sinha, 1983).[13] So, while he did not collect psychological data to establish the 'theory' of Advaita Vedānta, he nevertheless saw in experience (*anubhava*) an important authoritative, even self-guaranteeing mechanism for establishing saving knowledge. Though controverted, Śaṅkara appears to accord to *anubhava* the same status as a *pramāṇa*. More about this fundamental reflection on experience follows below.

Knowledge and the means of knowledge in Advaita

When we speak about 'knowledge' in Advaita, however, we quickly fall into language difficulties, many of which recall the later antinomies of Kant.

---

12 For example, 'Personal experience in this way is placed above the received knowledge of the Vedic revelation' (Flood, 1996: 82). Such a statement is tendentious, since it suggests a decontextualized programme for Buddhist enlightenment. 'Personal experience' in early Buddhism is, if anything, mental and affective events, which are highly conditioned by doctrinal and behavioural patterns.

13 Using Kantian and Husserlian heuristics, Sinha seeks to interpret experience not in terms of rationally conceived first principles, but with reference to 'the immanent structure of consciousness' (1983: xv). Sharma (1993a) takes a similar approach. I am most concerned with what and how we know through *anubhava*, if anything, although such questions in Advaita cannot be separated from its theory of consciousness.

Epistemology applies reasoned discourse on the cognizer (*pramātṛ*), the cognition (*pramā*), and the object of cognition (*prameya*). Advaita creates intellectual space for real-world philosophical and ethical discourse, the so-called 'relative standpoint' (*vyavahārika avasthā*). From this standpoint, its ultimate radical non-dualism notwithstanding, Advaita is decidedly realistic and pluralistic, admitting any number of metaphysical, epistemological and ethical distinctions – for example, subject, object, categories, whole–part relation, means of producing knowledge, merit, demerit, dharma and so on. The *vyavahārika*, in fact, is a necessary plank in the Advaita platform, for it allows the Advaita to meet on the philosophical pitch with the other schools and argue its position. Without the *vyavahārika*, the Advaitin cannot utter a word. With the *vyavahārika*, the Advaitin has a device to engage in debate, persuade or evoke a commitment to the ultimate non-dual metaphysic. Some unpersuaded disputants, however, may be dissatisfied with the trump card of the *paramārthika avasthā*, the standpoint from the absolute, for here no discourse is possible, by definition: 'and philosophy, which begins with the *pramāṇa-prameya-vyavahāra* comes to an end in respect of the *paramārthika*' (Balasubramanian, 1990: 22). The *paramārthika* (or *mokṣa* or Brahman or *Ātman*) is by definition transpersonal, transphenomenal, absolute. It has nothing to do with any common intercourse with the world. Indeed, Śaṅkara writes that the imperishable real (*akṣaram satyam*) is 'entirely beyond the scope of perception' (*atyantaparokṣatvāt*) (MU 2.1.1, 141). The knowledge which saves or is salvation, according to Śaṅkara, is not constricted by time or space.[14]

Although the ultimate standpoint reveals the non-dual real, getting there, as it were, involves a division by dichotomy: Self and non-self, whose fundamental differences, says Śaṅkara, are as opposed as the light and the dark.[15] In short, any object of perception is not-the-Self, or not-self (*anātman*). Anything known by the Self cannot be the Self. This means that the Self, by definition, *cannot* be known, for what is known is an object of knowledge. The Self is the supreme subject, not an object (BSB 1.1.4, Up. 1.16.10–14). In the simplest terms, the Self cannot 'know' itself because such would imply 'parts' and thereby confound non-dual truth. Instead, the Self is 'homogeneous' knowledge. 'Self-knowledge' in this view is not to be taken literally, but is used as a term of courtesy and suggests more the process of liberation than formal epistemology. But owing to the ultimate standpoint of non-duality, it seems that we lose purchase of the term 'knowledge' in any usual way of construing the term. Some thinkers prefer to use words such as 'awareness' or 'consciousness' to suggest a significant difference in the terms 'knowledge' and 'consciousness', but the troubles persist. A.B. Keith has suggested that this ultimate state, owing to its radical absence of subject and object, 'differs so entirely from the very nature of consciousness as not in our view to deserve the name at all' (Keith, 1989: 507).

14 ... *vidyāyāḥ kālaviśeṣābhāvāt aniyatanimittāt kālasaṅkocānupapattiḥ*.

15 Śaṅkara frequently uses the terms *ātman* and *anātman*; in his important discourse on superimposition, he chooses the terms *asmat* and *yuṣmat* – literally, I and you.

But this seems extreme. While from the standpoint of the supreme, distinctions for the Advaitin dissolve and the true Self shines in all its effulgent glory, there must be some degree of continuity between what we normally call consciousness and what is held to be this non-dual supreme consciousness. While the usual cognitive procedures may indeed be 'sublated' by realization, there must be a residuum in our *vyavahārika* processes that provide a window to the supreme. Otherwise, an interminable gap obtains between the phenomenal and the real, rendering impossible its connection to lived experience and, by extension, its 'connection' to saving experience; 'Thus, the utter non-duality is upheld, but at the cost, which to some would undoubtedly seem too high, of making reality unthinkable (*acintya*) and indescribable (*anirvacanīya*)' (Indich, 1995: 5). Indeed, not content with insisting on the *anirvacanīyatva* of the supreme, Śaṅkara holds that even *phenomenal* existence is beyond description, for it is neither real nor unreal (*na sadasat*): it is not ultimately real, for all duality is sublated upon the vision of the supreme; yet it is not absolutely unreal, for we do, in fact, behold generation, production, destruction and so on.

Śaṅkara is normally understood to operate out of a cognitive distinction which creates an unbridgeable epistemic chasm. Following the Muṇḍaka Upaniṣad, Śaṅkara appeals to two kinds of knowledge, higher and lower (*parā, aparā vidyā*), the former being knowledge of the supreme Brahman, the other, everything else. Eliot Deutsch holds that these two must be incommensurable, for *parā vidyā* is *sui generis* (Deutsch, 1969: 82). Yet, the fact of being incommensurable has the undesirable consequence, in my view, of having absolutely no relevance to lived experience whatsoever. It is hard to imagine even broaching the subject if it is utterly incommensurable with any ordinary conscious processes. And, in fact, closer analysis of Śaṅkara's consideration of the metaphysics of experience allows for important subtleties which make room for a hint of continuity between the *vyavahārika* and the *paramārthika*, and to this we shall now turn.

Anubhava *as a means of knowledge*

One of the most revealing passages concerning Śaṅkara's analysis of experience – and one which has provoked considerable debate – is his discussion of the second *sūtra* in the Brahma Sūtra which establishes Brahman as the source of the origin and dissolution of the world (*janmādyasya yataḥ*). In his gloss of this *sūtra*, Śaṅkara surveys the various means at our disposal for gaining knowledge of the supreme. Rejecting Sāṇkhya and Vaiśeṣika cosmologies, he affirms a particular method of appropriating *Brahmajñāna*: reflective appropriation of the import of upaniṣadic texts. While holding the standard *śruti* line here, however, he makes room for inference and reasoning as significant helps in this intellectual process, for scripture allows for argumentation and human understanding assists scripture. But he continues:

> In the inquiry into *dharma*, *śruti*, etc. are the only *pramāṇas*; but in the inquiry into Brahman, *śruti*, etc. and experience (*anubhava*), etc., are valid as far as possible, since knowledge of Brahman ultimately terminates in experience and since it has for its object an accomplished substance.[16]

This passage, tantalizing with its implications, has been a flashpoint for contemporary Indologists, drawing the attention of a number of scholars, including Sarvepalli Radhakrishnan (1989: 517), Wilhelm Halbfass (1990: 389), Satchidananda Murty (1959: 112), and most recently has been the subject of a lively exchange between Arvind Sharma (1992), Anantanand Rambachand (1994), and Kim Skoog (1989) in *Philosophy East and West*. There seem to be three approaches to this text by contemporary scholars. One approach appears to overemphasize this passage, thus minimizing the importance of scriptural exegesis in Vedāntic thought and casting *anubhava* as entirely decontextualized. Radhakrishnan is representative of this approach.[17] As Rambachand has pointed out elsewhere, *mokṣa* in Śaṅkara cannot be understood in isolation from his understanding of the nature and scope of the valid sources of knowledge and his affirmation that the Vedas constitute such a source (Rambachand, 1992: 33–46).

On the other hand, Rambachand, as well as Murty, represent another approach to this text – one that tends to minimize the significance of *anubhava* for Śaṅkara. While they are correct not to make the mistake of earlier scholars, they seem to err on the side of caution; after all, Śaṅkara, as seen above, clearly considers *anubhava* to be the definitive event on the path of self-knowledge and, indeed, such an event would be the definitive *ending* of the path. A third, more modest, approach tends to follow the middle path of these two extremes, properly recognizing the space that Śaṅkara accords for *anubhava*, yet focusing the tradition squarely where it belongs, in the exegesis of scripture and in the deft transmission of a teacher. Clooney, Halbfass and Potter seem to reflect this attitude; indeed, concerning the *pramāṇyatva* of *anubhava*, Potter says, 'And in some Pickwickian sense *anubhava* may constitute a "proof", but it is not a proof that will ever be used' (Potter, 1981: 98). Potter's reference to Dickens's Mr Pickwick is apt; as Pickwick tended to use terms in his own idiosyncratic fashion, so the term 'proof' here is peculiar. As Potter explains, 'When one has Self-knowledge one no longer has doubts or needs proof, and when one needs proof one is not in a position to have Self-knowledge, since one is under the sway of ignorance' (ibid.: 98).

A closer look at the terms *anubhava* and *pramāṇa* is in order. Sharma has determined at least three senses of the term *anubhava* in Śaṅkara's work: (1) to refer to experience in its widest connotation; (2) to refer to empirical experience; and (3)

---

16 *Na dharmajijñāsāyām iva śrutyādaya eva pramāṇaṁ brahmajijñāsāyāṁ kiṃ tu śrutyādayonubhavādayaś ca yathāsaṃbhavam iha pramāṇam anubhāvasānatvād bhūtavastuviṣayatvāc ca brahmajñānasya* (BSB 1.1.2, 8).

17 For a criticism of this approach and examples of other Neo-Hindu appropriations of Śaṇkara, see Rambachand's 1995 monograph.

to refer to non-dual experience (Sharma, 1992: 518). It is obviously this last sense of the term that subverts our ordinary notions of proof and illuminates Potter's literary allusion. Indeed, as Halbfass makes clear, Śaṅkara uses the term *anubhava* in accordance with his own hierarchy of conventional and absolute truth: 'there is "wrong" and "right", provisional and absolute experience' (Halbfass, 1990: 390). Yet, he adds:

> ... there is a common denominator; even false *anubhava*, which implies superimposition and false identification of self, is still *anubhava*, containing the element of immediate presence, in which being and knowing, subject and object coincide. Insofar, any act of perception or awareness can remind us of, and help us to approach, that absolute or ultimate experience which according to the upaniṣads coincides with the being of Brahman itself. (Ibid.)

To consider the epistemic value of *anubhava* – in the *vyavahārika* as well as the *paramārthika* – let us look afresh at the term *pramāṇa*. As we saw in Chapter 1, the nature and scope of authoritative knowledge-producing mechanisms have long been debated in Indian philosophy. Mysore Hiriyanna's study of the term arrived at three overlapping senses, the most common of which is the one we have been using – namely, a source of valid knowledge. But he identifies at least two other senses of the term, both rather general: 'a source of knowledge, without reference to its being either true or false; lastly, a means of scrutiny' (Hiriyanna, 1957: 69, in Sharma, 1992: 517). This last term is so general as not to merit any discussion, but the second one needs further clarification. Sharma makes the observation, however, that Śaṅkara is familiar with, and uses, all three senses of the term, although he most frequently employs the most common sense of the term (ibid.).

The most frequently used Sanskrit term for knowledge is *jñana*, but this term is perhaps best glossed as 'cognition' or even 'mental episodes', for the term is broad enough to include varying degrees of truth and certainty (*samyag jñāna*, *viparyaya jñāna*, *saṁseya jñāna*). *Pramā*, on the other hand, is the more precise term for knowledge. Needing no qualifiers, it is by definition valid knowledge. It is the cognitive output of the mechanisms of knowledge. And, as N.K. Devaraja reminds us, although Śaṅkara nowhere undertakes an exhaustive analysis of the *pramāṇas*, he is certainly familiar with standard use of the term in currency among the *darśanas*; moreover, Śaṅkara's discussion of *pramāṇas* is partly constrained by the absence of traditional Indian epistemology in the texts on which Śaṅkara bases his commentaries. Śaṅkara seems less interested in a 'theory' of *pramāṇas* than an assessment of their relative worth (Devaraja, 1962: 37). For Śaṅkara, the mundane *pramāṇas* function appropriately in the *vyavahārika*, but offer no insight into the divine; instead, *śruti* is the primary mechanism for 'producing' transcendent insight. Since Śaṅkara's 'formal' epistemology is overshadowed by his soteriological concerns, it was the work of a later Advaitin theoretician, Dharmarāja, to systematize Advaita epistemology. His terse definition of valid knowledge is simple and straightforward: *pramākaraṇam pramāṇam* (Sastri, 1971: 3).

Sharma, however, adds a twist in his rendition of *pramāṇa* – one that sheds light on Śaṅkara's gloss in BSB. He suggests that *pramāṇa* can mean either 'the means of valid knowledge' or 'the valid means of knowledge'. The distinction between these expressions is subtle and significant and sheds light on Śaṅkara's gloss. Let us consider it as a strong and weak sense of the term *pramāṇa*. The use of the strong sense of the term *pramāṇa* in this passage thus establishes *anubhava* as a mechanism for knowledge on the same footing as traditional Indian *pramāṇas*, such as perception, inference and testimony. But establishing *anubhava* as a *pramāṇa* in a strong sense is specious for several reasons. First, nowhere does Śaṅkara engage in a systematic analysis of the *pramāṇas*, and so, lacking such an account, it seems unreasonable to inflate the importance of *anubhava* in this manner. Not only are there limited intimations of the knowledge-producing power of *anubhava* in Śaṅkara's writings, there are limited concessions to the value and significance of the traditional *pramāṇas* under the domain, as they are, of the *vyavahārika avasthā*. Second, within the limitations of the *vyavahārika*, each *pramāṇa* has its own scope (*pramāṇa vyavasthā*). The standard expectation of a *pramāṇa* was that it operated only within its specific boundaries and produced new knowledge – that is, knowledge not already available through the proper functioning of other *pramāṇas*. Stock debates among the competing Indian philosophical schools over this issue include rejecting the *pramāṇic* status of *śruti* and *smṛti*, both of which have been held, by the Naiyāyikas, at least, to be finally derivative of perception or even equated with it, and thus not a genuine *pramāṇa*. Using this model, *anubhava* would apparently fall under the scope of *pratyakṣa*, perception, for whatever is perceived is experienced.

But this constricts *anubhava* to the scope of the *vyavahārika*, which is certainly is not the force of Śaṅkara's appeal to *anubhava* as a *pramāṇa*: 'because knowledge of Brahman *culminates* in experience'.[18] *Anubhava* can hardly mean mundane experience here. *Pramāṇas* by definition involve duality, which of course is the *pūrvapakṣa* negated by Śaṅkara's *a-dvaita*. So, at most, *anubhava* here must be read as a *pramāṇa* in a weak sense – that is, valid means of knowledge. Here, we are not committing the error of 'overpervasion' (*ativyāpti*) – in other words, extending the term too broadly, as Sharma does in his essays on *anubhava*. But a weak sense of *pramāṇa* – valid means of knowledge – suggests that *anubhava* is an appropriate mechanism for producing *jñāna*, a more general term which includes transcendent knowledge, a knowing beyond knowledge. Here we are concerned with a particular cognitive event, but one that does not necessarily imply duality, as does *pramā*. In this sense, *anubhava*, like *śruti*, is indeed an independent means of knowledge, drawing from, but extending beyond, the scope of mundane perception. By shifting the qualifier in the terms 'valid knowledge' (*pramā*) to 'valid means' of knowledge (*pramāṇa*), we avoid the duality implicated in the former expression and gain the

18 ... *anubhavāvasānatvāt* ... *brahmajñānasya*.

advantage of affirming Śaṅkara's value of *anubhava*. So, for example, while Rambachand is correct to illustrate and criticize the Indian and Western fixation on *anubhava* as *pramāṇa* in the traditional sense of the term, he unfairly minimizes its importance in Śaṅkara's thought.

In BSB 1.1.2 Śaṅkara first reminds the reader of the superiority of *śruti* and the significance of a teacher in effecting knowledge of Brahman. He then admits room for inferential reasoning, as long as such mental processes do not contradict Vedānta passages. He recognizes two transempirical realities – dharma and Brahman – inquiry into which require '*śruti*, etc. (*śrutyādayaḥ*)'. Halbfass translates this phrase as '*śruti* and other authoritative texts'. More correct, I think, is the suggestion of classical and contemporary commentators that 'etc. (*ādayaḥ*)' refers to the six ways of arriving at the import of a sentence, used as hermeneutical devices by both the Pūrva and Uttara Mīmāṃsā;[19] *śruti*, as sacred revelation, requires a hermeneutical strategy (*śrutyādayaḥ*) to determine its proper sense. And, as Francis Clooney has shown, despite their fundamental disagreements, both inquiries, *dharmajijñāsa* and *brahmajijñāsa*, depend on the correct exegesis of scripture and share significant interpretative strategies (Clooney, 1993: 25; 1992: 55–59). But this kindred relationship is shown elsewhere, for in the *vyavahārika* Advaita tends to follow Mīmāṃsā epistemology as illustrated by the maxim, *vyāvahare bhāṭṭanayah* (Balasubramanian, 1990: 24).

Despite their shared hermeneutical and epistemological strategies, there remain insuperable differences; *dharmajijñāsa* involves dualities – acts, agents and instruments – and, most significantly, produces a result at a future time. *Brahmajijñāsa*, on the other hand, while necessarily involving important propaedeutics, involves reflection upon an accomplished substance (*bhūtavastu*) which exists in the eternal now. Since the result of this inquiry is not produced by ritual action, experience is crucial, both in its mundane and transcendent aspects. In this passage, Śaṅkara clearly indicates the transcendent sense of *anubhava*, for it represents the culmination of *brahmajñāna*. Thus *brahmānubhava* is indeed special and lies at the very heart of Advaita soteriology. And, although the syntactical compound *brahmānubhava* consists of two elements, it should not be analysed as a genitive *tatpuruṣa*; such a reading would imply a subject–object split, 'experience of Brahman', thus generating two 'things' – experience and Brahman. A better rendering glosses the expression *brahmānubhava* as an appositional compound which reinforces the Advaita position: experience which *is* Brahman. Thus, numerous terms carry the same import in Advaita, which is not the case in other philosophical schools; here, *mokṣa*, *anubhava*, *anubhūti*, Brahman, *ātman*, even *saṃnyāsa* are all equivalent terms and point to the transcendent Self.[20] Brahma-

19 … *ṣaḍvidhatātpāryanirṇāyakapramāṇāni*. Padmapāda construes it this way; so does Thibault (1988: 17).

20 There is an important tendency in Śaṅkara which suggests the true *saṃnyasi* is a *jīvanmukta*. See Potter (1981: 34–35). Sawai introduces a further nuance to this consideration: he demonstrates a

knowledge culminates in experience, as Śaṅkara makes quite clear in Up. 1.5.5: 'Pure experience is the Supreme.'[21] Indeed, we *are* that experience. And Śaṅkara, maintaining his opposition to the ritual agenda of the Pūrva Mīmāṃsā, carefully and consistently emphasizes the fact that saving knowledge is never produced (*utpatti*), purified (*saṁskṛta*), modified (*vikāra*), or attained (*prāpti*), for such an admission ushers in such infelicities as acts and agents and entails the defeat of his fundamental premise: the fact of the eternal, immutable, one Self. Instead, 'I am perfect liberation (here and now).'[22] What testifies to this? 'Accept (the Self) as self-evident, which in turn is synonymous with being "self-knowable".'[23] But 'self-evident' and 'self-knowable' imply a critical epistemic evaluation of (*paramārthika*) Self-experience. This is facilitated by the intellectual and ethical programmes of Advaita which conduce to non-dual truth; however, Self-experience owes its ultimate validation to the experience of immediate perception (*aparokṣatva*) of the inner *ātman*. This is the crucial internalist criterion of Advaita, although, as we will see, it is supported in significant ways by external processes. Indeed, when Śaṅkara adds, in Up. 1.18.203, that 'for us, the experience (*anubhava*) of the one's Self is possible by the elimination of the ego',[24] this implies doctrinal and ethical inputs intended to refashion one's intellect and will accord with a particular view of reality, at least until that view of reality itself is 'sublated' upon realization. More about this process will be said in the next section.

Although Śaṅkara clearly implies *paramārthikānubhava* in his gloss on BSB 1.1.2, it is not improper to read *anubhava* from the *vyavahārika* as well. In this sense, even mundane experience is an effective component of *brahmajijñāsa*. On this reading, *all* mundane experience becomes an effective tool which eventually culminates in transcendent experience. Such mundane experience reveals, under the proper tutelage of a guru and in accord with proper Advaitin exegetical principles (*śrutyādayaḥ*, *sāmānādhikāraṇa*, *anvayavyatireka*), the eternal, unchanging, conscious nature of existence. Śaṅkara and later Advaitins employ a stipulative definition of the real – namely, that which perdures unchanging in the three periods of time (*trikāle abādhyatva*). More technically, what is real is not 'sublated' in past, present, or future. Now Rāmānuja and others have pointed out the weaknesses of such a stipulative definition: there is no *necessary* reason why being real should be indexed to eternality. Being real could be an ineluctable fact of empirical existence, however fleeting; or an entity could come into existence, become real, and thenceforth enjoy the fact of being eternal. Nevertheless, for Śaṅkara, that the non-

distinction between *vidvat-saṃnyāsa* and *vividiṣāsaṃnyāsa* in Śaṅkara's thought (Sawai, 1986: 371–87). See also the important work of Fort and Mumme (1996), particularly Lance Nelson's essay on Śaṅkara, and Roger Marcaurelle's (2000) illuminating study of renunciation in Śaṅkara.

21 ... *paraḥ so' nubhavo* (Up. 1.5.5, 11).

22 ... *siddho mokṣo' ham* (Up. 1.18.206, 109).

23 ... *svasaṁvedyatvaparyāyaḥ svapramāṇaka iṣyatām* (Up. 1.18.203, 109).

24 ... *nivṛittāvahamaḥ siddhaḥ svātmano' nubhavaḥ naḥ* (Up. 1.18.202, 109).

dual real is the eternal, unchanging substrate of the changing, phenomenal world of name and form is axiomatic. Following this basic foundation, the phenomenal world is unreal in any ontological sense. It is *māyā*, illusory, phenomenal, lacking any independent status apart from the supreme real, Brahman. Indeed, a standard Advaitin syllogism invokes perception as proof of the illusory nature of the world: this world is illusory, because it is an object of experience, like mother-of-pearl and silver.[25] Whatever is perceived is experienced, and objects of perception implicate the world of phenomena. But the ultimate real remains utterly beyond the scope of mundane perception.

Despite this axiomatic limitation of perception, the phenomenal or conventional real (*vyavahāra satyam*) is an important instrument on the path to *mokṣa*. For a phenomenological analysis of impermanent entities reveals the ground out of which these entities arise. In his commentary on the *Gītā*, Śaṅkara offers his interpretation of a well-known and challenging *śloka*:

> Of nonbeing there is no coming to be and of being there is no ceasing to be; the boundary between these two is perceived by those who know the truth.[26]

This is a difficult *śloka* because of the multiple ways of construing philosophically loaded terms. For example, the first term, *nāsataḥ*, could refer to a particular existent – for example, 'of what does not exist', or refer to a more abstract claim, 'of non-existence', or it could suggest an even more reified ontology, 'of the unreal', a choice that Śaṅkara makes which accords well with his assumptions. Śaṅkara wishes to engage in a kind of phenomenological as well as an epistemological analysis of impermanent entities to determine the ground out of which these entities arise – namely, *sat*, existence. But he indexes existence to reality. By observation and analysis we can determine the unreality of phenomena on account of their impermanence and transformation: the pot is, now is not; the cloth is, now is not. 'When scrutinized, these objects are not seen apart from clay and the like, their material causes. Therefore, as effects, they are unreal' (Warrier, 1993: 33). They are mere transformations (*vikāra*), with no independent status; they are, in fact, even, *unknown* apart from their material causes.

But a *pūrvapakṣa* worries about the *regressus* that ensues from this line of thought: complete negation, or absolute void (*sarvābhāvaprasaṅgaḥ*), the recurrent threat of Buddhist 'nihilism'. Śaṅkara responds in two important ways: he reinforces the importance of cognitive function, even in the most mundane observations, and he indexes the real to what is immutable:

> Your conclusion (of absolute void) is invalid, because throughout the sphere of

25 … *idaṁ jagan mithyā dṛśyatvāt śuktikārūpyavat.*

26 … *nāsato vidyate bhāvo nābhāvo vidyate sataḥ / ubhayor api dṛṣṭo' ntas tv anayos tattvadarśibhiḥ* (*Gītā* 2.16).

> experience we see two types of cognitions, the cognition of the real and the cognition of what is unreal. That object alone is real whose cognition is immutable; that object is unreal whose cognition proves mutable. Thus the distinction between the real and the unreal rests on cognitions. Throughout the sphere of experience the two cognitions with an identical substrate are perceived by everyone. This does not hold in the locution 'blue lotus'; proper locutions are 'the pot is', 'the cloth is', 'the elephant is', and so on throughout the sphere of cognitive experience. Of these two kinds of cognitions, the one whose content is the pot, etc., is mutable, q.e.d. Not so the cognition of reality or *sat*. Therefore, being mutable the objects of the cognitions of pot and the like are unreal; not so the object of the cognition of the real, it being immutable. (Warrier, 1993: 33)

In Śaṅkara's comment on the famous *sadvidyā* passage in CU 6.2.1,[27] he affirms the position that *sat*, existence or the real, is subtle, without distinction, all-pervasive, one, taintless, partless, conscious and, significantly, 'known from all the upaniṣads'. All 'this' (*idam*) is mere modification of name and form.[28] Thus, what *appears* to be real in the *vyavahārika* is ultimately cancelled out by a higher truth, just as the illusory snake is cancelled by the truth of the rope. Still, the phenomenon of the *vyavahārika* depends on *sat* for its apparent reality.

But the second half of CU 6.2.1 indicates a concern over an alternative ontology, suggesting not only Buddhist but Vaiśeṣika views, for both are considered proponents of *asatkāryavāda*, the view that the effect does not pre-exist in its cause. The CU text reads: 'Some say "in the beginning this was non-existence alone, one only, without a second. From that non-existence issued existence".'[29] Buddhists and Vaiśeṣikas would seem to be strange bedfellows here; the significant difference between them is, of course, their assessment of the reality of both cause and effect. For Vaiśeṣikas, from what exists, *sat*, something which did not exist previously (*asat*) emerges; in other words, something new, and real, emerges: the effect does not pre-exist in its cause, as it does in versions of Advaita and Sāṅkhya emanationism. For Buddhists, on the other hand, the cause is destroyed; hence what now exists emerges from what no longer exists (*asataḥ satiṁ jayate*); the effect emerges afresh, however momentary (*kṣaṇika*), for it is now destroyed, generating yet another momentary effect.

Śaṅkara rejects the Vaiśeṣikas for refusing to take seriously *ādvitīyam*, the fact that *sat* – which they surely recognize in the reality of substances, qualities and actions – was one only, without a second, before creation (*idam*). Śaṅkara's rebuttal of the Buddhists is twofold; first it is inconceivable to imagine, at a primordial moment, absolute non-existence having any association with time and number.

27 ... *sadevam idam agra āsīd ekam evādvitīyam.*

28 See Mayeda for a helpful discussion of Śaṅkara's tightrope-walking with *nāmarūpa*, the supersensible 'seed of the universe (*jagadbījabhūta*)', which of course cannot, according to his axioms, be considered an independent material cause *à la* Sāṅkhya (Mayeda, 1992: 22).

29 ... *āhur asad eva idam agra āsīd ekam evādvitīyaṁ tasmād asatsaḥ sajjāyata.*

Second, according to Śaṅkara, there is no proof of the 'non-existence' of existence before creation; for him, to imagine non-existence prior to creation is a direct affront to logic and therefore cannot be upheld.

Although informed by the upaniṣads, Śaṅkara establishes a crucial programme of phenomenological analysis, for the fact of an eternal, immutable real in the face of a universe of changing phenomena is hardly a transparent proposal. By reflecting on that which persists or perdures and out of which the world appears (*vivarta*) to emerge, one gains insight, a significant cognitive antecedent, into the *paramārthika satyam*. In other words, while Śaṅkara speaks of a culminating, transcendent *anubhava*, it is not unreasonable to employ the *vyavahārikānubhava* on the path of liberation. Mundane experience is inflected with infinite pluralities and distinctions. But by employing Śaṅkara's criterion of the real, one is able to perceive the undefeated real which persists in all impermanent events or entities. My use of the term 'perceive' is deliberate, for a common gloss of the term *dṛṣṭi* indicates both seeing and knowing.[30]

Important here is the obvious mental training that necessarily precedes the *paramārthikānubhava* which transcends all categories and distinctions. And this training naturally involves doctrine. Thus soteriology is invariably affected by doctrine. The question, of course, is which comes first – doctrine or experience? The prevalent view among apologists and scholars of religion holds that experience precedes doctrine. James, perhaps, is the most prominent advocate of this position early in the twentieth century, but many contemporary scholars are equally insistent that doctrine is derivative either of the 'immediate experience' of the virtuosi or of other historical or political phenomena. Thus, for example, Ninian Smart writes: 'The determination of metaphysics by forms of religious experience and practice occurs that way round, not conversely ...' (Smart, 1964: 144; quoted in Muller-Ortega, 1989: 5). And Karel Werner: 'experience is primary while doctrines, both philosophical and theological ... are derivative' (Werner, 1989: 2).

The relationship between experience and doctrine is much more complex than these scholars suggest, for ontologies and axiologies are deeply embedded in any spiritual practice. Robert Lester has illustrated this complex interrelationship in his analysis of Rāmānuja's reflections on yoga (Lester, 1976: xv). Moreover, the systematic study of soteriological texts may well be understood less as a direct preparation for spiritual training than for constructing a coherent universe in which these practices make sense – if such studies are done at all.[31]

---

30 Sanskrit root √ *dṛś; dṛṣṭi*, 'views'. Hence the importance of *samyag dṛṣṭi* (right views) as the important first step in the Buddhist Eightfold Path; Śaṅkara uses the term *samyag darśana* to distinguish Advaita from the opposing, erroneous views of various realists and dualists.

31 This point was made by Georges Dreyfus in a seminar, *Soteriology and Tibetan Scholastic Training*, at the University of Chicago, 31 January 1997. His analysis of two schools of Tibetan monastic training, the *Geluk pa* and *Nying ma pa*, determines that the *primary* use of the *mārga* literature in their curricula was to develop a coherent and consistent Vajrayāna world construction in which various ethical and ritual practices made sense. This is in striking contrast to a commonly held assumption that this genre of literature directly reflected and prepared one for particular kinds of meditative experience.

Thus, right doctrine is a necessary antecedent for liberation. But this is not to say that such transcendent experience must be gradual or cannot be spontaneous. Śaṅkara himself, while proposing a particular path to enlightenment, relentlessly asserts that *brahmajñāna* is always available, like the supposedly misplaced necklace draping the neck of a forgetful person. As such, *brahmajñāna* can be instantaneously realized. But that realization is largely, if not completely, advanced by a peculiar construal of the world, which in turn necessarily involves proper functioning mental apparatuses. This is best achieved, according to Advaita, by the correct appropriation of the meaning of the upaniṣads, a process gradually cultivated in a dynamic relationship between text, tradition and teacher. But it can be spontaneous or at least come close to being spontaneous, as suggested in the case of the so-called 'sage of pure experience', Ramaṇa Maharṣi. In any case, no programme of liberation can do without the functioning of the mind, however much the mind may be devalued or deconstructed. It is with this 'in mind' that we now consider the role of mental functioning in Advaita soteriology.

Mental equipment in the programme of liberation

Recalling Plantinga's emphasis on proper mental functioning in his epistemology of religious experience, I shall make the Advaitin case for the importance of mental cultivation as a necessary antecedent to enlightenment. Although the mind is often represented as the primary stumbling block to liberation, the use of the mind to get beyond the mind is clear in Advaita. The 'problem' of the mind, however, is its material constitution. Only the supreme *ātman* is spiritual, immaterial, unimplicated in material flux (*prakṛti*). While Advaita ultimately rests on a non-dual metaphysic, it borrows Sāṅkhya categories for its *vyavahārika* cosmology and anthropology. Significant in this regard are the three constituents (*guṇas*) of *prakṛti*: the luminous (*sattva*), the active (*rajas*), and the dull (*tamas*). While some Western philosophical anthropologies have often considered the mind to be somehow immaterial or spiritual, mind in the Vedānta, although extremely subtle, is still constituted by matter. A twofold problem thus develops.

First, since the mind is material, it is inherently afflicted by the play of *guṇas*, which constitute nature; the mind is calm (*sāttvika*) now, agitated (*rājasika*) later. The dispositional tendencies of an embodied soul (*jivātman*, *liṅgātman*) are shaped by karmic patterns (*samskāras*, *vāsanas*) of previous births; moreover, the inherent proportions of the *guṇas* interact with the *guṇas* of the surrounding environment. An interplay occurs which affects the equilibrium of *sattva*, *rajas* and *tamas* in the subject. In addition to this, the mind as the premier sense organ, according to Indian physiology, has the function of organizing data from the senses, which in turn are naturally structured to reach out to their objects and 'appropriate' sensory stimulation. So the mind itself is a flux of dispositions and is almost irresistibly drawn into sensation and stimulation; this 'outgoing' process creates and establishes mental and behavioural tendencies and further implicates the *jīva* in the transitory rounds of birth and rebirth. It is for this reason that traditions of yoga insist on reverse processes of 'withdrawal' (*pratyahāra*) – that is, a process of turning 'within', by various programmes of concentration – to eliminate sensory contact and its consequent troubles.

But a tension exists in the Vedānta. A famous antagonism to the mind is clear in the upaniṣads and in the great *ācāryas* of Advaita. The Kaṭha, for example, holds 'this self is unobtainable by discussion, nor by reflection, nor by many texts';[32] the Muṇḍaka repeats this conviction in MU 3.2.3 and adds that the divine form is unthinkable (*divyam acintyaṁ rūpam*). Gauḍapāda, the putative grand-teacher of Śaṅkara, affirms that 'this moving and immoving duality whatsoever is perceived by the mind'[33] and counsels establishing the mind in the state of non-mind (*amanobhāve*) in which duality no longer arises.[34] Indeed, in a parallel to Nāgārjuna, Gauḍapāda suggests the dichotomizing[35] tendency of the mind is the primary flaw of the human condition: 'when the mind does not dichotomize, in virtue of the knowledge of the Self, it goes to the state of non-mind; and, in the absence of something to be cognized, there is no cognition'.[36] Śaṅkara himself follows Gauḍapāda's lead and extols the supreme state beyond all mundane mental (and bodily) states: 'I am without mind and pure ... Freedom from mind and freedom from change belong to Me, who am bodiless and all-pervading' (Mayeda, 1992: 133).

This supreme state transcends all subject–object dualities constructed by the mind. For Śaṅkara, superimposition (*adhyāsa*) is the *sine qua non* for the functioning of both *laukika* and *vaidika* activities, for both presume the mundane state of being a knower (*jñātṛtva*). The state of being a knower, however, is unreasonable without an embodied 'I', for the *pramāṇas* cannot operate without a knowing agent, endowed with sense faculties. Prior to Self-realization, the *jīvātman* is a knowing agent; afterwards, it is disembodied awareness (*aśarīracit*). Indeed, the *Jīvanmuktiviveka* of Vidyāraṇya, the great fourteenth-century Advaitin, dedicates an entire chapter to 'The Dissolution of the Mind' (*manonaśoprakaraṇam*) (Sastri and Ayyangar, 1978: 303). He first reiterates the usual Yogic and Vedāntin antagonism to mind. Quoting from various texts dear to Advaitins, such as the *Laghuyogavasiṣṭha*, he marshals support to confirm the troubling nature of the mind – for example, 'The mind is, as it were, the root of the tree of *samsāra* ... I believe it to be none other than imagination (ibid.: 303–304).' The unpredictable nature of mind is attested in the *Gītā* as well: 'For the mind is verily restless, O Kṛṣṇa! It is impetuous, strong, and difficult to bend. I deem it as hard to curb as the wind.'[37] The

32 ... *nāyam ātmā pravacanena labhyaḥ na medhayā na bahunā śrutena.*

33 ... *manodṛśyam idaṁ dvaitaṁ yat kiṁcit sacarācaram.*

34 ... *manaso hyamanībhave dvaitaṁ naivopalabhyate.*

35 *samkalpayate*: categorizing, constructing, imagining.

36 ...*ātmasatyānubodhena na saṁkalpayate yadā amanastāṁ tadā yāti grāhyābhave tadagraham.*

37 ... *cañcalaṁ hi manaḥ kṛṣṇa pramāthi balavad dṛḍham / tasyāhaṁ nigrahaṁ manye vāyor iva suduṣkaram* (6.34).

consequences of such lack of control are clear: 'The impossibility of peace in the absence of "mindlessness" is thus set forth: Neither friends, nor relatives, neither teachers, nor others can help him, who has no power over his mind, which obsesses him like a *yakṣa*' (ibid.: 309).

Ramaṇa Maharṣi follows in this tradition. Although using a different practical method, he nonetheless carries many of the same Advaitic presuppositions and goals, including viewing the mind and its operations with grave suspicion. Like Vidyāraṇya, he too counsels 'destruction of the mind (*mānasam naśam*)' (Sastri, 1989: 31). Yet while these exponents of non-duality place no ultimate value on the functioning of the mind and are quick to point out the usual habitual mental troubles it generates, all of them recognize its significant provisional importance. For while the tradition articulates the ultimate beatitude which is beyond the mind, it necessarily imputes a crucial role for the mind. The Kena Upaniṣad, for example, reminds the adept of the significant role of the mind in liberation: 'Now, the Supreme Self. It is this toward which the mind moves, as it were.'[38] Moreover, it is through the mind's powers of recollection and decision that one 'moves' towards the Supreme Self: 'through it this (individual) remembers constantly, likewise volition'.[39] And, following a warning of what ensues from failing to follow the surely counterintuitive position of Advaita,[40] the author of the Kaṭha upaniṣad assures 'by mind alone is this to be obtained: there is no plurality here at all'.[41]

Finally, despite Śaṅkara's insistence on the utter inaccessibility of the unmanifest Self to the mind and senses, he nevertheless carefully acknowledges the importance of mental activity and sets out the externalist aspect of his agenda. So, in his comment on BG 2.21 he represents a *pūrvapakṣa* who insists that no one can acquire the knowledge 'I am the Self' precisely for the reason Śaṅkara adverts to later, 'because the Self is beyond the range of the senses'.[42] But this is unacceptable for Śaṅkara, for it flies in the face of BU 4.4.19[43] and other *śruti* which clearly indicate the importance of cultivating and directing mental processes: 'The instrument for perceiving the Self is the mind, purified by serenity, restraint, etc., the instruction of a teacher, and scripture.'[44] The use of the past participle *samskṛtam* is telling. Meaning 'refined', 'remade', 'perfected', it suggests a complete refashioning of the mind, an overhaul of mental processes oriented toward a particular content – the identity of the Self and Brahman.

Thus an ambivalent attitude towards the mind is evident in Advaita; it contributes to bondage, yet, when disciplined, conduces to liberation: 'The mind itself is the

---

38 ... *athādhyātmam yadetat gacchatīva ca manaḥ* (KeU 4.5).

39 ... *anena caitad upasmaraty abhīkṣnaṁ saṁkalpaḥ* (KeU 4.5).

40 'Who perceives plurality here goes from death to death (*mṛtyos sa mṛtyum āpnoti ya iha nāneva paśyati*)' (KU 2.1.10).

41 ... *manasaivedam āptavyaṁ neha nānāsti kiñcana* (KU 2.1.11).

42 ... *karaṇāgocarātvāt* (BGB 47).

43 ... *manaivānudraṣṭavyam.*

44 ... *śāstrācāryopadeśaśamadamādisaṁskṛtaṁ manaḥ ātmadarśane karaṇam* (BGB 47).

cause of both bondage and liberation for humankind.'[45] Less ambivalent is the role of appropriate mental content: the doctrine and teaching of non-dualism. Within the doctrinal universe, it is absolutely crucial to be invested with the right views (*samyag darśana*), a term that recurs frequently in Śaṅkara's commentary on the *Gītā*. To put this another way, one could be more or less *wrong* in the view one holds. Potter nicely details this hierarchy of increasingly correct positions. For example, those thinkers, say the Naiyāyika or Bauddha, holding an *asatkāryavāda* theory of causality are in deeper cognitive and metaphysical waters than the *satkāryavādin*. And, of the latter, the real-change theorists (*pariṇāmavāda*) come up short against apparent-change theorists (*vivartavāda*) – that is, *kevalādvaita*, pure non-duality (Potter, 1981: 7). No egalitarian relativism operates here (although the Jains produced a version of it in their *syādvāda*); all beliefs are not alike, and there are serious consequences for wrong ones. One can, however, be more or less wrong, with commensurate ills attending. The same demand for right views (*samyag dṛṣṭi*) is, of course, foundational to Buddhism, but it implies a cognitive overhaul which includes the categorical rejection of wrong views. This is important to remember, especially since Buddhism is sometimes represented as supremely tolerant – albeit a tolerance that can be interpreted as a kind of equanimity in the face of the absurd cognitive perversion of others. Ananda Coomaraswamy reminds us that early Buddhist texts indicate that 'heresy is a damnable sin, to be expiated in the purgatories' (1988: 158);[46] moreover, among the heretical views, Ājīvakas apparently merited special condemnation by the Buddha, owing to their strict determinism which seemed to subvert moral responsibility. What these examples illustrate is that, for both Buddhists and Advaitins, the mind needs to be 'trained', as it were, by a particular construal of reality; thus doctrine and its transmission, in mutually reinforcing patterns of learning and practice, establish important external mechanisms that set the stage for liberation. It is to these doxastic practices in Advaita that we now turn.

The culture of liberation in Śaṅkara

Śaṅkara's strategy for appropriating the right views of Advaita involves both external and internal mechanisms of transmission and appropriation. We have highlighted the significant internalist dynamic – reflecting on sacred and profane experience to arrive at indubitable, self-guaranteeing saving knowledge. Internalism in its technical sense indicates privileged access to criteria of truth which in turn

---

45 ... *mana eva manuṣyānam kāraṇam bandhamokṣayoḥ*.

46 Coomaraswamy refers to an observation of the Buddha in the *Anguttara Nikāya*: only one Ājīvaka in 91 aeons attained heaven, let alone *nirvāṇa*. Diatribes against those holding 'wrong views' seem reserved for the benighted non-Buddhists and not necessarily Buddhists holding different opinions. See Gombrich (1984: 13).

impacts on the justification of the beliefs that follow from this process. I argue, on the basis of Śaṅkara's primary metaphysic and his analysis of experience, that internalism as the process of introspection (Śaṅkara prefers the terms *viveka* or *vicāra*) is the dominant epistemology of religious experience in Śaṅkara. It is dominant because this process terminates in a self-validating and indubitable conclusion: 'consummate' or liberating experience. In a less technical sense, however, internalism suggests internalization – that is, a process of appropriating material presented to the subject by external means. This in turn implies a culture of liberation with certain socially established patterns of doxastic practices. In Advaita these doxastic mechanisms are first and foremost the Veda, the *adhikāra*, and the teaching of a guru.

These traditional Advaitin institutions constitute powerful belief-forming mechanisms, an 'external circuitry' which the adept taps into and through which his transformation is facilitated. The question, as always, is the extent to which the 'circuitry' is necessary for the experience of liberation. If it appears to be absolutely necessary, then the externalism of Advaita decisively indexes its soteriology to local culture. If, owing to a dominant internalist dynamic, the 'circuitry' is relativized in significant ways and therefore not absolutely necessary, then greater space opens in Advaita for a transcultural, universalist approach to its tradition. In the Advaita of Śaṅkara, an electric engagement exists between these two poles of internalism and externalism: in theory, the 'external circuitry' is relativized owing to its ultimate insubstantiality; in practice, however, it is highly valorized, which appears to 'lock' Advaita into its unique subculture – one must be a (male) Brahmin, schooled in Vedic lore, and prepared for *mokṣa* by a recognized adept. The Advaita of Ramaṇa Maharṣi, however, is decisively internalist, both in theory and in practice, and this paves the way for a coherent universalism.

It will be our task to evaluate the relative weight of the 'external circuitry' in Śaṅkara. Although I have argued that internalism is the primary mechanism for producing saving knowledge in Śaṅkara, a very prominent role is given to external mechanisms, presented here in cultural and institutional settings. The question of the relative prominence of these mechanisms in Śaṅkara's Advaita has implications in evaluating versions of neo-Hindu apologetics. The universalism or inclusivism represented by some apologists may be viewed as incoherent by a balanced reading of Śaṅkara that properly includes these external mechanisms. A more radical form of Advaita, however, might be considered properly universalist if it relativizes 'external circuitry' and relies with less ambiguity on an internalist epistemology of religious experience. Ramaṇa Maharṣi, I suggest, represents precisely such a radical form of Advaita.

There is good reason, however, why apologists such as Radhakrishnan and Sharma have appealed to Advaita as a universalist tradition. Indeed, Śaṅkara propounds a view which in the end negates all distinctions – caste, stage of life, merit, demerit and even, by extension, orthodoxy and heterodoxy – as mere *upādhis*, limitations or superimpositions upon the real:

> The different castes, such as Brahmana or Kṣatriya, the various orders of life upon which rites depend, and which consist of actions, and their factors and results, are objects of notions superimposed on the Self by ignorance – i.e., based on false notions such as that of a 'snake' in a rope.[47]

Nevertheless, we must not presume that Śaṅkara is unconcerned with the status of phenomenal reality, especially in the areas of social institutions and ideologies. Indeed, it is not for nothing that Śaṅkara is sometimes viewed as the champion of Brahmin orthodoxy. The phenomenal world may be illusory, but there are varying degrees of illusion. We saw above the problem of the 'downward spiral' not only in Buddhism but also in Advaita that can result from varying degrees of error within the doctrinal universe.

So, unless we are a Ramaṇa Maharṣi and experience a radical moment of realization, the Advaita adept needs a programme of deepening interiorization.[48] The state of realization may consititute our nature, after all, but a tall stack of obstacles (*karma, kleśa, saṁskāras, avidyā*) prevents us from appropriating this birthright. This deepening interiorization implicates an important externalist dimension in Śaṅkara's soteriology, for certain practices constitute belief-forming mechanisms which begin the transformation of intellect, will, and affect, and prepare for liberation. The experience of liberation itself is, according to Śaṅkara, immediate and self-evident; it needs no further justification. It is, in an important sense, known through introspection. But this experience is prepared for by numerous practices which constitute, in Advaita, reliable belief-forming mechanisms. The external means we are most concerned with here are the Veda, the *adhikāra* and the guru.

The Veda

Another formulation of process of interiorization indicates the importance of the Veda: *śravaṇa, manana, nididhyāsana*. Hearing (*śravaṇa*) of course presumes content and context, namely the Veda, especially the *vedāntavākyas*, a well-schooled pupil and an extraordinary teacher, himself skilled in exegesis, hermeneutic strategy and reasoning. All of this further implicates our 'external circuitry' in Śaṅkara's Advaita. But this process, when properly assimilated, holds promise; Śaṅkara is insistent that release instantly follows upon knowledge of Brahman, 'Moreover, various *śruti* declare that release follows directly upon knowledge of Brahman, and not from an intermediary action, e.g., "the one who knows Brahman becomes Brahman", "Rites are destroyed upon perceiving the Supreme, who is higher and lower, etc."'[49] However, when realization 'fails', owing

---

47 ... *brahmakṣatrādi karmanimittaṁ varnāśramādilakṣaṇam ātmanyavidyādhyaropitapratyayaviṣayaṁ kriyākārakaphalātmakam avidyāpratyayaviṣayaṁ rajjvām iva sarpapratyayaḥ* (BUB 2.4.5, 193).

48 And despite his profound initial experience, Ramaṇa Maharṣi also needed to further interiorize his non-dual awareness.

49 ... *brahma veda brahmaiva bhavati* (MU 3.2.9). ... *kṣīyante cāsya karmaṇi tasmin dṛṣṭe parāvare*

to a variety of moral and cognitive flaws, a deepening process of interiority is needed to establish the metaphysic – to sink it in, as it were. This process is suggested by reflection, *manana*, usually construed as removing doubts about non-duality, and *nididhyāsana*, 'meditation' or 'sustained reflection'. 'Hearing' obviously involves receiving some sort of content from an external source; however, for the person prepared and ready, this content is confirmed by immediate experience. But this process also occurs for others who are less prepared mentally or morally and, in this case, a process of introspection is necessary to reflect on the truths of scripture and the nature of reality and to confirm gradually the truth of non-duality in the inner reaches of one's own being.

In his long polemic against Mīmāṃsā, Śaṅkara argues for the *pramāṇic* status of *śruti* on the path to *brahmavidyā*. Among his numerous concerns, he emphasizes the cognitive content of *śruti*, 'that all knowing, all powerful Brahman, cause of the origin, subsistence, dissolution of the universe, is known through the Vedānta parts of the scripture'.[50] The Mīmāṃsā, vitally concerned with dharma and, by extension, proper exegesis of scripture, streamlined the salvific force of *śruti* to injunctions (*vidhi*), thus valorizing a performative hermeneutic over a cognitivist.[51] Such an approach is anathema to Śaṅkara, for it involves agents, ends and acts at every level; in a word, it involves plurality.

In the second *sūtra* (*janmādyasya yataḥ*), he argues for the primary status of *śruti*, and even initially dismisses the value of the other *pramāṇas*, such as the inference that 'the comprehension of Brahman is completed through the determining, through reflection, the meaning of the sentence, not through any other *pramāṇas*'.[52] On the other hand, while the Vedānta passages declare the origin of the world, inference is not to be excluded as long as it does not contradict scripture, for scripture admits (*abhyupetatva*) the help of reasoning. Still, although Brahman is a real entity (*bhūtavastu*), the identity of Self and Brahman cannot be grasped without the aid of *śruti*.[53]

So an apparently 'external' mechanism, *śruti*, conveys indispensable information about the Supreme. I say apparently, because, in the end, the Vedas, as with every other distinction, must fall away. While the Veda has cognitive import, and a necessary hermeneutic is required to make sense of that import, the Vedas themselves have a relative – though high – value. And, indeed, because Śaṅkara's ultimate position advocates the *nirguṇatva* of Brahman, they cannot point to Brahman as this or that object, however much they reveal a content. One cannot

(MU 2.2.9) ... *ity evam ādyāḥ śrutayo brahmavidyānantaraṁ mokṣaṁ darśayantyo madhye kāryāntaraṁ vārayanti* (BSB 1.1.4, 14–15).

50 ... *tad brahma sarvajñaṁ sarvaśakti jagadutpattisthitilayakāraṇaṁ vedāntaśāstrād evāvagamyate* (BSB 1.1.4, 11).

51 See Lipner's discussion of the 'performative' use of language in Mīmāṃsā (Lipner, 1986).

52 ... *vakyārthavicāranādhyasānanirvṛttā hi brahmāvagatir na anumāna* (BSB 1.1.2, 7).

53 ... *brahmātmabhāvasya śāstram antareṇa anavagamyamānatvāt* (BSB 1.1.4, 11).

grab hold of Brahman as one grabs the horns of a cow (*śṛṇgah grāhika*). Instead, the 'scripture culminates in the cessation of all differences constructed by ignorance. It does not intend to represent Brahman as this (or that) object; instead, since Brahman is the inner Self, not an object, scripture destroys the distinctions of knowledge, knower, and knowable which are constructed and established by ignorance.'[54]

Now, even though the Vedas themselves are, from the ultimate standpoint, illusory, Śaṅkara, and later disciples such as Maṇḍana and Sureśvara, are quick to point out that even illusions can produce effects: the misguided fear of the illusory snake could induce a heart attack out of fear; the dream tiger can produce a beastly sweat in the dreamer. In any case, for Śaṅkara, *śruti* assumes a surgical role, removing the mortal flaw of dualism: 'The one who sees plurality here goes from death to death.' Since, we are 'already liberated', the Veda and all other practices merely remove the obstacles that prevent us from realizing or experiencing Brahman.

But if we are, in an absolutely crucial sense, already free, or if release is 'nothing but being Brahman',[55] how does this come about for Śaṅkara? He is exquisitely nimble at remaining consistent with his premises in his discussion of realization and meditation. Knowledge is the mechanism for liberation; even meditation and rites are misguided and doomed to fail if they are entered into as some programme to 'attain' Brahman, for this assumes plurality and change, as well as differences of acts, agents and products. Brahman-realization is not a product; if it is something to be attained, it is also something to be lost, and hence is not eternal. Instead, *śruti* testifies that 'liberation is of the nature of the eternally free Self, and liberation cannot be impugned with the defect of impermanence'.[56] At most, the programme of salvation reveals what is already within, and does not construct something afresh.

On the other hand, there is no liberation by the word 'Brahman' alone, a point taken up by Rāmānuja as a criticism of Śaṅkara, albeit an unfair one: certainly mere words do not save, as Rāmānuja holds, but Śaṅkara no doubt would agree with him. There is a world of difference between an intellectual or theoretical understanding of the identity of the Self and Brahman and a felt experience of it. A superficial hearing does not save; some process of interiorization is necessary, itself situated in a culture of liberation. This process is usually comprehended in the threefold formula *śravaṇa*, *manana*, *nididhyāsana*, a gradual process which firmly establishes what otherwise may have been known only through glimpses and intimations: the reality of the one, true, Self. This can occur through 'hearing' for those particularly prepared for it, but not for one who superficially 'hears' the truth of non-duality.

This concern with 'mere hearing' notwithstanding, Śaṅkara makes it clear that

---

54 ... *avidyākalpitabhedanivṛttiparatvāt śāstrasya / na hi śastram idaṁ tayā viṣayabhūtaṁ brahma pratipipādayiṣati / kiṁ tarhi pratyagātmatvena aviṣayatayā pratipādayadavidyākalpitaṁ vedyaveditṛvedanādibhedam apanayati* (BSB 1.1.4, 16).

55 ... *brahmabhāvaḥ ca mokśaḥ* (BSB 1.1.4, 18).

56 ... *nityamuktātmasvarūpasamarpaṇān na mokṣasyānityatvadoṣaḥ* (BSB 1.1.4, 16).

there exist adepts who can realize the truth of the Self immediately upon the cognition of Brahman, an assertion which suggests the Vedānta's characterization as 'leap philosophy'.[57] Neverthless it is still the threefold process of *śravaṇa*, *manana* and *nididhyāsana* that probes the boundaries of the culture of liberation, and Śaṅkara suggests that each of these individual processes is mutually implicated, and must be viewed as a unified project: 'When these three are combined, then only true realization of the unity of Brahman is accomplished, not otherwise, e.g., not by hearing alone.'[58] Śaṇkara here attempts to avoid, I think, the problems of a superficial 'hearing' and recognizes the need for a deepening process of interiorization. The usual Advaitin gloss on these terms is the following: hearing can issue in spontaneous enlightenment (as Sureśvara holds) but it is more likely to be the case that reflection and meditation are needed to remove doubts and distractions respectively. This process presumes an entire culture of liberation: a qualified candidate, a superior teacher, 'received' instruction – the Veda and its interpretation – and pedagogical methods that eliminate doubts and permit the insight into the Self to be firmly established. This culture of liberation is implied in the threefold process of *śravaṇa*, *manana*, *nididhyāsana*, which, taken together, constitute a powerful set of doxastic practices. Śaṅkara's comment on the well-known BU text is telling:

> Therefore, the 'Self, my dear Maitreyi, should be realized,' is worthy of realization, or should be made the object of realization. It should be first heard of from a teacher and from scriptures, then reflected on through reasoning, and then steadfastly meditated upon. Thus only is it realized – when these means, viz., hearing, reflection and meditation, have been gone through.[59]

It remains for Advaita, and for all traditions, I think, to establish a culture of liberation in which doctrine, value, text and interpretation weave together a coherent circuit of doxastic practices. These belief-forming mechanisms have a variety of internal checks – norms of exegesis, standards of argument, the coherence of a received tradition, and, as we will see, the examples of extraordinary teachers and saints. When these mechanisms function properly, they contribute to reliable cognitive outputs. And in the case of Advaita, although liberation ultimately negates

---

57 Potter's term (Potter, 1991: 236). He applies it to Sureśvara, who, as we will see, unfolds and extends Śaṅkara's thought. The same might be said of Ramaṇa Maharṣi; indeed, both Sureśvara and Ramaṇa are interpreted as holding to *ajātivāda*, the doctrine that nothing is ever created, including liberation. Śaṅkara, of course, holds this position, although his *vyavahārika* discussions occasionally suggest gradualism in cosmology and soteriology.

58 ... *yadaikatvam etāny upagatāni tadā samyagdarśanaṁ brahmaikatvaviṣayaṁ prasīdati nānyathā śravaṇamatrena* (BUB 2.4.5, 193).

59 *Tasmād ātmā vā are draṣṭavyo darśanārho darśanaviṣayam āpādayitavyaḥ śrotavyaḥ pūrvam ārcāryata āgamataś ca / paścān mantavyas tarkataḥ / tato nididhyāsitavyo niścayena dhyātavyaḥ / evaṁ hy asau dṛṣṭo bhavati śravaṇamanananididhyāsanasādhanair nirvarvitaiḥ* (BUB 2.4.5, 193). See also BUB 4.5.7, 380–81, in which Śaṅkara uses the following glosses for the three terms in the process of interiorization: *ācāryāgama*, *tarka*, *mata*.

all constructive discourse, various cognitive inroads are nevertheless made to understand, communicate and evoke the truth and experience of Brahman. Teachings, texts, practices, and the examples of saints and gurus, thus help constitute the 'cognitive environment' of a subject. Combined with the subject's own 'properly functioning' mental equipment – in a mundane sense, but also with respect to the doxastic practices of the particular culture of liberation – the cognitive outputs of these processes may enjoy *prima facie* justification. We see, therefore, in addition to traditional Advaita's internalism, a deeply implicated externalism in its epistemology of religious experience.

While Śaṅkara's persistent theme is that saving knowledge is never produced, numerous conditions nevertheless appear necessary for liberation. His comment on the famous BU text above indicates conceptual content (there is a Self) and implies the need for its explication (what is the nature of the Self?); moreover, the concept has value (it is worthy of being realized), is revealed by sacred text, and must be explicated by appropriate teachers. This in turn implies a tradition of teaching and exegesis. Patterns of reasoning also factor in this circuit as well: in Advaita, in addition to using *yukti* where necessary (and where it does not conflict with *śruti*), methods of de-superimposition (*adhyāropa-apavāda*) are employed to peel away false identifications and establish saving knowledge. Thus the culture of liberation presumes as necessary certain externalist processes that conduce to the highest good. In this case, the Veda is given pride of place among the external processes, but the Veda needs teachers and students. Let me now show the contribution of *adhikāra* and gurus to the external circuitry of Śaṅkara's Advaita.

Adhikāra

Another important external dimension is the *adhikāra*, the qualification for the *Brahmajijñāsa*. Theoretically, any sincere person, regardless of caste or stage of life, should be qualified for this programme, since all phenomenal categories are mere superimpositions on to the divine, as we saw above. Superimposition is the *sine qua non* of phenomenal interaction. It is a congenital or natural (*naisargika*) mental process, triggered, of course, by beginningless ignorance. Śaṅkara's introduction to the Brahma Sūtra, the commentary on superimposition (*adhyāsa bhāṣya*) lucidly details this process:

> Since object and the subject, whose scope includes the notions of 'you' and 'I', whose natures are as opposite as darkness and light, cannot be established, nor can their respective attributes. So it follows that it is wrong to superimpose on the subject, whose nature is awareness, and whose scope the notion of 'I', the object and its attributes, whose scope is the notion of 'you'. Similarly it is improper to superimpose the subject and the qualities of the subject on to the object ....[60]

60 *Yuṣmadasmatpratyayagocarayor viṣayaviṣayinos tamaḥprakāśavadviruddhasvabhāvayor*

Through this process any number of qualities attributed to the mind–body complex are ascribed to the Self. So one says, 'I feel whole', 'I'm fat', 'I'm blind', 'I'm anxious' and so on. The endless superimposition appears in the form of 'wrong conception' – and it is with the goal of refashioning that conception that Śaṅkara undertakes his study of the Brahma Sūtra.

Since superimpositions are by definition limitations, it might be assumed that Śaṅkara would accord little importance to social and cultural institutions. But this is not the case. In his exegesis of the first *sūtra*, he engages in an important polemic against the Pūrva Mīmāṁsā concerning the eligibility of inquiry into Brahman. The reading of the Veda, he says, is the common antecedent to both Mīmāṁsās, but specially qualified aspirants need not enter into the comprehensive study of ritual action and instead may proceed directly to the study of the knowledge portion of the upaniṣads. But, in this Brahmin-centric world-view, access to the Veda was limited to twice-born males, and in practice, usually only to Brahmin males.[61] Although he concedes in BSB 3.4.36–38 that extraordinary persons outside the *āśrama* system may indeed qualify or even exemplify knowledge of Brahman, Śaṅkara makes clear the soteriological value of the *āśrama* system in BSB 3.4.39. The *sūtra* aphorism 'better than this' means 'a better means to knowledge is living within the *āśramas* "than this", i.e., than being without an *āśrama*, since it is prescribed in *śruti* and *smṛti*'.[62] Śaṅkara recognizes the *āsrama* as valuable epistemological institution; it is a 'better means of knowledge (*jyāyo vidyāsādhanam*)'. The reason for this is clear: it is the vehicle by which doctrine, ritual and reasoning practices work the intellectual and affective transformation of the *āśrami* and prepare him for transcendent experience. But how necessary is the *āsrama* in the economy of liberation? Śaṅkara cites an ominous *smṛti* text: 'Let a Brahmin not reside for even one single day outside the *āśrama*; having stayed outside for a year, he goes to utter ruin.'[63] Moreover, in BSB 4.4.40 he argues, on the basis of restrictive rules, scripture and the 'custom of the good (*sadācara*)' that 'ascent' into higher *āśramas* is permanent. Once the 'higher' path has been commenced, there is no returning to 'lower' stages (BSB 3.4.40, 451).[64]

The significance of these considerations is that the Brahmin world construction is affirmed in these 'external' institutional settings. Revelation, *śruti*, the 'premier

---

itaretarabhāvānupapattau siddhāyāṁ taddharmāṇam api sutarāmitaretarabhāvānupapattir ity ato'smatpratyayagocare viṣayiṇi cidātmake yuśmatpratyayagocarasya viṣayasya taddharmāṇaṁ cādhyāsaḥ tadviparyayeṇa viṣayiṇas taddharmāṇāṁ ca viṣaye' dhyāso mithye' iti bavituṁ yuktam (BSB intro., 1).

61 Exceptions are represented in the upaniṣads.

62 ... *atas tu antarālavartitvād itaradāśramavartitvaṁ jyāyo vidyāsādhanam / śrutismṛtisaṁdṛṣṭatvāt* (BSB 3.4.39, 451).

63 ... *anāśramī na tiṣṭheta dinam ekam api dvijaḥ / saṁvatsaram anāśramī sthitvā kṛcchram ekam caret* (BSB 3.4.39, 451).

64 For a detailed study of the historical developments in the ideology and theology of the *āśrama* system, see Olivelle (1993).

pattern and guide' of religious experience, is transmitted in particular social and cultural contexts, which further privilege those who adopt a more rigorous lifestyle. Still, while affirming these orthodox cultural constructions, Śaṅkara nonetheless makes room for the particularly gifted student who may bypass the study of ritual texts in favour of the correct exegesis of the upaniṣads.

In addition to the Vedic requirement, Śaṅkara adds the following four requisites, all of which imply mental training and a particular kind of culture which reinforce certain intellectual and ethical values:

1 the discrimination of the eternal from the non-eternal (*nityānityavastuvivekaḥ*);
2 the renunciation of the fruit of action, both now and hereafter (*ihāmūtrārthabhogavirāgaḥ*);
3 the practice of restraint, introspection, and other virtues (*śamadamādisādhanasampat*);
4 the intense desire for liberation (*mumukṣatvam*).

Śaṅkara makes it clear that this fourfold preparation is antecedent to the inquiry into Brahman. In short, it frames a comprehensive set of virtues – cognitive, affective and conative – which indicate the refashioning of human personality in preparation for realization.

None of these values is, of course, particularly original to Śaṅkara; all are included in a well-resourced stock of spiritual values that gained prominence in *brāhmaṇa* and *śramaṇa* cultures since the sixth century BCE. The principal cognitive virtue among these values, *viveka*, has long been esteemed in the history of soteriology in India; the upaniṣads illustrate various processes of discrimination, and later upaniṣads, such as the Śvetāśvatara and Maitrī, adopt yogic methods to develop the intellectual and mental qualities of discrimination, concentration, and tranquillity. The hero of the Yoga Sūtra is the *vivekin*, and YS 2.26 offers this method for attaining the yogic goal of cessation: 'the means of cessation is the unceasing vision of discernment',[65] a mental virtue seen in the *Sāṅkhya Kārikā* as well (Sastri, 1948: 3).

Moreover, detachment (*vairāgya*), while primarily a virtue belonging to the affect (or perhaps better, a virtue which *resists* affect), also presumes a cognitive element: there must be *reasons* for developing indifference to the objects of enjoyment – reasons which quickly (and thickly) implicate various Indian world-views and doctrines. *Vairāgya* has also enjoyed long currency in Indian thought, perhaps quintessentially advocated in Chapter 2 of the *Gītā*, where Kṛṣṇa advocates *niṣkāma karma*, action free of desire. *Vairāgya*, along with *abhyāsa*, constitute the foundation of yogic practice as represented by Patañjali.[66]

65 ... *vivekakhyātir aviplavā hānopāyaḥ*.

66 ... *abhyāsavairāgyābhyāṁ tannirodhaḥ* (YS 1.12) (Feuerstein, 1989: 34). See also *Sāṅkhya Kārikā* 45, *vairāgyāt prakṛtilayaḥ* (Sastri, 1948: 76).

The virtues further shaping the mind and will are included in the 'riches of practice', *sādhanasampat* – namely, calm, restraint, renunciation, forbearance, collected meditation and faith. Lastly, a virtue in which intense affect is expected as requisite for *brahmajijñāsa* is the desire for liberation, *mumukṣutvam*. Again, intensity is seen in other Indian traditions; the Yoga Sūtra reports that only those aspirants who are 'extremely vehement' or energetic (*tivrasamvegānām*) attain the highest states of *samādhi*. Feuerstein points out that Hemacandra glosses *samvega* as 'the desire for liberation' (*mokṣābhilāsa*); he adds that *samvega* 'has nothing to do with excessive asceticism or pathological mortification. It is enthusiasm in the best sense of the word' (Feuerstein, 1989: 41). *Samvega* is further qualified in the YS as soft (*mṛdu*), medium (*madhyama*), and 'beyond measure' (*adhimātra*). *Mumukṣatva* has the same sensibility as *adhimātra*: an often repeated anecdote by contemporary *ācāryas* uses the image of a guru holding the head of his disciple under water until the disciple instinctively, involuntarily thrashes about for air; such should be the intensity of the desire for liberation.

What is important for our purposes are the cognitive dimensions and the epistemic implications of eligibility and its constitutive virtues. I use these terms deliberately, for the term 'epistemic' tends to shade into evaluation and justification – precisely our concern here. The cognitive dimensions include, again, a mutually reinforcing association to the culture of liberation; the *adhikāra* presumes an entire host of concepts, the most important in this case being non-dual truth, but others as well – assumptions about mind and body, karma, transmigration, merit, demerit and so on. The virtues associated with *adhikāra* also have cognitive dimensions – values imply an understanding of a world-view and the highest good. Following Alston, the epistemic implications of the 'external circuitry' of Advaita suggest that, in the absence of contraindications, the claims which follow Advaita religious experience may be *prima facie* justified. One check on potential contraindications is the role of the guru, a constitutive element in the 'external circuitry' of Advaita, examined below.

The guru

So far we have addressed two external factors in the culture of liberation, the Veda and the *adhikāra*. First, an authoritative text, the Veda, is transmitted in a particular context, the *varṇāśramadharma*. Second, as an element of that context, the qualification (*adhikāra*) for *brahmajijñāsa* contributes to and reinforces a quite specific cognitive and social environment. A third constitutive element in this process is the role of the teacher. A useful starting point is MU 1.2.12, which addresses the 'existential' state of the *adhikāri*, a preliminary round of intellectual and affective training, and the need for a realized teacher:

> Having examined worlds constructed by rites, let a Brahmin arrive at complete indifference, for action cannot but make what is made. For the sake of this

> knowledge, let him approach, firewood in hand, a teacher well-versed in the Vedas and established in Brahman.[67]

This verse emphasizes a comprehensive world-view with appropriate intellectual and axiological dimensions. Specifically, it highlights the importance of renunciation, detachment, the futility of ritual action and the instrumental role of a teacher – all central themes in the process of gaining saving knowledge for Śaṅkara. Śaṅkara's initial comment on this passage summarizes our earlier discussion of *vairāgya*: 'this is stated for the purpose to illustrate the eligibility for supreme knowledge for one who is indifferent to this (world) of ends and means which constitutes *samsāra*'.[68]

Śaṅkara's gloss expands on these themes. In vivid language, he describes the heavenly and hellish worlds 'won' by proper or improper attention to ritual action; he expects the student to make full use of the powers of observation, analysis and scripture (*pratyakṣānumanopamānāgama*) to ascertain the impermanence of all worlds constructed by ignorance and desire. Arriving at their ultimate illusory nature, comparable, say, to dreams, mirages or castles in the air, Śaṅkara adds, significantly: 'The Brahmin is mentioned because he alone is particularly eligible for the knowledge of Brahmin by renouncing all.'[69] But such renunciation needs the strict direction of a superior: 'the Brahmin (disgusted with the insubstantial nature of phenomenal existence) should go only to a teacher who is blessed with mental and physical self-control, mercy, etc., for the sake of fully understanding that state which is fearless, auspicious, unproduced, and eternal'.[70] Lastly, and most significantly, he glosses the emphatic particle *eva*; the phrase 'only to a teacher (*gurum eva*)' implies that 'although he may know the Veda, the Brahmin should not attempt to make an independent inquiry into the knowledge of Brahmin'.[71]

This passage is important for it highlights the tension between internalist and externalist structures in Śaṅkara. The axioms of Advaita suggest that we are constituted to access the divine through our powers of introspection. Moreover, once we do access it, the knowledge that shines forth is self-certifying and self-luminous. Here, however, Śaṅkara explicitly warns against independent programmes of realization, instead advocating a programme strictly conditioned by the transmission of a teacher. The guru must be available to those who properly approach him. The *Upadeśasāhasrī* is even more specific about the traditional programme of transmission:

---

67 ... *parīkṣya lokān karmacitān brāhmaṇo nirvedam āyān nāsty akṛtaḥ kṛtena / tad vijñānārthaṁ sa gurum evābhigaccet samitpāṇiḥ śrotriyaṁ brahmaniṣṭham* (UPB: vol. 1, 139).

68 ... *asmāt sādhyasādhanarūpāt sarvasmāt samsārād viraktasya parasyāṁ vidyāyām adhikārapradarśanārtham idam ucyate* (UPB: vol. 1, 139).

69 *brāhmaṇasyaiva viśeṣato' dhikāraḥ sarvatyāgena brahmavidyāyam* (UPB: vol. 1, 139).

70 *abheyaṁ śivam akṛtam nityam padaṁ yattat vijñānārthaṁ viśeṣanādhigamārthaṁ sa nirviṇṇo gurum evācāryaṁ śamadamadayādisampannam abhigacchet* (UPB: vol. 1, 140).

71 ... *śāstrajño' pi svātantreṇa brahmajñānānveṣaṇaṁ na kuryat* (UPB: vol. 1, 140).

> The means to final release is knowledge. It should be proclaimed repeatedly – until it is firmly grasped – to a pupil who is indifferent to everything transitory, achievable through (various) methods, who has abandoned the desire for sons, wealth, and worlds and has reached the state of *paramahaṃsa* ascetic; who is endowed with tranquillity, self-control, compassion, etc.; who is possessed of qualities of a pupil which are well known from scripture; who is a Brahmin and pure; who has approached the teacher in the prescribed manner; and whose caste, profession, behaviour, knowledge, and lineage have been examined.[72]

This passage highlights many of the intellectual, affective, and conative virtues which we saw in BSB 1.1.1. Moreover, an intellectual process of interiorization is suggested here and then exemplified in the back-and-forth dialogue between guru and disciple in the prose section of the *Upadeśasāhasrī*. This passage clearly emphasizes the importance of the guru–*śiṣya* relationship and certain social conditions, despite their phenomenality. I have already discussed the former above, but it is worth seeing again how the prerequisites clearly function in a Brahmin context, no matter how much caste and so on are *upādhis*. Indeed, distinctions continue despite programmes of renunciation as well: we see here that Śaṅkara recognizes a hierarchy among ascetic orders in addition to the social order. Of four groups of renunciants – *kuṭicaka, bahūdaka, haṃsa, paramahaṃsa* – the last has the most prestige for Śaṅkara and represents the stage at which one is fit for knowledge of Brahman. A conflict in Advaitin theory and practice can be seen in this section of the *Upadeśasāhasrī*, for Śaṅkara first insists on these social prerequisites in the candidate for liberation, then immediately begins deconstructing the disciple's self-understanding as 'Brahmin', 'renunciant' and so on.

On the other hand, prerequisites are not lacking for gurus either:

> The guru is endowed skill in reasoning, understanding, memory, tranquillity, self-control, compassion, favor, etc.; he has mastered the scriptures; unattached to all enjoyments visible or invisible; he has abandoned rituals and their requisites; he is a knower of Brahman, established in Brahman; he leads a blameless life, free from faults such as trickery, arrogance, deceit, dishonesty, fraud, jealousy, falsehood, egotism, self-interest, etc.; he wishes to apply his knowledge with the sole purpose of helping others.[73]

For Śaṅkara, the role of teacher cannot be underestimated. This important role, clearly contributing to an externalist epistemology, raises challenging questions

---

[72] *Mokṣasādhanaṁ jñanaṁ sādhanasādhyād anityāt sarvasmāt viraktāya tyaktaputravittalokaiṣaṇāya pratipannaparamahaṃsapārivrājyāya śamadamadayādiyuktāya śāstraprasiddhaśiṣyaguṇasampannāya sucaye brāhmaṇāya vidhivadupasannāya jātikarmavṛttavidyābijanaiḥ parīkṣitāya śiṣyāya brūyāt punaḥ punar yāvadgrahaṇaṁ dṛḍhībhavati* (Up. 2.1.2, 121).

[73] ... *ācāryaś cohāpohagrahaṇadhāraṇaśamadamadayānugrahādisampanno labdhāgamo dṛṣṭādṛṣṭabhogeṣv anāsaktas tyaktasarvakarmasādhano brahmavit brahmaṇi sthito' binnavṛtto dambhadarpakuhakaśāṭhyamāyāmātsāryānṛtāhamkāramamatvādidoṣavivarjitaḥ kevalaparānugrah-aprayojano vidyopayogarthī* (Up. 2.1.6, 123).

about the nature of the religious experience which is cultivated and transmitted by the teacher. Michael Peterson, William Hasker *et al.* have clearly illustrated this point in their study of religious experience. Recognizing that our prior beliefs, formed by the interaction of our religious tradition, shape our religious experience 'by pre-forming the schema in terms of which the experience is perceived and understood', they continue:

> As confirmation of this position, note the role of gurus and teachers of mystical tradition. The relevant wisdom is closely held by small groups of devotees, led by a master or teacher who instructs them in a specific method for achieving the desired goal. Hence, the mystic experience itself is conditioned by the methods and beliefs instilled by the teacher. *The attainment of genuine mystic insight is sanctioned, if not determined, by the master.* (Peterson, *et al.*, 1991: 24; my italics)

There is no doubt that the methods and beliefs instilled by the teacher serve as necessary conditions for the possibility of the experience, but what the phenomenal content of the experience is remains unclear. In any case, the role of teacher is dominant in ancient, classical and modern India and, at least in ancient and classical India, was deeply shaped by Brahmin ideology. Minoru Hara has made a study of the Hindu concept of teacher and notes that, as far back as Atharvaveda 11.5, the '*ācārya* is said to seek out a Vedic student (*brahmacārin*), to take (a student) as a pupil (*upanayamāna*), to bring about the rebirth of this student ...' (Hara, 1980: 93). This tradition is seen in the upaniṣads as well, especially the Chāndogya, Taittirīya and Muṇḍaka. In many cases, the details of a Brahmin world-view are affirmed; the teacher ushers the student into rebirth, guides him in the recitation and study of the Veda, and, finally, sets the stage for esoteric, saving knowledge. One the one hand, the teacher appears as an 'institutional instructor of intellectual and objective knowledge' (Hara, 1980: 95), which establishes fundamental beliefs and practices – the external circuitry that prepares an extraordinary pupil for knowledge of Brahman. But in addition to the 'institutional instructor' of Brahmin culture, the teaching of a realized one (*brahmavit*) appears to be the *sine qua non* for the acquisition of saving knowledge – see, for example, CU 6.14.2: 'One who has a teacher knows'[74] and CU 4.9.3: 'The knowledge which has been learned from a teacher best helps to attain his end.'[75]

These last two verses are significant because they are included in the prose section of the *Upadeśasāhasrī*, which emphasizes the essential role of the teacher in the plan of liberation and models an ideal exchange between teacher and student. Although Śaṅkara cites CU 6.14.2 to stress the implications of the teacher–student relationship, his comment on the verse is worth quoting in full for it weaves together teacher, student, beliefs and, finally, realization. Śaṅkara considers the Chāndogya

74 ... *ācāryavān puruṣo veda.*
75 ... *ācāryavāddhyaiva vidyā viditā sādhiṣṭhaṁ prāpatīti.*

parable of the lost man of Gāndhāra; in a metaphor for the burdens and trials of *samsāra*, the traveller undergoes numerous humiliations before finally encountering a realized guru and, through his efficacious instruction, experiences liberation himself:

> Somehow, through very great merit arising from past deeds, while crying out thus, he manages to find refuge in some supremely compassionate person who has direct knowledge of the fact that his own real Self is pure Being of the Absolute, who is established in the Absolute, and who is free from bondage. From this supremely compassionate person of perfect enlightenment, he receives instruction in noting the defects attaching to the objects encountered in transmigratory life. Eventually, when he has become indifferent to the objects of the world, he is taught, 'Thou art not a denizen of the world, with worldly characteristics such as "being the son of so-and-so". Thou art pure Being.' In this way he becomes released from his bands of ignorance and delusion and reaches his own true Self, as the inhabitant of Gāndhāra reached Gāndhāra, and becomes happy.
>
> This is what the text means when it says, 'One who has a Teacher acquires knowledge.' It is of such a person only, who has a Teacher, and whose bonds of ignorance have been removed, that it is said, 'In his case the delay will only extend until he is released from the body.' It means (the delay in) realization of Brahman, one's own true nature. (Alston, 1989: 272–73)

There are actually two teaching moments in this passage. The first is the 'life experience' of the lost soul. While it is clear from this passage that the encounter with a teacher is a necessary condition for liberation, so too is the 'existential' crisis of the lost soul. We see this dynamic in the despair of Arjuna on the eve of battle in the *Gītā* and also in young Gautama's confrontation with suffering in the legend of the 3 Passing Sights as well. What this tells us is that life experience is meant to be used as a source of reflection on meaning and truth. But the deepest truth is, according to Śaṅkara, transmitted in important ways by one who testifies to it by his own example, the *brahmavit*.

So, while the event that defines liberation and its certainty, *anubhava*, is arrived at in a relevant sense by the internal access of a subject, this process is clearly facilitated by a culture of liberation that includes text, teacher, student and, we should add, rites as well. For while it is clear in his discussion of BSB 1.1.1 and elsewhere that Śaṅkara holds that knowledge, not action or rites, is the efficient and proximate cause of liberation, ritual nevertheless plays an important role in the economy of salvation. Once again implicating the importance and need for a Brahmin world-view, he holds that rites are necessary as purifying agents. While they do not produce liberation, they produce a moral and psychological state which conduces to liberation; in short, rites are meant to diminish accumulated sins and set the stage for the 'arising' of knowledge. Indeed, as an end to this, Śaṅkara admits even the propriety for praying for wealth: 'The prayer for prosperity dealt with in this context of knowledge is for the sake of wealth. Wealth is needed for rites; and rites are meant to diminish accumulated sins; precisely on the exhaustion of these, knowledge becomes revealed.'[76]

Rites and auxiliary instruction are intended for '(creating the proper) tendencies in a person',[77] so that 'knowledge of the Self arises clearly to one (whose mind is) refined and whose being is purified'.[78] Again, as pointed out in an earlier discussion, the use of the term *samskṛta* is telling: its semantic range includes 'remade', 'refined', 'purified', 'perfected'. The term indicates that an adept enters into a process of reworking or refashioning one's mind and heart; this is done by tapping into the 'external circuitry' of the entire range of doxastic practices, including the Veda, social institutions, the instruction of a guru and ritual actions to set the stage for the internal access of the one true Self.

And while Śaṅkara always privileges the threefold process in the economy of liberation, certain meditations (*upāsana*) are helpful in this regard as well, for they represent a kind of intermediate state between action and knowledge. In BSB 1.1.1 Śaṅkara notes the significant difference between knowledge and meditation: knowledge results from its appropriate *pramāṇa* and depends on its object, the thing itself; knowledge possesses intrinsic validity (*svataḥ prāmaṇyatva*) and does not depend on human will. Meditation (*upāsana*), however, depends on human will and mental constructions; its object is not a 'real thing' (*bhūtavastu*). Inferior to knowledge and not ultimately necessary, meditation can nevertheless assist in the plan of salvation much in the same ways as rites; this is not surprising, for the oldest form of *upāsana* was associated with Vedic ritual. As with rites, 'meditations contribute to the final understanding of the metaphysical truth by purifying the mind, and are in this sense auxiliaries to knowledge of non-duality' (CU 1.1.1).[79]

So, a complex world construction is reinforced by social dogmas (*varṇāśramadharma*), doctrine (Advaita theory) and ritual programmes. This 'world construction' has validity until saving knowledge dawns, when all rites and rituals are forsworn as contradictory to ultimate truth. Until then, duties of caste and stage of life enjoy a relative importance as part of a broader programme of mental and affective transformation.

But all the practices inscribed in this programme conduce to liberation; they do not produce it. These various sets of intellectual, social and ethical practices constitute the so-called 'indirect means' to enlightenment (*bahiraṅga*). But these indirect or 'external' mechanisms nevertheless loom large in the transformation of the *mumukṣu*. By reinforcing a particular world-view, a particular kind of

76 ... *śrīkāmo' smin vidyāprakaraṇe 'abhidhīyamāno dhanārthaḥ dhanaṁ ca karmārthaṁ karma copāttaduritakṣayāya tatkṣaye hi vidyā prakāśate* (TUB 1.4.3, 391).

77 ... *puruṣasamskārarthtvāt* (TUB 1.11.1, 420).

78 ... *samskṛtasya hi viśuddhasattvasya ātmajñānam añjasaivotpadyate* (TUB 1.11.1, 420).

79 For extended discussion of *upāsana* in its Vedic context and of Śaṅkara's discussion of *upāsana* as a propaedeutic to saving knowledge, see Gambhirananda (1992a: 375–85), Bader (1990: 32–64), Alston (1989: 1–80), and Rambachand (1991: 81–83).

experience is theorized which both conforms to, and confirms, it. Given the tight circle of inner and external mechanisms here, the cognitive outcomes of this process, *nirguṇatva* notwithstanding, minimally enjoy at least *prima facie* justification.

Concluding remarks

In this chapter I have examined the dynamic of internalism and externalism in Śaṅkara's Advaita. I have argued that Śaṅkara's definitive mechanism is internalism, on the basis of his metaphysical axioms and the introspective process of accessing, indubitably and in a self-justifying manner, the inner Self. Despite this non-dual metaphysic and the internalism it suggests, the process of accessing saving knowledge is profoundly supported by a broad 'external circuitry' of Advaita, an interwoven process of text, tradition and teacher which presents and reinforces a particular construal of reality in its broadest context.

These observations bear on our discussion of justification in Chapter 1. While the decisive experience of saving *anubhava* effectively issues in justification, its scope is limited to the subject of the experience; however, for one who has an experience of *mokṣa* such epistemological niggling may be moot. Still, while the experience of *anubhava* may be 'self-established', the combination of Advaitin internalism with the various externalist processes which I have highlighted confer far stronger theoretical justification on the beliefs which precede and follow the Advaitin 'religious' experience. This justification, following Alston, may be 'mere' *prima facie* justification, but it is justification nonetheless – a conclusion which has profound implications for the philosophy of religion and the practice of spirituality.

There is a final observation which shades into the social implications of the epistemology of religious experience. We see the sustained interplay of metaphysics and epistemology in Advaita, and, with regard to the latter, the tension between internalism and externalism. But the relatively high value placed on these external mechanisms locks early Advaita into its local context; here we see a tradition which appears to be universalist, on the basis of its premises, instead limited in striking ways. How later Advaitin thinkers 'tip the scales' in favour of internalism or externalism also impacts on the theoretical universalism of Advaita. The next chapter examines the tension of externalism and internalism in the thought of the immediate heirs of Śaṅkara's intellectual and spiritual legacy, Sureśvara and Padmapāda.

CHAPTER 3

Later Advaita on religious experience

Sureśvara, Padmapāda, the *Vivekacūḍāmaṇi*

Advaita is a school of Indian thought that commanded much intellectual attention in the centuries following Śaṅkara, an evolution that has been well documented elsewhere.[1] It is not the purpose of this study to repeat the historical evolution of all things Advaita, but to stay within the framework of my objectives, namely to consider the epistemology of religious experience particularly as it pertains to classical Advaita and the Advaita of the twentieth-century Tamil saint, Ramaṇa Maharṣi. The rationale for selecting Ramaṇa as a case study of twentieth-century Advaita will be explained in Chapter 4. For now, some explanation for choosing Sureśvara, Padmapāda, and the *Vivekacūḍāmaṇi* as representations of 'later Advaita' is in order.

Of course, certain traditional Indian *paṇḍits* or Western apologists for non-dualism might consider the more monistic upaniṣads to be the quintessential expressions of Vedānta. But the interpretation of the upaniṣads defies unanimous agreement, as evidenced by the competing readings among Vedāntin *ācāryas*. So while there are clearly monistic passages found in the upaniṣads, even a cursory reading of the text, apart from any ideological analysis, subverts the notion of a homogeneous non-dualism as the sole voice in the text. Indeed, their very ambiguity and esoterica were the engines driving the various interpretative communities in medieval south India.

In any case, the earliest formal formulation of Advaita probably begins with Gauḍapāda (*c.* 600 CE), which was then expanded and systematized by Śaṅkara.[2] But even Śaṅkara seemed occasionally unconcerned with terminological and other inconsistencies in his presentation – explanations for which usually focus on Śaṅkara's axiology[3] – and such gaps led to increasingly formal developments in later Advaita. However, rather than surveying the whole of these developments, let me choose a more modest objective: examining the reflections on religious

1 For example, Dasgupta (1988), Sharma (1960: 239–334), Potter (1981), and Radhakrishnan (1989: 445–658) Murty (1959: 445–658). Murty's study has a specific focus, though his method is as sweeping as Dasgupta's. Radhakrishnan's survey focuses on Śaṅkara, but he often refers to many later Advaitins as well.

2 As is the case with so many authors in Indian literature, answers to who Gauḍapāda was and when he actually lived (assuming he is a genuinely historical figure) are difficult to pin down. See King (1995), Fox (1993: 3–7), and Karmarkar (1973: i–x).

3 See, for example, Devaraja (1962); Eliot Deutsch considers the 'axio-noetic' dimensions of the *sattātrāyavāda* (Deutsch, 1969: 17). Daniel H.H. Ingalls suggested this in an earlier study (1953: 72).

experience found in Śaṅkara's two immediate disciples, Sureśvara and Padmapāda and a later Advaita text, the *Vivekacūḍāmaṇi.*

Concerning the former authors, while no necessity guarantees that proximity to the master conduces to significant intellectual continuities, the Indian pedagogical tradition is, if anything, conservative,[4] so in this case the closer to the source the better. J.M. van Boetzelaer is rather blunt, however, in his assessment of the work of Sureśvara: drawing upon Paul Hacker's analysis of the use of key technical terms in Śaṅkara's Advaita, he concludes that 'Sureśvara's doctrines do not differ from Śaṅkara's, at least not as regards the main points' (van Boetzelaer, 1971: 6). Mahadevan concurs (1972: xiv–xv). While these observations are correct, I wish to suggest that Sureśvara and Padmapāda extend Śaṅkara's thought and unfold its deepest implications. In doing so, they do not merely repeat what was taught to them, but shape the contours of an emerging Advaitin tradition of thought and practice. This is particularly the case concerning the nature of experience and the necessary conditions for liberating experience, our primary concerns here.

Some scholars have already reviewed the work of Sureśvara. Balasubramanian, for example, takes pains to assure his readers that Sureśvara is not slavish in his repetition of his guru's ideas, and insists that Sureśvara offers his unique contributions to developing strands of Advaita.[5] A.J. Alston, one of the first Western translators and scholars of Sureśvara, identified three of these intriguing reflections in the *Naiṣkarmyasiddhi* alone.[6] Padmapāda, on the other hand, was the first Advaitin thinker to consistently use the so-called 'reflection theory' (*pratibimbavāda*) as a model for understanding the relationship between *ātman* and *jīva* – a model that has enjoyed long currency in Advaitin treatises, doxographies and popular representations. In addition to this, Padmapāda significantly advanced Śaṅkara's lucid, but relatively brief, reflections on superimposition; indeed, over half of his *Pañcapādikā* is taken up with his interpretation of the *adhyāsa bhāṣya.* Many of his comments here are more epistemologically refined than Śaṅkara's and have served as a resource for later Advaitin thinkers such as Dharmarāja Adhvarin, author of the manual *Vedāntaparibhāṣā.* The nuances concerning knowledge and religious experience in Padmapāda and Sureśvara will be the focus of this chapter. While the premises of Advaita promise a privileged access to the one true Self, the 'pendulum' of the emerging tradition seems to swing from a peculiar form of externalism (Sureśvara) to a modest internalism (Padmapāda). Both of these

4 Francis Clooney notes this tendency in the Śrīvaiṣṇava tradition after the fourteenth or fifteenth century; '… it became the *ideal* that very little in the way of new insight should ever occur, particularly if it proceeds by a new style or from new presuppositions. Even today, it seems to remain the highest praise of a Śrīvaiṣṇava speaker to observe, "He was magnificent, he said nothing new"' (Clooney, 1996: 253–54).

5 These seem finally reserved to exegetical distinctions, for 'there is no difference between them in the basic philosophical standpoint' (Balasubramanian, 1984: 10–14).

6 Nuances concerning the injunction to meditate, the concept of the *ahaṃkara*, and the magic power (*mahimā*) of the *mahāvākyas* (Alston, 1959: i–ii, cited in De Smet, 1961: 256).

positions, seemingly in conflict, nevertheless have their roots in Śaṅkara's epistemology of religious experience, which also dances between the poles of internalism and externalism.

In addition to Sureśvara and Padmapāda, I shall examine the *Vivekacūḍāmaṇi*, a text that traditionally has been ascribed to Śaṅkara. Few Indologists accept that the text is Śaṅkara's, although a few Western and Indian scholars champion Śaṅkara's authorship of it. Paul Hacker, for example, has claimed at least a provisional status of authenticity for the *Vivekacūḍāmaṇi* on the basis of the text's colophons (Hacker, 1995: 50). However, the fact that the text lacks the usual commentarial apparatus suggests that even traditional Advaitins consider it spurious. The most intriguing literary analysis of the text is Robert Gussner's 'stylometric' analysis (Gussner, 1977). His penetrating study concludes that the text bridges a period between the philosophical *prakaraṇas* and a later period of Vedānta more disposed to devotion. While one may quibble with certain elements of his analysis,[7] the overall weight of his presentation seems conclusive: the text represents a later development of post-Śaṅkara thought. How much later, of course, is another question. Gussner makes the intriguing suggestion, if not altogether persuasive, that stylometrics may link the text to Sureśvara. In any case, while it may be 'spurious' in terms of authorship, the *Vivekacūḍāmaṇi* nonetheless contains important philosophical considerations which also reflect continuities and discontinuities with Śaṅkara's thought concerning religious experience.

Although few Western scholars consider the *Vivekacūḍāmaṇi* to be written by Śaṅkara, the text is appropriate for a study such as this for a number of reasons. First, following Gussner's analysis, it is a text whose internal evidence reveals itself to be later than Śaṅkara; thus we are able to discern patterns of thought which recur and develop in post-Śaṅkara Advaita. The text, moreover, compares well to two other important philosophical dialogues, Śaṅkara's own *Upadeśasāhasrī* and the *Bhagavad-Gītā*. These latter two texts share a striking similarity of style. Strip away the political machinations and impending martial catastrophe on Kurukṣetra and the two texts simmer to a single shared genre: an extended philosophical discourse between guru and *śiṣya*. This style is adopted by the author of the *Vivekacūḍāmaṇi* as well. Above all, these three texts share the same didactic strategy: they each seek to extend the awareness of the student beyond the confines of egocentric boundaries.

In addition to these reasons for including this text as an object for study, two others recommend themselves. First, it has been a text of immense popularity for both popular and professional Vedāntins. Various translations into Indian and European languages, usually sponsored by the Ramakrishna Mission, have continuously been available for most of the twentieth century. Two English translations have enjoyed numerous reprintings and a third has recently been

[7] The strength of his presentation may be its weakness: the computer-like analysis seems mechanical and deterministic, leaving little room for novelty on the part of an author.

published as well: the text 'travels well', so to speak (Prabhavananda and Isherwood, 1978; Turīyānanda, 1992; Mādhavānanda, 1992). Moreover, despite its dubious authorship, the *Vivekacūḍāmaṇi* has often been used by gurus in their homilies, lectures and popular presentations of Advaita to Indian and Western audiences. So, rather than operating out of an intellectual snobbery which scoffs at a 'non-canonical' text, this study recognizes the need to take seriously a text which has had a commanding perennial appeal for gurus and seekers across cultures.

A final reason for examining the *Vivekacūḍāmaṇi* recommends itself. Ramaṇa Maharṣi (1879–1950), whose life and works we will examine in Chapter 4, composed a slim, though significant, body of work in Sanskrit and Tamil. Included among his writings is a rather free Tamil translation of the Sanskrit *Vivekacūḍāmaṇi*. So, while Ramaṇa's primary teaching 'method' was his so-called silent *upadeśa*,[8] his writings, including his translation of the *Vivekacūḍāmaṇi*, will shed light on just how closely his thought agrees with that of Śaṅkara. For now, let us return to Sureśvara and explore his own continuities with Śaṅkara.

Sureśvara

The exact dates of Sureśvara are uncertain, as are the dates of so many authors and texts in Indian history; moreover, precisely when Sureśvara lived depends on the dates of Śaṅkara, which are by no means unambiguous (Potter, 1991: 420).[9] However, since most contemporary scholars of Advaita hold that Śaṅkara lived sometime between 700 and 750 CE, we can at least tentatively hold that Sureśvara lived in the middle of the eighth century. With regard to Sureśvara's biography, although we know much about his thought by virtue of the texts he wrote, we know little with any certainty about his life. In any case, most traditional accounts consider Sureśvara to be a contemporary, and perhaps initial disputant, of Śaṅkara. Early work on Sureśvara, uncritically accepting Anantānandagiri's biography of Śaṅkara, *Śaṅkaradigvijaya*, assumed that Sureśvara was the post-conversion name of the famous Mīmāṃsaka, Maṇḍana Miśra.[10] However, there are considerable differences between the Advaita of Miśra and that of either Śaṅkara or Sureśvara; for our purposes, the most outstanding is Miśra's insistence on the need for

8 A method worth considering and comparing: Halbfass cryptically – and properly – notes that Ramaṇa's silence is equally important as what he said (Halbfass, 1990: 384); cf. Ramaṇa's silence to the literate verbosity of Aurobindo Ghose (1878–1950) and to the Socratic intellectualism of J. Krishnamurti (1895–1986).

9 Traditional accounts, *paramparās*, and the *maṅgala* verses all indicate that Sureśvara followed Śaṅkara.

10 Balasubramanian reviews the *digvijayas* and their construction of Sureśvara's identity; he then summarizes the reasons for deconstructing the traditional equation of Maṇḍana and Sureśvara (Balasubramanian, 1983: 11–18). See also M. Hiriyanna (1972: 2–5); on the *Brahmasiddhi* itself, see Biardeau (1969).

prolonged meditation (*prasaṅkhyāna*) on *mahāvākyas* such as '*tat tvam asi*' in order for saving knowledge to take root and have its ultimate effect. This reasonable position is rejected by Sureśvara for it compromises a fundamental Advaita tenet: one need not, must not, *do* anything for liberation; one *is* liberation: 'all action is prescribed for a result that is not the Self; since the Self has already been attained, action should not be employed to attain it'.[11] Liberation, like the Self, has an 'unchangeable' nature.[12] In the end, 'liberation, say the wise, is the abiding of the Self in its own nature'.[13] It is our real nature, however veiled by ignorance.

However, another problem would trouble Sureśvara: acts involve plurality, a clear affront to non-dual truth. Moreover, while liberation is eternal and unchangeable, ritual acts – and their fruit – are temporary and fleeting. The worrisome implication here is that if one 'achieves' liberation through action, one can 'lose' liberation as well. Sureśvara on this account is the standard-bearer of his master's teaching, repeating Śaṅkara's argument in BSB 1.1.4 and elsewhere: 'If (release) were the fruit of action, it would be non-eternal, like heaven, etc.' (TUBV 1.24).[14] Instead, according to Sureśvara, liberation occurs spontaneously and permanently from the hearing of the word.

While Sureśvara probably was not the former Mīmāṃsaka Miśra, there is a good chance he came to Advaita from the ritual school after all, for much of the *Naiṣkarmyasiddhi* (NS) and the *Bṛhadāraṇyakopaniṣadbhāṣyavārtika* (BUBV) show detailed and unstereotyped understanding of the presuppositions and argument of Mīmāṃsā. Sureśvara's principal philosophical effort, following Śaṅkara, repeatedly involves demonstrating the superiority of knowledge over ritual action in the plan of salvation. To this end, he frequently marshals the Mīmāṃsā *pūrvapakṣa* with considerable expertise before deconstructing it. And, although we do not know precisely who Sureśvara was, intratextual evidence suggests that he was indeed a disciple of Śaṅkara – both the TUBV and the NS indicate that Sureśvara's motivation to write owed its origination and inspiration to the 'direction' (*anuśikṣa*, NS 1.3) and 'favour' (*ācāryaprasāda*, TUBV 1.3) of his guru. Indeed, de Smet adds that Sureśvara's reference to Bhagavān Pūjyapāda (Śaṅkara) 'constitutes, along with Padmapāda's, the only really trustworthy information we have on the great Vedāntin' (de Smet, 1961: 256). His relationship with Śaṅkara apparently was not without filial devotion as well; although both the TUBV and NS offer the usual *maṅgala* hyperbole by extolling the shining qualities of Śaṅkara ('by

11 ... *yaddhyanātmaphalaṁ tasmāi karma sarvaṁ vidhīyate / āptatvād ātmanaḥ karma naiva syād āptaye tataḥ* (Balasubramanian, 1984: 219). Henceforth abbreviated according to chapter and verse, e.g., as in this case, TUBV 1.1.18. Translations are mine, although I have consulted available translations of Sureśvara's work, including those of Balasubramanian, Mahadevan, J.M. van Boetzelaer and A.J. Alston.

12 ... *mukteḥ kauṭasya svarūpāt* (TUBV 1.1.24).

13 ... *svarūpaḥ ātmanaḥ sthānam āhur niḥśreyasaṁ budhāḥ* (Mahadevan, 1972: 59). Henceforth abbreviated according to verse, e.g. here, SV 109.

14 ... *svargādivad anityā syād yadi syātkarmaṇaḥ phalam* (TUBV 1.1.24).

the axe of whose speech the opinions of the logicians are hewn'), there is no reason to think that such homage was not genuine.

This devotion to the master is evident not only in *what* he said – for example, explicitly in the benedictory verses and implicitly in his philosophy – but also *how* he said it. For example, apart from the NS, an independent Advaita treatise, all his works were elucidations (*vārtikas*) on Śaṅkara's commentaries (*bhāṣyas*). A *vārtika*, according to the *Kāvyamīmāṃsā*, a tenth-century text on poetics by Rājāśekhara, examines 'what is said, unsaid, and poorly said (*uktānuktaduruktacintā vārtikam*)' (Mahadevan, 1972: 2).[15] Sureśvara wrote *vārtikas* on Śaṅkara's commentaries on the Bṛhadāraṇyaka and Taittirīya upaniṣads in addition to the NS. He also is the putative author of two further commentaries on texts ascribed to Śaṅkara, the *Mānasollāsa* (on the *Daksināmūrti Stotra*) and the *Pañcīkaraṇavārtika* (on the *Pañcīkaraṇa*), although both his and Śaṅkara's authorship of these texts have been strongly disputed. This section will pay most attention to those texts generally agreed to be genuinely written by Sureśvara – namely, the BUBV, TUBV and the NS. This narrows the field somewhat, though not by much; the *Pañcīkaraṇavārtika* and *Mānasollāsa* are slim volumes while the BUBV is a massive text consisting of nearly 12 000 *ślokas*, which 'approximates to half the Rāmāyaṇa', as Mahadevan enthusiastically notes (Mahadevan, 1972: xiii). It had been one of the few Vedānta texts left untranslated until 1982, when Shoun Hino and his Sanskrit mentor, K.P. Jog, began methodically publishing sections of it every two years or so. A narrower, more philosophically interesting portion of the BUBV, the *Sambandhavārtika*, has been available since Mahadevan published his critical edition of the text in 1958. This edition is an important contribution to the work on Sureśvara, although Mahadevan's notes occasionally reflect his neo-Vedāntic bias.

In the SV, Sureśvara comments on Śaṅkara's introduction to the Bṛhadāraṇyaka Upaniṣad and repeats many of the same anti-Mīmāṃsā arguments as his mentor. Both Śaṅkara's introduction to the BU and Sureśvara's commentary on it are less constrained by exegetical gymnastics and permit more systematic exposition. This is also seen in the *Naiṣkarmyasiddhi*, the one 'independent' treatise of Sureśvara, and the text that I shall refer to most frequently. In the NS we are able to see clearly how Sureśvara follows Śaṅkara, but also the manner in which he unfolds the implications of his teacher's thought. Concerning the epistemology of religious experience, both thinkers operate out of a presumption of internalism, but Sureśvara emphasizes, to a even greater extent than his teacher, the principal doxastic mechanism of Advaita, *śruti*.

The NS is organized into four chapters, perhaps in imitation of the structure of

---

[15] The Sanskrit definition is an irresistibly catchy phrase. Most scholars of the *Vārtikakāra* appeal to it in their work but often make a rather literalist application of Rājāśekhara's poetic gloss. Van Boetzelaer is more circumspect; he thinks the definition, strictly speaking, does not apply to the TUBV since its connection to the TUB is often loose, especially in Chapter Two, suggesting that 'Sureśvara was more inspired by Śaṅkara's commentary than actually commenting on it' (van Boetzelaer, 1971: 43).

the Brahma Sūtra. Each chapter consists of approximately one hundred verses, interconnected by a prose commentary (*sambandhokti*). The first chapter rejects theories of *karma* and *jñānakarmasamuccaya* in the economy of salvation, just as Śaṅkara's first extended comment in the BSB (1.1.1) refuted these theories as well. The second chapter engages an analysis of experience to peel away the insubstantial mind–body complex from the Self and prepare for realization by the culture of liberation: text, tradition and teacher. The third chapter carries this project to its conclusion by an exegesis of the principal *mahāvākya*, '*tat tvam asi*', and the fourth recapitulates his themes and offers citations from Śaṅkara, Gauḍapāda and others to demonstrate the continuity of Sureśvara's view with those of his predecessors. Now let us turn to the principal ideas which recur in Sureśvara's work, first by setting the philosophical context of Advaita during his lifetime.

Philosophical context

The intellectual climate of Advaita following Śaṅkara produced several budding schools of thought characterized by an increased focus on logic and argumentation. This increasing emphasis in Vedānta dialectics eventually culminates in *Khaṇḍanakhaṇḍakhādya* of Śrīharṣa, a twelfth-century Advaitin text which uses a destructive method of argument not unlike that of Nāgārjuna (Dasgupta, 1988: 126–27). At the time of Sureśvara, however, two principal schools of thought in Advaita began to develop, coalescing around decisions concerning the locus of ignorance, the number of selves afflicted with ignorance, and the structure of the relationship between the *jīva* and *ātman*. These schools found their most popular, if not clearest,[16] expressions in the *Bhāmatī* of Vācaspati Miśra (*c.* ninth CE) and the *Pañcāpādikāvivāraṇa* of Prakāśātman (*c.* thirteenth CE). Thus they eventually came to be known as the Bhāmatī and Vivāraṇa schools.

The Bhāmatī school takes the position that there are many selves (*jīva*) afflicted with two kinds of ignorance, first a fundamental ignorance (*mulāvidyā*), a kind of congenital cognitive error built on the basic misconception (*abhimāna*) of plurality. This primal ignorance, generating the perception of independent selves, is then compounded with a secondary ignorance (*tulāvidyā*), the ancillary errors burgeoning from original misconception. These include desire and aversion, two reified categories dependent on an ego subject ('This is good; I want it'). The relationship of *jīva* to *ātman* found in the Bhāmatī is usually characterized as *avacchedavāda*, the doctrine of limitation. Here, the argument runs, there are entities that are not normally understood to break into 'parts' even when they are limited by other entities. The often cited example here is *ākāśa* and *ghaṭākāsa*. Space is space and remains one and the same whether 'limited'

---

16 For example, concerning *avacchedavāda* and *pratibimbavāda*, discussed below, Potter notes that 'we find Vācaspati in the *Bhāmatī* itself using the language of limitation and of reflection indiscriminately (Potter, 1991: 173).

by a pot or not.[17] Similarly, blueness remains blueness whether 'limited' on a page or not.

The Vivāraṇa school accepts many of the presuppositions of the Bhāmatī, but draws different conclusions with regard to the above questions, taking the striking position that Brahman itself is the locus of ignorance. This seems peculiar, for, as Rāmānuja notes, how could the self-effulgent pure consciousness (*cit*) be in any way ignorant?[18] Moreover, if Brahman is ignorant, non-dualism seems to fail, for there are now two states, pure consciousness and ignorance. The usual Advaitin response returns to its basic premise: there is only one real. All else, including ignorance, is unreal. The structure of this unreal relationship between the *jīva* and the *ātman* in the Vivāraṇa is called *pratibimbavāda*, the doctrine of reflection. The idea works on an analogy: a reflection in a mirror appears to be an animated, independent entity, but exists only as a 'borrowed' life, so to speak. It survives only upon the accidental proximity of face and mirror. Similarly, the *jīva* appears to be an independent unit only upon the accidental proximity of the *ātman* and the inert psychophysical unit. What we call the *jīva* is merely a reflection of the Self in the highly refined or subtle (*sukṣma*) intellect (*buddhi*).

Where Sureśvara stands concerning the locus of *avidyā* is clear enough: Brahman, not the *jīva*, is the locus of ignorance.[19] Moreover, concerning the theories of the relationship of the *jīva* to the Self, he weaves a third position, a variation of the reflection theory. In this case, the individual soul is the mere *appearance* of consciousness (*cidābhāsavāda*), which is destroyed upon realization. Of course, elements of this 'theory' have roots in Śaṅkara's thought (BSB 2.3.49–50, CUB 6.3.2, Up. 1.18.29–32), although, as with other themes in Śaṅkara's writings, his position here is not unambiguous. For our purposes, the principal issue in the *pratibimba* and *cidābhāsa* theories is the value of 'mundane' consciousness in the economy of liberation. Sureśvara, as we will see, looks with some suspicion on it, while Padmapāda sees it as a 'window' to the supreme.

Sureśvara occasionally shows little patience with his intellectual rivals. In NS 2.85, he confidently asserts that his demonstration of the Self's immutable nature will be found faultless 'by the dogs of logicians (*tarkikaśvabhiḥ*)'. In the main, however, Sureśvara's intellectual efforts were not directed to Nyāya or even to intra-Advaitin

17 Sureśvara makes this point in NS 2.62: 'When smoke rises, do you suppose the sky is divided or not?' (*ūrdhvaṁ gacchati dhūme khaṁ bhidyate svinna bhidyate*). The metaphor offers a parallel to the Self, which also is ubiquitous and immutable, although it appears to change just as the sky (*kham*) appears to change (Balasubramanian, 1988: 173).

18 The so-called *āśrayatirodhānānupapatayaḥ*, two of seven challenges to Advaita by Rāmānuja. Here, the Supreme Brahman can hardly be considered ignorant, nor can its supremacy allow it to be 'covered'. See his *mahāsiddhānta* in the *Śrībhāṣya* (Thibault, 1988: 111). Modern responses to Rāmānuja's challenges can be found in John Grimes (1990a), Balasubramanian (1978), and Wilson (1970).

19 See Sureśvara's prose introduction (*sambandhokti*) to NS 3. Since there is only the Self, 'the fact of being ignorant belongs to the Self alone (*ātmana evājñānatvam*)'.

polemics, but to an energetic and sustained criticism of Mīmāṃsā. Thus we find in the BUBV and in the NS Sureśvara's repeated arguments against the assumptions, goals and exegetical practices of the Mīmāṃsā *darśana*. This is important because it reflects Sureśvara's central value: salvation comes through intellectual scrutiny of Self and not-self (*ātmānātmaviveka*) and culminates through the hearing (*śravaṇa*) of the word. His work in the NS analyses the nature of action and knowledge and the correct interpretation of scripture. It follows therefore that to properly hear the word one must be equipped with the correct hermeneutical method. Sureśvara's sophisticated intrepretative strategy also takes its inspiration from his teacher, but he offers a tighter technical exposition than Śaṅkara. By doing so, he establishes the method and standard for exegesis in Advaita (Mayeda, 1980). In the NS, Sureśvara labours to construct his method to interpret the principal *mahāvākya* of Advaita, '*tat tvam asi*'.

Sureśvara on religious experience

There are numerous concerns as we reflect on the teachings of Sureśvara, a corpus which van Boetzelaer describes as 'primarily a doctrine of salvation' (1971: 5). First and foremost, as suggested above, is the power of sacred revelation. Unlike Padmapāda, who pursues a phenomenology of experience to arrive at the one true Self, Sureśvara warns of the ambiguity of the *lokaprasiddhi*. NS 1, for example, includes an extensive analysis of mundane experience, shot through, as it is, with ignorance and relentless misidentifications. Indeed, for Sureśvara, '*anubhava* which is not guided by scripture does not speak for its own truth, as the experience of the conch-shell as silver exemplifies ...' (Halbfass, 1990: 391). There is too great a scope for error concerning *lokaprasiddhi*, not least due to its faulty foundation, *avicāritasiddhadvaitavastu*, duality 'established' through non-discrimination. So Sureśvara urges caution in any appeal to mundane experience for evidential testimony to the Self. But while Padmapāda examines the character of immediacy present in all perceptions, mundane experience, as interpreted by Sureśvara, is actually *indirect*, since it is processed through the senses and *antaḥkaraṇa* (NS 2.98). These faculties, according to Advaitin physiology, are inert and insentient, once (in the case of the *antaḥkaraṇa*) and twice (in the case of the senses) removed from the Self. Our so-called 'direct' perceptions of external objects are thus highly filtered and cannot be counted on to reveal anything of *real* significance (since they themselves are the product of unreal processes according to Advaita). Instead, immediacy belongs to the Self alone; the cognitions of mental states (pain, pleasure) or external objects epistemically 'come to life', as it were, as 'direct' perceptions due to the reflection of the Self in the intellect. But their apparent immediacy is in fact derivative or second-hand. Sureśvara could not be more clear about this: 'Intellect, body, and (external objects such as) pot are known mediately; since the Self is the Self, what could possibly count as a "medium"' (for it)?[20]

---

20 ... *vyavadhīyanta evāmī buddhidehaghaṭādayaḥ / ātmatvād ātmanaḥ kena vyavadhānaṁ manāg āpi* (NS 2.98).

Nevertheless, as Balasubramanian notes, while the *lokaprasiddhi* cannot serve as a *pramāṇa* of the Self, it can still serve as a 'pointer to its existence', for mundane experience depends upon the existence of the Self (1988: 10). How so? Because the world is *known*. That we know means there must be a knower; but mind, body, universe, are all unconscious (NS 2.99); therefore there must be a consciousness transcendent to these. On this construal, the Self is *pratyagdharma*, 'characterized by interiority', or 'having an inward nature'. Thus to attain this inward state a rigorous programme of introspection is needed, a 'negative dialectic', as Potter calls it, to peel away not-self from the Self. This discrimination is an essential move in the programme of realizing the Self, which ultimately 'rests in the experience of itself'.[21] This discrimination, however, is finally completed by the hearing of a *mahāvākya* and liberation is spontaneous and irrevocable. Let us examine in closer detail notions of immediacy, interiority, and discrimination, and finally the definitive mechanisms for producing saving knowledge in Sureśvara.

Immediacy, interiority and discrimination

Sureśvara holds several important basic assumptions – the supreme Self is immediate or direct (*sākṣāt, aparokṣāt*), self-established (*svataḥ siddaḥ*), self-luminous (*svaprakāśa*), and, relative to the manifold universe, inward (*pratyak*). These are terms used frequently by Śaṅkara, and Sureśvara seems quite at home in adopting them. The second and third terms are closely related and mean that the Self is an objective entity not dependent on any other entity for its being, for it exists of itself (*svataḥ siddhaḥ*) and shines by its own light (*svaprakāśa*). Sureśvara writes, 'the Self is established through itself; the non-self, through another'.[22] There is an important cognitive implication here as well. Since the Self, whose nature is knowledge, is already established, it illumines all cognitive processes which establish the intellect, external objects, pot and so on: 'Since it itself constitutes all effective knowledge, what (proof) does the Self, the Knower, require (to establish it)?'[23] Here we begin to see a role for introspection that we shall consider below; for now, let us suggest that an analysis of the act of knowing itself allows the *mumukṣu* to make considerable headway in the programme of salvation.[24] The third term in our initial series, *svaprakāśa*, of course, must not presume an 'activity' of illumination, for action implies change and Sureśvara relentlessly maintains the Advaitin drumbeat of Brahman's constant (*avyabhicārin*) and unchanging (*akriyaḥ*)

21 ... *svātmānubhavasaṁśraya* (NS 1.7).

22 Sambandhokti to NS 2.101: *ātmānātmanoḥ svataḥ parataḥ siddhayor*; ignorance and superimposition (*adhyāropa*) 'establish' the not-self, 'as in the mundane example of the superimposed snake in the rope' (*laukikrajjusarpādhyāropavata avidyopāśraya*).

23 ... *anubhūtiphalārthitvād ātmā jñaḥ kim apekṣate* (NS 2.99).

24 It is noteworthy that *anubhūti* and *anubhava* can mean both 'knowledge' and 'experience'. Although Sureśvara is rather harsh in his estimate of the worth of mundane experience, an analysis of it has the potential for revealing the Self. Padmapāda seems to have noticed this; see 'Padmapāda', p. 98.

nature. Brahman *is*; the fact that it apparently 'reveals' is occasioned by various objects proximate to it (NS 2.68). The *svaprakāśatva* of Brahman is another way of saying that Brahman is not dependent (*nirāpekṣa*) on any other entity for its illumination. Instead, 'it is the witness to all cognitions'.[25]

The terms 'immediate' and 'direct' are also significantly related. 'Immediate' of course means 'without media' – that is, without filter or mechanism of transmission or reception. As we saw in NS 2.98, the Self alone is without any 'screen', 'cover', or 'intermediary', all various glosses on the Sanskrit term *vyavadhānam*. Extending the logic of immediacy further, the Self is void of qualities (*nirdharmaka*), form (*ākāra*), or imagination (*niṣprapañca*), since mental constructs are modes of knowing conditioned by various degrees of *avidyā*. They are, above all else, filters, more or less transparent, depending on the severity of one's cognitive dysfunction. Possessing none of the physical or mental conjuncts (*upādhis*) which inflect the world with particularity, the Self, eternally free, exists in state of 'pure' experience (*anubhava*): in other words, the Self 'resides in its own experience' (*svātmānubhavāśraya*). The conclusion of this thinking is, as Mahadevan notes, the axiom that 'There can be nothing more immediate than the Self ... the Self by its very nature is the direct and immediate reality' (Mahadevan, 1972: xxiv). Such thinking recalls Śaṅkara's own insistence in BSB 1.1.4 on the transcendent character of *anubhava*. In short, the Self *is* consummate experience. If this is the case, then to have an experience of the Self is to share in that consummation. Since the Self is immortal and eternal, it is to share in immortality here and now.

This poses interesting questions for us, not the least of which is the issue of immortality here and now. The theoretical possibility of the *jīvanmukta* has been a controverted topic in historical Vedānta and the subject of considerable contemporary research as well.[26] More germane to our concerns is the interrelationship of experience and knowledge, and a careful analysis of this relationship will shed light on the question of what the *jīvanmukta* knows. Mundane experience, by definition, involves the input of sense faculties and the organizing schema of the intellect. These processes, workable on the relative plane, are cancelled at the dawn of liberation. Why? A higher truth (*paramārthika*) cancels them just as a valid cognition cancels an erroneous one, a process, Sureśvara says, that is quite clear (*prasiddaḥ*) to cowherds, shepherds, and scholars (*āgopālāvipālapaṇḍitam*, NS 2.104). Extending this epistemic relationship of 'canceller and cancelled' (*bhādakabhāditabhāva*) to metaphysics, Sureśvara, following Śaṅkara, says, 'as the "rope" is cancelled by the snake, so knowledge of

---

25 ... *niḥśeṣadhīsākṣiṇam* (TUBV 1.1).

26 See, for example, Fort and Mumme (1996), Fort (1991), Sawai (1986), and Warrier (1981). The articles by Sawai and Fort (1991) are excellent summaries of the central issues. Sawai correctly notes that renunciation is *mukti*, that is, for the *vidvat-saṁnyāsin*. Fort offers much useful information, and appropriately recognizes that Śaṅkara's characterization of a *jīvanmukta* is implicit, though 'the Gītā's *sthita-prajña* or the *Upadeśasāhasrī*'s *ācārya* seem close approximations' (1991: 334).

the Self cancels notions of body, etc'.[27] In the Advaita of Śaṅkara and Sureśvara, the ultimate truth of the non-dual real exhaustively cancels all conventional categories comprehended in space and time, including the body, for liberation is equated with bodilessness (NS 1.95).[28] This is largely a negative move for Sureśvara, for the fundamental cognitive distortion which projects the manifold universe is, upon liberation, finally eliminated. Indeed, 'liberation is merely the destruction of ignorance' (NS 1.24).[29]

What remains is the effulgent Self. We note, then, two uses or appeals to experience in Sureśvara: absolute or consummate experience of the Self, mundane experience (*lokaprasiddhi*) which is both fundamentally flawed by apparent (*ābhāsa*) duality and which even on its own terms (*pramāṇa vyavasthā*) all too often issues in error anyway. Such problems in mundane experience compare to the *vyavahārikasattā* and *pratibhāsikasattā* of Śaṅkara.

But Sureśvara refines his thoughts on the scope of experience. Apart from common mundane misperceptions such as the 'rope–snake', he notes, with some exasperation, the usual course in philosophy: rational arguments rarely yield unequivocal adjudication. Philosophical defeat seems only to invite more precise counterarguments. All philosophies are vulnerable to criticism; moreover, no 'path' (*vartma*) exists which definitively adjudicates disputes. But there is a path, says Sureśvara: experience (*anubhava*). He writes as follows:

> Such a path can confidently be established, because the foundation of all thinkers is the appeal to experience alone.
>
> Those afflicted with the fever of debate delude each other with the web of deceptive reasons. But it is to this experience that they make their appeal.[30]

These are fascinating comments, for they reveal an argument that is remarkably contemporary. *Anubhava* here clearly means 'consummate experience', but such experience also implies a host of mundane experiences including proper reading of texts, listening to a teacher and abiding by the moral, ritual and social expectations of a tradition. All of this creates a culture of liberation with its own internal

27 ... *ahirajjvādivad bādho dehādyātmamates tathā*. Some thinkers have shown concern over the *ācāryas*' leap from epistemology to metaphysics, but this complaint has been handled many times by Advaitins. See D.M. Datta (1972). Sureśvara specifically uses the term *bādhyabādhakabhāva* in NS 1.55. In this case, knowledge is the *bādhaka* and ritual action is the *bādhya*.

28 As Fort notes, 'But bodilessness does not mean being without a physical body; being liberated/bodiless means being utterly detached, untouched by dharmic activity or likes and dislikes' (1991: 374). Balasubramanian takes *aśarīratva* to mean the end of identification with the 'gross' body (1988: 59).

29 The complete quote: 'since liberation is merely the destruction of ignorance, ritual action is not the means' (*ajñānahānamātratvānmukteḥ karma na sādhanam*), an anti-Mīmāṃsā *siddhānta*.

30 *Visrabdaiḥ saṃbhāvyatām anubhavamātraśaraṇatvāt sarvatārkikaprasthānānām / tad abhidhīyate / imaṁ prāśnikam uddiśya tarkajvarabhṛśāturāḥ / tvācchiraskavacojālair mohayantītaretaram* (*Sambandhokti* and NS 2.59).

coherence; in this case, the Advaitin culture of liberation creates the conditions for the possibility for a knowing beyond knowledge. While we may be able to say precious little about this experience, since words implicate an impoverished dualism, one verbal outcome does has epistemic merit. The very givenness of the experience, in the context of the intellectual and moral integrity of socially established Advaitin doxastic practices, suggests that the claim that 'there is a knowing beyond knowledge' is *prima facie* justified, a central argument of this book. While Sureśvara's concerns hardly include quibbling over the merits and measure of epistemic justification, he is nonetheless quite aware of the persuasive power of consummate experience. This is why he appeals to *anubhava* as the impartial 'umpire' (*praśnika*) of philosophical disputes and confidently assumes that it will resolve conflicts (and apparently justify the claims of Advaita). But this is curious, for Sureśvara seems to suggest (to use an anachronism) an Ottovian programme of evocation: once you've *had* this experience, you will see its truth. But this assumes that the 'sacred experience' of thinkers in competing schools is everywhere the same – something of a classical Indian version of the perennial philosophy. But Sureśvara recognizes the importance of mundane experience in the preparation for consummate experience. Indeed, in the verses which follow the one just mentioned, the opponent admits Self-as-*anubhava*, but disputes the nature of the Self. Consummate experience everywhere may be the same; nevertheless, Sureśvara takes no chances: text, teacher and tradition play critical roles in the economy of liberation and constitute, for him, the necessary conditions for experience of realization.

Sureśvara makes use of another sense of the term 'experience', an appeal to the 'experience of the wise' as an important example for seekers. Although the experience of the wise is not apodictic, it serves as an important plank in the cumulative case of Advaita, for it establishes both a 'model of' and 'model for' a particular kind of experience which in turn has important social, as well as soteriological, consequences.[31] The positive and negative implications of such appeals is obvious.[32] What is important is that criteria are established which either directly or obliquely allow the seeker to evaluate his paradigm for spiritual growth.[33] Thus, considerable room is given philosophically and socially to the spoken or unspoken testimony of the guru's own experience of the real. This permits the possibility not only of an epistemology of religious experience, but an epistemology

31 See the testimonies of devotees concerning their experience of the contemporary Śaṅkarācāryas of Dwaraka and Kāñcī in Cenkner (1983: 168–70).

32 For an eloquent and sensitive discussion of the virtues and vices of this spiritual pedagogy, see Kornfield (1995: 228–43). Bharati (1976) had direct experience of this pedagogy and professional training as an anthropologist to help him discriminate between saints and 'the lunatic fringe', as he calls it.

33 See Śaṅkara's list in Up. 2.1.6; cf. Dhammapada 208: extolling the compelling virtues of a 'wise one', the verse concludes, 'With such a one as this, one would associate, as the moon the path of the stars' (Carter and Palihawadana, 1987: 259).

of holiness. That is, the quality of human presence, human 'being', modelled by a teacher's or saint's own experience of transformation, testifies or bears witness to the claims and beliefs that precede and follow that experience. In the manner of mundane epistemology, warrant is conferred to the claims on the basis of this testimony, just as witness claims of a person of good character also enjoy warrant. The importance of the testimony of holiness as an intrinsic, if unspoken, element in the teaching of a guru is particularly acute in Sureśvara's Advaita, for an electric relationship exists between guru and *mumukṣu*. According to Sureśvara, after the preliminary training of the disciple, it is finally the guru's articulation of the *mahāvākya* which spontaneously triggers the consummate experience. A poetic flourish often used by Sureśvara serves to heighten the intensity and spontaneity of this experience: knowledge is a consuming fire; the *mahāvākyas* themselves 'burn all ignorance and indeed make known the unconditioned' (TUBV 2.657).[34]

But what do we 'know' in an experience 'beyond concept, (form, etc.)' (*nāmādibhyaḥ paro*, NS 2.57)? And how do we access something that is actionless (*akriyah*, NS 2.57), already accomplished (*bhūtavastu*), and which transcends time and space? Sureśvara's strict answer to the first question must be 'we know nothing at all' or, more precisely, 'we perceive but we do not know', for 'knowledge' implies plurality – namely, objects that are known. The answer to the second question is, according to Sureśvara, provided by a programme of discriminating internalism, or as Balasubramanian nicely captures it, a 'rigorous regressive inquiry'. We will not only see that these questions are intimately related, but will also see that such salvific 'perceiving' cannot be without cognitive implications which are not exclusively indexed to the 'interpretation' following the experience. Instead, these can be found in the experience itself, making possible a knowing beyond knowledge.

Let us take the first question and segue into the second. Sureśvara is quite clear about what he means by 'Self-knowledge', but his use of the term must be considered idiosyncratic. We are frequently reminded that the nature of the Self is knowledge.[35] Yet, at the same time, the Self is never an object of knowledge, not even of itself. 'Since "being a seer" properly belongs to the Self, it itself cannot be seen.'[36] Although this seems clear, because it preserves the cherished non-dualism, it does make the use of the term 'knowledge' idiosyncratic. What I wish to do is salvage something of the empirical use of the term 'knowledge' and apply it to the Advaita metaphysic. In this way, we will be able to speak meaningfully of 'Self-knowledge' or 'knowledge of Brahman' or even, as in the Western context, 'knowledge of God' without sacrificing what we typically mean by knowledge. The

---

[34] cf. *Gītā* 4.37, 'As a blazing fire reduces wood into ashes, so, Arjuna, does the fire of knowledge reduce all karma to ashes' (*yathaidhāṁsi samiddho 'gnir basmasāt kurute 'rjuna // jñānāgniḥ sarvakarmāṇi bhasmasat kurute tathā*).

[35] NS 2.105, TUBV 2.90, 2.178, etc.

[36] … *draṣṭṛtvenopayuktatvāt tadaiva syān na dṛśyatā* (NS 2.27).

way to do this is to consider the notion of 'perceiving the real' through immediacy and interiority.

But, to rework and to contest Steven Katz: there are no programmes of pure internalism although there can be experiences of pure consciousness, and even these are, in some sense, cognitive. With regard to the former, if we leave aside more contested debates in sociology and anthropology, the fact that humans are physically and socially structured to receive input from external sources seems unremarkable and obvious. Beginning with training from parents and continuing with teachers, texts, institutions or disciplines, we are genetically and socially built to experience reality through various external inputs. This claim seems beyond dispute. Concerning the latter, however, the combination of external input and internal discipline can lead to extraordinary events which have been called 'pure consciousness events', surely initiated by various media which themselves need not necessarily be implicated in the phenomenal event. This event, I wish to argue, can still be considered cognitive in important ways: clearly in the cognitive construction (or deconstruction) preceding and following the event, but also in the experience of liberation itself; for, at the very least, if one knows one is liberated, one knows something after all. Perhaps we can discover more than this, but to establish this requires further analysis of the mechanisms of religious knowing, so, with that in mind, let us return to Sureśvara's epistemology of religious experience.

The philosophical anthropology of Sureśvara (and Śaṅkara) suggests that a profound interiority leads to the supreme. But the radically skewing problem of *avidyā* so fundamentally contorts one's mental functions that only inwardness conditioned by external mechanisms – training, scripture, grace of guru – can 'accomplish the accomplished', to borrow Rambachand's (1991) apt phrase. These external media all strongly shape the mental world of the *mumukṣu* and prepare the way for spontaneous enlightenment. What is fascinating about the life of Ramaṇa Maharṣi is that these media were highly minimalist. He apparently experienced enlightenment without the traditional supports of the *svasampradāya*. This in turn leads to questions concerning the possibility for a universalist spirituality decisively grounded in an internalist epistemology – one which intimately weaves a synthesis of theory and practice. In this case, the external mechanisms contructed around, and on behalf of, religious experience are minimized. This in turn liberates Advaita from its local context.

In the case of Sureśvara, we see a 'peculiar' form of externalism. It is peculiar, because Sureśvara begins, as does Śaṅkara, with a strong epistemological presumption of internalism – in his primary metaphysical assumption, the privileged access it presupposes, and its principal method of analytical introspection. Despite the independence or universalism these characteristics might suggest, Sureśvara, as Śaṅkara, decisively indexes them to a particular culture of liberation. This is most clearly seen in his analysis of the role of *śruti* in the economy of liberation – a role which is even more decisive and unambiguous than found in Śaṅkara. Thus we see a growing complexity in the epistemology of religious experience in Advaita, and Sureśvara's own dance between internalism and externalism contributes to it.

We recall that the Self has an inward nature; to access the one true Self, a deepening interiority is demanded – Balasubramanian's regressive inquiry. This interiority is profoundly conditioned by the mental training of the *mumukṣu*. We first note that Sureśvara adopts the dichotomy of Self and not-self introduced by Śaṅkara in his *adhyāsa bhāṣya*. This seems reasonable; since the world of duality is 'established' through non-discrimination (*avicārita*), inquiry (*vicāra*) or discrimination (*viveka*) is the proper programme for cognitive correction. The *ātmānātmaviveka* thus indicates at once a metaphysic and a programme for salvation. As a metaphysic, it accounts for the nature of reality in its most complete context; as a 'programme' for salvation it presumes that internalizing this truth establishes liberation. We have here a *summum bonum* (*ātman*), a particular problem (*anātman*), and a method for both solving the problem and attaining the highest good (*viveka*). In the SV, Sureśvara writes, 'Knowledge of the real nature of inner Self alone fashions the destruction of ignorance concerning it.'[37] Indeed, here and elsewhere, he insists that the process of liberation is destructive, not constructive. Nothing new is created, only ignorance is destroyed – for example, 'destruction of that constitutes liberation of the Self'.[38]

But while knowledge of the non-dual real is the 'simple' antidote to ignorance, it comes packed with any number of intellectual decisions about the nature of person, society, philosophy and even grammar. This is inescapable. The Advaitin programme of salvation cannot be construed as merely urging 'knowledge by acquaintance', a favourite appeal of many twentieth-century Advaitins. Rather, it must be understood as a fundamental reconstruction of the intellect upon the foundations of Advaitin theory. In fact, the work of Advaita *sādhana* amounts to replacing one intellectual foundation – naive realism – with another, a highly sophisticated and certainly counterintuitive non-dualism. In order to defeat the overwhelming realist patterns of thought generated by the senses and mental faculties, discrimination must begin to refashion the mind. This discrimination, of course, must be sustained by significant intellectual and behavioural support mechanisms – the 'external circuitry' of Advaita. The intellectual support includes the cognitive content of Advaita doctrine and its many arguments offered to defeat the realist or dualist opponent. His disparaging comments on the net worth of reasoning notwithstanding, Sureśvara clearly gives a crucial role to argument (*yukti*) in his texts; indeed most of the NS and SV are packed with arguments to defeat various *pūrvapakṣas*. The behavioural supports, on the other hand, include the culture of liberation, especially text, teacher and tradition, all of which reinforce the Advaitin construal of reality in its most complete context.

In addition to the Advaitin training in doctrine and reasoning, the programme of

37 ... *pratyagyāthātmyadhīr eva pratyājñānahānikṛt* (SV 18).

38 ... *tannāśo muktir ātmanaḥ*.

discrimination peels away the changing from the unchanging, seeking to reveal the absolutely real within the universe of fleeting appearances. To this end, Sureśvara employs dialectics which accomplish the negative task of destroying the unreal. Through the methods of *anvaya-vyatireka* and *adhyāropa-apavāda* the horizons of the *mumukṣu* are gradually and, in the case of the *jīvanmukta*, permanently altered. No scope remains for the substantial reality of senses, mind, body, objects or categories. Only one real exists, the supreme Self. Through an intellectual process of 'inward turning', the *mumukṣu* analyses both conventional experience and the experience of his mental world. It is not surprising, therefore, that Sureśvara chooses to comment on the Taittirīya Upaniṣad, for much of that text engages in a discriminating analysis of the 'sheaths' (*kośa*) which envelop the Self. Such intellectual analysis has the Self as its goal and prepares the way for the consummate experience. This intellectual, rational process of discrimination, fuelled by a particular intellectual content, thus completes a negative process of eliminating not-self. But liberation is not 'secured' until this negative move is completed by a positive one – namely, the hearing of the word. For Sureśvara, 'reason prepares the way, but scripture accomplishes the goal' (Balasubramanian, 1988: xl). So, although Sureśvara is not a fideist, neither is he a radical internalist; for although his metaphysical assumptions and initial programme of liberation conduce to internalism, he holds that scripture in the end is the ultimate 'producer' of liberation.

We see in our discussion so far numerous themes and arguments that we have encountered in Śaṅkara. It is with good reason, then, that De Smet, Balasubramanian, Alston and van Boetzelaer have emphasized the continuity of thought between Śaṅkara and Sureśvara. But it is my suggestion that Sureśvara (and Padmapāda) extend the thought of Śaṅkara, and unfold various implications of it, especially concerning the nature of experience and the 'conditions' of Self-realization. For example, Sureśvara stresses the role of *śruti* and its immediacy in stronger terms than Śaṅkara, and his more technical discussion of exegetical methods sets the standard for Advaitin justifications of a non-dualist interpretation of *mahāvākyas* (Mayeda, 1980: 152). Moreover, there also appears to be less equivocating concerning *ajātivāda* in Sureśvara than in Śaṅkara; Śaṅkara, after all, takes pains in BSB 1.1.2 to ensure Brahman as the material cause of the universe, although *vivartavāda* looms in the background of all his cosmological speculations. Sureśvara, on the other hand, seems less willing to concede intermediary positions, and this applies to soteriological discussions, our primary concern here. *Ajātivāda* is a theory of causality – 'non-causality', to be precise. Applied to religious experience, liberation cannot be caused, but only spontaneously realized. This means that liberation is sometimes viewed in negative terms for Sureśvara; Śaṅkara, we recall, often interpreted liberation in positive terms – that is, in the realization of the identity of Self and Brahman. Sureśvara, on the other hand, 'takes enlightenment to consist in the absolute destruction of even the appearance of not-Self' (Potter, 1991: 243). Thus, for example, 'Since this entire universe, including ego, appears and then disappears in the Self, which is supreme consciousness, it is transitory, like a pot. It is like the "hair" (that falsely appears before someone with an eye problem and disappears when that problem is cured)'.[39]

Both thinkers can be interpreted as operating out of an 'internalist' epistemology of religious experience, owing to the principal axiom of Advaita, the privileged access it presupposes, and its method of introspection. But the internalism of Śaṅkara and Sureśvara is supported in profound ways by externalism as well: it presupposes among the necessary conditions for liberation certain socially established doxastic mechanisms – texts, methods of reading texts, patterns of reasoning, the guru – all of which constitute the 'external circuitry' of this tradition which the adept taps into and begins the reconstruction of mind and heart. With that in mind let us examine the premier doxastic, and ultimately salvific, mechanism, *śruti*, and certain auxiliaries in the economy of liberation for Sureśvara.

Śruti, upāsana, *and* karma

Sureśvara is quite clear about the value of the sacred word. It is the *kāraṇa par excellence* of liberation. It alone is the source of saving knowledge. The reason for this is the same as for Śaṅkara. Brahman is trans-empirical and consequently inaccessible by ordinary means of knowledge. Our senses and ordinary reasoning processes are not constituted to receive or to process information concerning the supreme. At most, reasoning proves the falsity of not-self and offers a presumption of transcendent consciousness; reasoning cannot, according to Śaṅkara and Sureśvara, unequivocally demonstrate what exactly the Self is. This can only be done through an 'external' mechanism which reveals the nature of the Self – namely, *śruti*.

So, according to Sureśvara, the Self is inward, interior, and thus concealed or hidden. Mental training and ritual practices prepare the student for the hearing of a 'great saying', which has no small 'effect' for him. The *mahāvākyas* have a particularly potent efficacy according to Sureśvara, who even suggests that these sentences possess a magical power (*mahimā*) of transformation. We now see the internalism of his epistemology of religious experience shifting to the pole of externalism – sets of socially established practices that prepare for a particular kind of experience. These include various reading and exegetical practices and, under specific conditions, the 'transmission' of saving knowledge through them. Thus the external mechanisms loom large in the production of 'religious' knowledge. If we are beginning to see internalism invariably buttressed by external programmes – scripture reigning supreme among them – then how are we to adjudicate the claims about the nature of reality that entail from different scriptures and their communities of interpretation and worship? Must the different claims stemming from various

---

39 ... *avagatyātmano yasmād āgamāpāyi kumbhavat / sāhaṁkāram idaṁ viśvaṁ tasmāt tat syāt kacādivat* (NS 2.95).

scriptures produce an imbroglio of competing revelations? How are we to reconcile these claims?

While Sureśvara obviously did not encounter the extent of the contemporary global interpenetration of 'world religions', he was, of course, faced with the theoretical dilemmas of competing scriptures on the subcontinent. Although he and Śaṅkara make cavalier comments about the empty value of *nāstika* scriptures, they recognize the necessity of reasoning to judge the coherence of 'non-orthodox' soteriological systems. And, concerning 'orthodox' systems, the proper method of interpreting *śruti* is the primary agenda for these Advaitins. Appropriating the correct interpretation makes all the difference for Sureśvara. He makes abundantly clear the power of scripture for effecting liberation; indeed, as we have already mentioned, *śruti* possesses a 'magical' quality for transforming the *adhikārin*.

Earlier we spoke of the immediacy of the one true Self. If one wished to generate a list of appropriate qualifications of the divine, 'immediacy' seems to be a reasonable candidate. It suggests a construal of the divine as radical self-presence, with no barriers to that presence, such as cognition or emotion. However, according to Sureśvara, not only does the Self enjoy the fact of being immediate (*aparokṣatā*), but the *knowledge we gain from scripture* is immediate as well. This claim seems fantastic until we understand how Sureśvara conceives the nature of scripture. What we have is an apparently external mechanism of knowledge revealing something profoundly internal to ourselves. Thus we have a profound identity, and not merely of Self and Brahman; as Guy Maximilien writes, 'The Word is therefore the Self itself' (1975a: 18).[40] In other words, *śruti*, for Sureśvara, is an external mechanism which triggers an internal awareness of supreme consciousness. A revelation occurs, triggering the final moment of liberation. But this internal awareness is not to be confused with a Christian concept of revelation, as Maximilien points out. While it is eternal and without human (*apauruṣeya*) origin, it is not supernatural in a dualist sense; instead, 'far from being supernatural, it is a Word simultaneously conforming to the provisional human condition and to its eternal essence, simultaneously relevant to the order of objective knowledge and to the order of pure Consciousness' (ibid.: 18).[41] Although Maximilien's phrasing here is tendentious, his point is clear. *Śruti* is not about the revelation of external realities; instead, it is a revelation of the innermost dimension of human experience.

In his study of Sureśvara, J.M. van Boetzelaer concludes that the outcome of Sureśvara's method yields a peculiar cognitive event which cannot be considered 'empirical knowledge, but a mystical intuition' (van Boetzelaer, 1971: 6). I am not entirely happy with this description for two reasons. First, 'mystical intuition' harks back to so many imprecisions and confusions over what exactly counts as either

40 'La Parole est donc le Soi lui-même.'

41 'Loin d'être surnaturelle, c'est une Parole simultanément conforme à la condition provisoire de l'homme et à son essence définitive de toujours, relevant simultanément de l'ordre de la connaissance objective et de l'ordre de la Conscience pure.'

mysticism or intuition. In addition, it is not so much that such intuition is not empirical but that the empirical is penetrated, dissected and analysed in building to the moment of enlightenment. Sureśvara is clear about the limits of the *tripuṭī* system – the 'triple form' of 'knower', 'object known' and 'process of knowing' in the end is to be discarded 'like faded flowers'. Still, if intuition means some sort of cognitive *je ne sais quoi*, one can sympathize with Sureśvara – the supreme is pure consciousness, purged of all phenomenal content. It is somehow supremely conscious, but not discursive. Discursive reasoning, the *anvayavyatireka* method, discriminates between Self and not-self. The hearing of the word, under suitable conditions, transmits the experience of the Self. Despite the difficulties latent in the term, Potter also considers Sureśvara's method to provoke a 'mystical intuition' (Potter, 1991: 225).

Let us consider in more detail Sureśvara's reliance on scripture to provoke such an 'intuition'. Keeping in mind the central premise of Advaita, scripture is informative, not productive. It is informative because its object is real: and knowledge, we are repeatedly told by both Śaṅkara and Sureśvara, depends on its object (*vastutantram*). This seems to approximate traditional Western theories of correspondence; Rāmānuja also has a version of correspondence operating in his epistemology, although he combines this theory with a more literalist method of interpreting scripture. For Rāmānuja, scripture is informative, and informative in a rather radical fashion. Not only are we informed of a supramundane real who is a 'person'; we benefit further from revelation and learn that Viṣṇu is blue, lies on a sofa in Vaikuṇṭha, sports with Lakṣmi and so on.[42] Such literal renderings of scripture are unacceptable for Śaṅkara and Sureśvara because of their obvious betrayal of non-dual truth. Any exegesis of *mahāvākyas* such as *tat tvam asi* 'which would result in a final residue of duality is therefore inappropriate' (De Smet, 1961: 257).

At best – and this is sufficient indeed – the information we gain from scripture is absolutely simple, in a philosophical sense. The knowledge we gain from scripture is immediate (*aparokṣa*), non-propositional (*avākyārtha*) and non-relational (*akhaṇḍārtha*). This means that the primary hermeneutical strategy for Advaita must be implication (*lakṣaṇā*). A literal exegesis of '*tat tvam asi*', the 'archetype of the upaniṣadic Word' (Maximilien, 1975: 6), devolves into an absurd conclusion: the identity of the supreme Brahman and the empirical self. Instead, by proper exegesis – in this case, the appeal to the implied meaning of the two terms – the mutually incompatible determinants of each term are removed, leaving the common element, namely consciousness. In this manner, texts such as these convey 'a sense of identity, a unitary unrelated content' (Balasubramanian, 1988: 38). Since words circumscribe a mental universe, limiting it by category, class-characteristic and other markers, they cannot be applied denotatively to Brahman, for Brahman is void

42 See his *Vedārthasaṅgraha*. I will return to Rāmānuja's cognitivism in Chapter 5.

of quality, class, action or part. The usual spoken sense (*vācyārtha*) of words fails. Instead, by resorting to the implied sense of scriptural terms we negatively but asymptotically approach Brahman until the power of scripture spontaneously has its effect. Maximilien captures this eloquently:

> The word here is not notional information – there is no notion of Brahman – it is an indication, that is to say that it has the same informative value as a gesture which turns someone's glance to an object and causes him to directly apprehend it. The word here does not name the object, it causes an immediate contact between the object and our power of direct apprehension of the object.[43]

These considerations – the immediacy of the knowledge from scripture, the non-propositional sense of scripture, and the fact that knowledge depends on the reality of the object (*vastutantram*), not on the effort of the knower – have direct application to concerns over meditation (*upāsana, bhāvanā*). That Sureśvara takes issue with the Mīmāṃsā emphasis on action is not surprising. Action by definition indicates change; yet, if anything is certain, according to Advaita, it is the unchanging, eternal Self. Since this Self is one and non-dual, ritual action for ultimately salvific ends is out of the question. The usual four states that Śaṅkara describes in BSB 1.1 – origination, production, purification, modification – are commented on by Sureśvara in his attack on Mīmāṃsā. All these have a beginning and an end; ritual action can have nothing to do with the eternal Self, except as a 'remote aid' to salvation.

More surprising is Sureśvara's contention with Advaitin disputants over the merits of meditation. Two views are represented in the NS and, although Sureśvara does not refer to them by name, medieval and contemporary exegetes have identified them as Maṇḍana Miśra, the author of the ***Brahmasiddhi***, and Brahmadatta, a more obscure contemporary of Miśra (Alston, 1959: 46). These Vedāntins represent what appear to be eminently reasonable views concerning meditation. One view, apparently that of Brahmadatta, held that *mahāvākyas* do not directly issue in release, but indirectly and through the efficacy of meditation; it is meditation which 'improves upon' the knowledge in scripture and transforms it into saving realization. The other view, apparently represented by Miśra, adds that the upaniṣadic sayings are relational and do not penetrate to the real nature of the *ātman* (De Smet, 1961: 258); however, for one engaged in repeated meditation, 'another kind of knowledge arises, void of propositional content; this alone eradicates the entire darkness of ignorance'.[44]

---

43 'La parole ici n'est pas une information notionnelle – il n'y a pas de notion du Brahman – elle est une indication, c'est-à-dire qu'elle a la même valeur informative qu'un geste qui tourne le regard de quelqu'un vers un objet et le lui fait appréhender directement. La parole ici ne nomme pas l'object, elle cause un contact immédiate entre l'objet et notre pouvoir d'appréhension directe de l'objet' (Maximilien, 1975a: 12).

44 ... *evāvākyārthātmakaṁ vijñānāntaram utpadyate / tad evāśeṣājñānatimirotsārīti* (NS 1.67).

Sureśvara is remarkably consistent in rejecting these plausible positions. The first is unacceptable because it implies that knowledge depends on the effort of the knower; however, this cannot be the case since knowledge depends on the object, not the knower. Second, since the so-called 'improved' knowledge depends on the diligent effort of the meditator, it implies that liberation is a result of such effort. If liberation is a result, it is non-eternal. As Sureśvara writes, 'If you say, "repeated mental cultivation completely removes bondage", no; not complete cessation, because that, arising from mental cultivation, would be a result.'[45] Moreover, in no analysis of *pramāṇas*, says Sureśvara, do we see that 'repetition' produces 'new' knowledge. Instead, 'the knowledge derived from *śruti* demolishes at once ignorance which appears in the form of the instruments of action. Therefore there is no combination of these two (knowledge and action, including meditation).'[46]

Against the view supposedly held by Miśra, Sureśvara rejects the notion that *śruti* texts are relational or propositional. Here again he follows the inspiration of Śaṅkara, whose principal method of textual interpretation is seen in the *Upadeśasāhasrī*. But Sureśvara offers a more detailed, systematic analysis of proper exegetical methods; in addition, he develops the doctrine of the non-propositional content of scripture. *Śruti* surely promises a cognitive content, but it is immediate, non-propositional, and non-relational. Miśra apparently argued that scripture was fundamentally relational, but that, owing to the instrumentality of sustained meditation, scripture developed a non-relational, non-propositional content. According to Sureśvara, this cannot be the case, in part because of the same defect associated with the Brahmadatta's position: meditation is an act, and no action can produce an eternal result.

More significantly, Miśra's position rests on an unsound foundation – namely, the assumption of a relational and denotative understanding of scripture. To counter this, Sureśvara extends Śaṅkara's discussion of the *anvaya-vyatireka* method and strengthens Advaitin theory concerning scriptural exegesis. More specifically, he analyses the *mahāvākya*, '*tat tvam asi*', both semantically and syntactically, using, in addition to the *anvaya-vyatireka* method, the theoretical support of *sāmānādhikaraṇya* (appositional relation), *viśeṣaṇa-viśeṣyabhava* (qualified–qualifier relationship) and *lakṣana-lakṣyasambandha* (theory of implication) (Mayeda, 1980: 152). The implication theory he develops also has three stages: *adhyāropa*, *apavāda*, and *paramartha-lakṣanā*. In the first, the student superimposes the 'relational' content of scripture; in this case, the ego is identified with Brahman. Next, the student negates (*apavāda*) the mutually incompatible content of the identity statement. Not accepting the primary meaning of the word 'I', the student looks for the implied or secondary meaning. After this extended

[45] ... *abhyāsopacitā kṛtsnaṁ bhāvanā cen nirvartayet / naikāntikīnivṛttiḥ syād bhāvanājaṁ hi tat phalam* (NS 3.91).

[46] ... *sakṛtpravṛttyā mṛdnāti kriyākārakarūpabhṛt / ajñānam āgamajñānaṁ sāṅgatyaṁ nāsty ato 'nayoḥ* (NS 1.67).

process, the student assumes the 'elevated meaning' (*paramārthalakṣaṇa*). The conclusion of these hermeneutical developments in Sureśvara is the rejection of the primary, relational content of scripture. Instead, the knowledge 'generated' by scripture is non-relational, non-propositional, and immediate (De Smet, 1961: 258). According to Sureśvara, this knowledge, 'stimulated' by *māhāvakyas* such as '*tat tvam asi*', is immediate (*sākṣāt*) and extends beyond the expressed meaning (*avākyārtha*) of the sentence (NS 3.9).

If much of this sounds familiar, it is with good reason: an incipient theory of implication is found in Śaṅkara and a process of negation is seen in the famous '*neti neti*' text of the BU. But Sureśvara extends the discussion and establishes the principles of Advaitin exegesis to which later thinkers appeal, such as Sarvajñātman (*c.* tenth century CE), Vidyāraṇya (fourteenth century CE), and Sadānanda (*c.* sixteenth century CE). Thus we see the development of a sophisticated and consistent hermeneutic: an implicatory sense of scriptural terms which indirectly 'name' the Self, a method which has its culmination in the immediate and direct knowledge of the Self. This is why Maximilien interprets Sureśvara's theory of scripture so conclusively: 'The Word therefore is the Self itself.' *Śruti* is not a 'text' *per se* – that is, a mere collection of ideograms – but a living transmission of a penetrating word, the teaching of a guru and, above all, the truth of the *ātman*–Brahman equation. In short, we are 'word', we are 'guru', we are 'Brahman'.

To realize this truth we must take the inward path. But the process of interiority only reveals what we already are; it amounts to attaining what we already have. It is attainment 'as it were'. Yet, this interior path comes packed with many behavioural and social supports. Among these supports is ritual action. Since Sureśvara's analysis of meditation closely follows his broader analysis of ritual action, I will close my discussion of him with a brief review of his position on *karma*.

As mentioned earlier, much of Sureśvara's polemics are directed to the Mīmāṃsakās. A good place to examine his views in this regard is the *Naiṣkarmyasiddhi*, whose special theme, especially in chapter one, is the antagonism of *karma* and *jñāna*. Although the *Naiṣkarmyasiddhi* engages the harried ground of anti-Mīmāṃsā polemics, it also serves as 'compendium of essential Advaita',[47] which compares well with Śaṅkara's own *Upadeśasāhasrī* and later Advaita texts such as the *Pañcadaśī* of Vidyāraṇya and the *Vedāntasāra* of Sadānanda. His writing is clear and straightforward; interestingly, Alston, Potter and Hiriyanna all use the terms 'charm' or 'charming' when referring to Sureśvara or describing the NS. Such a description may be due to Sureśvara's passionate style, which drives its point home forcefully yet in eminently memorable phrases. For example, rendering the paradox of seer and seen in eloquent *śloka* verse, Sureśvara writes:

47 Sureśvara's *sambandhokti* to NS 1.1 is more elaborate: *aśeṣavedāntasārasaṁgrahaprakaraṇam*.

> not seeing, the seer perceives the seeing mind;
> not hearing, the seer perceives the listening mind;
> not desiring, the seer perceives the craving mind;
> effortless, without action, lucid, the seer perceives.[48]

Without doubt, the importance of the *śloka* verse here lies not just in its doctrinal content but in its ability to be easily committed to memory, thereby facilitating the internalizing of important Advaitin doctrines.

An obvious clue to the goals of Sureśvara's *Naiṣkarmyasiddhi* may be found in its title, which is taken from *Gītā* 18.49: 'the self-controlled one, with mind unattached, who in every quarter has conquered ambition, achieves supreme freedom from activity through renunciation'.[49] Freedom from activity here means both ritual activity (*karma*) and its consequences (*karmaphala*). In short, it means freedom from the endless cycle of embodiment, fuelled by desire. This ideal is addressed at length in the *Gītā*, especially in chapter two which extols the need for *niṣkāma karma*, action free of desire.

Desire is a considerable flaw in the human personality according to Sureśvara, as it is according to the author (or authors) of the *Gītā*. A concise summary of the existential situation of all creaturehood is offered in the opening verse of the *Naiṣkarmyasiddhi*, which, paraphrased, can be characterized in the following manner: there is fundamental desire shared by all creatures – namely, avoiding suffering – but the measure of suffering apportioned to creatures arises from merit and demerit, themselves the result of the performance (or not) of ritual action; but the fundamental motivating dynamic of ritual action is none other than desire. Hence the trap of *saṁsāra*. This introductory section thus actually marks out two central problems, desire *and* ritual action. Ritual *karma* merely produces ontological *karma*; it does not save. The solution to such a dilemma is, of course, knowledge.

Sureśvara's arguments against Mīmāṃsā follow Śaṅkara fairly closely: ritual action engages pluralism as its intellectual foundation. As a *product* of such faulty intellectual foundations, ritual action can hardly be employed to deconstruct them. Moreover, as actions have both an origin and end, if liberation were the result of action, it too would be impermanent. Finally, as stated above, action exhaustively includes objects of production, purification, transformation or attainment. But, as Balasubramanian observes:

> Release is not something to be produced, since it is eternal (*nityatvāt*). It is not something to be purified, for it is bereft of all qualities and impurities (*nirguṇatvāt, nirdoṣatvāt*). Further, only a thing that serves as a means can be purified, like the sacrificial vessel ... Since release is not a means (*asādhana-*

48 ... *apaśyan paśyatīṁ buddhim aśṛṇvan śṛṇatīṁ tathā / niryatno' vkriyo' nicchan nicchantīṁ cāpyaptaṛk* (NS 2.71).

49 ... *asaktabuddhiḥ sarvatra jitātmā vigataspṛhaḥ / naiṣkarmyasiddhiṁ paramāṁ saṁnyāsenādhigacchati.*

> *dravyātmakatvāt*), it cannot be purified. It is not something to be transformed, for it is immutable (*kuṭasṭhatvāt*). It is not something to be attained, for it is already attained as the Self of every one (*ātmatvena nityāptatvāt*). (Balasubramanian, 1988: xlix)

Although Sureśvara rejects the ultimate salvific efficacy of *karma*, he nevertheless concedes a role to it in the economy of liberation. In NS 1, he argues for the efficacy of saving knowledge but nonetheless proposes various ritual practices, especially the *nitya* and *naimittika* duties, as 'remote aids' to liberation. These practices 'purify' the mind and help to generate dispassion, *vairāgya*, an important affective disposition which we reviewed in the last chapter. While *vairāgya* is a disposition of the will, it nonetheless includes important cognitive implicates. It is a disposition or virtue profoundly informed by broader metaphysical principles, reading, teaching and ritual practices. Vedic chanting (TUBV 1) also contributes to 'mental purification', which in turn conduces to a student's understanding of the upaniṣads (TUBV 1.50). One can imagine how, in an Advaitin culture of liberation, chanting discreetly internalizes formative doctrines that continue the work of cognitive and affective transformation.

We see, then, a combination of the intellectual and behavioural supports in Sureśvara, as we did in Śaṅkara. While both were adamantly opposed in theory to *jñānakarmasamuccaya*, the entire mental and behavioural culture which their writings address constitutes an inevitable combination of knowledge and action. If exegesis of scripture and various deconstructions of *pūrvapakṣas* constitute important intellectual supports of Sureśvara's Advaita, then the place he confers to ritual actions and ethical practices constitutes significant behavioural supports. All this contributes to the 'external circuitry' of emerging Advaita. They indicate powerful sets of socially established practices that facilitate the transformation of the *adhikāri*. It is for this reason that Sureśvara, while operating out of internalist presuppositions, nevertheless, like Śaṅkara, includes a culture of liberation which emcompasses important externalist dimensions. However, although Sureśvara follows his teacher in important ways, by extending and unfolding the implications of Śaṅkara's thought, he makes his own important contribution to Advaita. I have highlighted some of these developments in this section and will close with a brief comparison of their views of *adhikāra*.

We recall that, in theory, Śaṅkara is open to any qualified aspirant, but in practice this meant only Brahmins. The reason for this is that, as just stated, however much actions conduce to liberation, they do not produce it. In the culture of liberation we have reviewed, Brahmins alone were eligible to perform the *nitya* and *naimittika* duties. It is for this reason that Śaṇkara, as Yoshitsugu Sawai notes, 'appears to have allowed only *brāhmaṇas* to become members of the Śṛngeri Maṭha, which he is traditionally said to have founded' (Sawai, 1986: 381). While the precise historical development of the *maṭhas* – and Śaṅkara's role in it – is controverted, we saw how Śaṅkara favours the Brahmin in the *Upadeśasāhasrī*. Sureśvara, on the other hand, following the 'social' logic of Advaita's metaphysic, departed from his teacher in this regard. In the BUBV he writes, 'Since according to *śruti* renunciation pertains to all three *varṇas*, [Śaṅkara's] comment that it pertains only to Brahmins is wrong.'[50] Sureśvara takes the term 'Brahmin' to indicate the *kṣatriya* and *vaiṣya* as well. He reasons that if knowledge *removes* the eligibility for ritual practices, why should one *impose* a limitation to renunciation (Sawai, 1986: 381)? Sawai drily notes that 'There is no evidence that this opinion of Sureśvara was ever accepted as authoritative in Śṛngeri Maṭha' (1986: 381).

What is important for our purposes is the suggestion here of a greater harmony of theory and practice concerning eligibility. However much the 'externalism' of early Advaita constitutes a necessary culture of liberation, its primary metaphysic and the internalist assumptions of privileged access and introspection implied by that metaphysic in theory should 'liberate' eligibility from the culture of liberation. In other words, eligibility in theory should be available to all, and not merely to members of the three classes. Sureśvara's position here is radical, although it appears not to have been accepted. Nevertheless, he indicates a broader context for the programme of liberation than does Śaṅkara. Ramaṇa Maharṣi follows the metaphysic and internalist methodology to their logical conclusion: a genuine universalism which liberates Advaita from its local context. Before we examine his position, let us turn to the 'modest internalism' of Padmapāda, whose analysis of mundane experience provides a window to the supreme. This 'optimistic' assessment of experience is adapted by Ramaṇa and contributes to universalist programme of liberation.

Padmapāda

Dasgupta reminds us that Padmapāda is 'universally reputed to be a direct disciple of Śaṅkara' (Dasgupta, 1988: 102). According to his reasoning, since Padmapāda's *maṅgala* verses indicate a *śiṣya* relationship with Śaṅkara, and since no evidence external to written texts contradicts this, 'it may safely be assumed that he was a younger contemporary of Śaṅkara' (Dasgupta, 1988: 102). However, as in the case of Sureśvara, we know very little about the life history of this important successor to Śaṅkara. Of the many *digvijayas* of Śaṅkara, that of Vidyāraṇya offers interesting accounts of the career of Padmapāda, although how much of these stories actually represent historical events is questionable.

While, as with Sureśvara, we do not have substantial reports of Padmāpada's life or career, we do have his *Pañcapādikā*, one of the most important texts of Advaita.[51] He apparently wrote another treatise, no longer extant, called the

50 ... *trayāṇām api varṇānāṁ śrutau saṁnyāsadarśanāt / brāhmaṇasyaiva saṁnyāsa iti bhāṣyam virudhyate* (BUBV 3.5.1, quoted in Sawai, 1986: 381). My translation differs slightly from Sawai's.

51 In this section, I use Venketaramiah's (1948) translation with some minor modifications.

Ātmabodhavyākhyāna, but the importance of the *Pañcapādikā* cannot be overstated, and there are many reasons for the prestige it commands in Vedāntic literature. First, it is one of the first texts, if not the first, to comment on Śaṅkara's *Bhāṣya* on the Brahma Sūtra, thus initiating a long tradition of critical reflection on foundational Advaita. Second, as mentioned in the introductory section to this chapter, the *Pañcapādikā* contains important ideas concerning the nature of the *jīva* and its relationship to the *ātman* that shape the thinking of one important school of thought in Vedānta, the Vivāraṇa. Although seminal ideas of the Vivāraṇa school are found in the *Pañcapādikā*, a later advocate of the school, Prakāśātman, appears to read into Padmapāda's occasionally ambiguous reflections his own decidedly univocal positions. Nevertheless, as Dasgupta points out, 'the doctrines of *avacchedavāda* and *pratibimbavāda* ... are also at least as old as Padmapāda's *Pañcapādikā*, ... both Padmapāda and Prakāśātman seem to support the reflection theory (*pratibimbavāda*), the theory that the *jīva* is but a reflected image of Brahman' (Dasgupta, 1988: 106).

A final reason stands out for the premier status of the *Pañcapādikā* among Vedāntic texts – one which will occupy our reflections here: Padmapāda carefully unpacks the implications and the potential rebuttals to Śaṅkara's discourse on superimposition in BSB 1.1.0, which constitutes a lucid tract on Vedānta. Padmapāda astutely recognized this and introduced the *pūrvapakṣa* of the Bhāṭṭa and Prābhākara Mīmāṃsakās, the realist positions of the Nyāya-Vaiśeṣika, as well as versions of Mādhyamika and Yogācāra Buddhism. In engaging these objectors, Padmapāda developed a more refined epistemology than his famous predecessor and created a model for later Vedāntins concerned with consciousness and the operations of the mind. His thought in this regard will be the focus of our reflections here.

Padmapāda on experience: introduction

First, I will cite reflections on Padmapāda by two prominent philosopher–Indologists, Karl Potter and the late Wilhelm Halbfass. Both recognized important nuances in Padmapāda's thought which are germane to my discussion of his epistemology of religious experience. Potter, for example, recognized the potential for considering Padmapāda's work as cognitive in an important sense:

> Padmapāda and his followers would like to see philosophy as utilizing a peculiar method of cognition, unlike that of science and ordinary affairs but for all that rational. Such a method would be a kind of direct experience, not necessarily conceptual or expressible but at least in some sense cognitive. This, Padmapāda thinks, is what Śaṅkara has in mind rather than the more mystical intuition which Sureśvara found in Śaṅkara's pronouncements. (Potter, 1991: 225)

The way to understand the cognitive aspect of direct experience is to return again to the structure of the relationship between the *jīva* and *ātman*. In our brief recounting of the Bhāmatī and Vivāraṇa schools we saw competing metaphors which illustrated this relationship, the *avacchedavāda* and *pratibimbavāda*. Sureśvara, in keeping with his rigorous theory of the non-production (*ajātivāda*), has a slight variance of *pratibimbavāda*, namely *cidābhāsavāda* – that is, the doctrine of appearing as consciousness. We recall that he took a dim view of mundane mental processes, considering their cognitive outcome to be derivative and indirect. Only the knowledge 'generated' from scripture is direct or immediate.

Padmapāda, however, is more generous to the psycho-mental organism. We recall that in the *pratibimbavāda* and *cidābhāsavāda*, the psycho-mental unit reflects pure consciousness but is itself inert. Padmapādaī, however, holds that localized selves are reflected images of the pure witness (*sākṣin*); these selves are not the pure witness, since they are unfree, but they are essentially the same as the witness. So, while the psycho-mental unit (*antaḥkarana*, *buddhi*) is *acit*, since it is spawned by ignorance, the new localized selves, although apparently 'born' through the reflection of divine consciousness in the subtle equipment, do not become inert like that equipment (Potter, 1991: 176). This suggests an opening in the analysis of cognition and experience *per se* which promises dividends in our analysis of religious experience.

Another helpful direction for this analysis is suggested by Halbfass in his discussion on Śaṅkara in his acclaimed study *India and Europe*. Among the many fascinating reflections in that book are Halbfass's observations concerning the use of 'experience' in the rhetoric of the twentieth-century neo-Hindu revival. Briefly examining several passages in Śaṅkara's *Bhāṣya*, he accurately points out that the great *ācārya* never used the term subjectively; he never appealed to his personal experience as an apodictic proof of non-dualism. In Halbfass's discussion of this theme, he makes a cursory but important reference to Padmapāda, noting that 'Padmapāda pursues the phenomenology of immediate awareness (*anubhava*) further than his master' (Halbfass, 1990: 391). Rather than appealing to any extraordinary 'mystical' experiences for confirmation of the one, true, Self, Padmapāda analyses the notion of immediacy (*aparokṣatā*) and finds that it is one and the same in any act of perception, whether directed to external objects or to inner experience. He adds:

> Accordingly, experience (*anubhava*) itself, which is of the nature of immediacy, is one and the same with regard to all individuals (*anubhavo'parokṣatayā sarvān pratyaviśiṣto' pi*); and it must ultimately be identical with the self-luminous (*svayaṃjyotis*) 'witness' or self (*ātman*). (Halbfass, 1990: 391)

Keeping in mind the observations of Halbfass and Potter on these nuances in Advaita theory, let us look closer at Padmapāda's reflections on experience.

Anubhava *in Padmapāda*

In Padmapāda's *Pañcapādikā*, we are able to discern at least three central reflections on experience (*anubhava*) of increasing importance. They are not, of course, systematically presented according to my value scale, but are embedded in various discussions of Śaṅkara's thought and in the various debates with *āstika* and *nāstika* opponents. Our first consideration of experience in Padmapāda's reflections concerns his comment on BSB 1.1.4; here, we remember, Śaṅkara briefly makes the case that *anubhava* enjoys a status not only comparable, but eventually superior, to the mundane *pramāṇas*. This, as we know by now, is because *anubhava* is the ultimate terminus of the inquiry into Brahman. The second reflection on experience focuses on the relation of *experience* to the Self. Is experience a separate event, somehow independent of the Self? How does experience work? Does experience illumine both the Self and the object? If so, how? These questions are considered in the last half of Padmapāda's discussion of superimposition. This last area of discussion of experience for Padmapāda – namely, his phenomenology of immediacy – is most significant of all. Let us consider each of these areas of reflections. The first two we may consider with reasonable dispatch since Padmapāda's discussion of them is fairly limited.

The Self is anubhava *(I)* There are three ways in which Padmapāda argues that the Self is of the nature of experience. The first which we will examine is the last one Padmapāda discusses, and unfortunately all too briefly. Padmapāda's view of *anubhava* here amounts to a cursory repetition of Śaṅkara's words in BSB 1.1.2. We recall Śaṅkara's insistence on retaining the compelling power of *anubhava*, and establishing its authority as a saving *pramāṇa*, if not precisely a mundane *pramāṇa*. We also saw that *anubhava* or experience is authoritative in the realm of the Self. Padmapāda takes up this theme and repeats it, but unfortunately offers little additional expatiation. In the fifth *varṇaka*, he explains the import of *śravaṇa*, *manana* and *nidhidhyāsana*. While *śravaṇa*, he agrees, is 'stated to be the means in the acquisition of Brahman knowledge', he agrees with Śaṅkara that 'human reasoning assists scripture'. Padmapāda takes the term *śrutyādayaḥ* as the hermeneutical method of the Mīmāṃsakās – direct statement (*śruti*), potency of words (*vākya*), syntactical relation (*liṅga*), context (*prakaraṇa*), position (*sthāna*), and name (*samākhyā*). However, he adds the following:

> It is not that only these alone which are the right means in the cognition of Brahman, but on the contrary, experience (*anubhava*) as well, in corroboration of which the *bhāṣya* says, 'because *anubhava* is the culmination of the knowledge regarding Brahman, and because that knowledge has as its object an accomplished entity'. (Venketaramiah, 1948: 269–70)

Padmapāda reworks Śaṅkara's explanation without adding anything new: 'To explain: this is so, since experience concerns something that already exists, and because the consummation of the desire for the knowledge of Brahman is experience' (Venketaramiah, 1948: 270). One wishes that he had added further comment, but this minimal repetition at least shows that he is in agreement with Śaṅkara. To have an experience means to be engaged with a *bhūtavastu*, 'something that already exists', at least phenomenally and therefore ephemerally. Or it could mean to be engaged with a *bhūtavastu* transcendentally – that is, engaged with 'existing' consciousness which is a condition for the possibility for any mental event, with or without phenomenal content.

Mundane experience clearly suggests intentionality to experience: one has an 'experience of' something. Consciousness 'grasps' an object but, according to Śaṅkara, Sureśvara and Padmapāda, ultimate experience dissolves the subject–object relationship; *anubhava*, here, is the realization of the unqualified substrate of all acts of consciousness. In the end, there is something compelling about 'experience', certainly in its ultimate sense, but also in its mundane sense, for both intimate a lively presentation to consciousness. In Advaita *sādhana*, however, the particular presentations of mundane experience are peeled away, leaving only indeterminate, contentless experience. This *regressus*, however, is liberation, for in the end Self and experience are one and the same.

The Self is anubhava *(II)* Our concern in this section is Padmapāda's understanding of the Self and whatever it is we call *anubhava*, rendered as experience or even as we have said before, 'knowledge following experience'. Padmapāda is careful here to protect the self-conscious nature of the Self, but recognizes challenges from the schools of Kumārila Bhaṭṭa and Prabhākara. The former holds that the Self can be both subject and object in the same knowledge (Venketaramiah, 1948: xviii). While this position has an attraction for those who wish to preserve something of the common-sense notion of 'knowing oneself', it entails unacceptable consequences for non-dualists, since objects are insentient, insubstantial and, finally, unreal. Knowing oneself, according to this view, implies that the Self is both sentient and non-sentient, for objects that are known are insentient. Moreover, if the self-consciousness of the Self is construed this way, not only does the Self 'know' an unconscious element of itself, but it is now obviously composed of parts. And entities, as we are reminded by the stock example in Indian logic, which are composed of parts are also subject to dissolution – 'like a pot' (*ghaṭavat*). Consequently, they are not eternal.

Prabhākara holds that the Self is actually inert, though somehow still an agent (*kartā*). In keeping with the Mīmāṃsā emphasis on agency, the act of knowing reveals both the object known (*prameya*) and the knower (*pramātā*). This position is also unacceptable to Advaita, for it suggests that self-consciousness is dependent on the accidental proximity of objects, which in any case possess no substantial reality. As we have seen earlier, the Self is self-luminous (*svaprakāśa*) and independent (*nirāpekṣa*); the self-consciousness of the Self is innate or self-established (*svataḥ siddhaḥ*) and is not an accident occasioned by the act of knowing.

And yet, both Śaṅkara and Padmapāda hold that 'it is not the case that the *ātman* is absolutely a non-object (*aviṣaya*), because it is an object of the "I-notion" (*aham pratyaya*)' (Venketaramiah, 1948: 56). Padmapāda's discussion here expands on Śaṅkara's classic consideration of 'I–Thou', *asmat* and *yuṣmat*, in his introduction to the BSB and in Up. 1.10–14 by representing a *pūrvapakṣin* who understandably wonders how the eternal subject, pure awareness, can become an object. Objects are external and somehow appropriated by the mental faculties. '*Idam*' ('this') is the upaniṣadic term which indicates the external world of objects appropriated by the mental faculties. Opposed to this is the subject (*viṣayi*), the inner self; this 'entity' is the self-luminous 'not-this' (*anidam*) element. It is inward (*pratyak*), inaccessible to language and thought, and unavailable to the senses. How then, asks the Mīmāṃsaka, could these mutually hostile properties, subject and object, coexist in the *ātman*, which is one and devoid of parts?

The answer lies in the 'ego-notion' (*asmat-pratyaya*), taken by Padmapāda to include the inner faculty or the *antaḥkaraṇa*. It is through the ego-notion that one can speak of 'knowing the Self', however ultimately erroneously. That the ego-notion embraces both the '*idam*' and '*anidam*' elements – that is, objectivity and subjectivity – is 'a matter of universal experience' (ibid.). The Self, *reflected* in the *antaḥkaraṇa*, becomes adapted to mundane reality (*vyavahārayogya*) and manifests itself indubitably. This is why Śaṅkara could speak so confidently about the existential fact of the Self in BSB 1.1.1: 'The existence of Brahman is established on account of being the Self of all, for everyone admits the existence of the Self; no one ever says "I am not".'[52] Although for Śaṅkara, while the fact of the Self is indubitable – even doubt presumes consciousness, as Descartes reminded us many centuries later – *what* this Self is is quite another thing. But to predicate objectivity of the Self means to recognize the manifestation of the Self in the *antaḥkaraṇa*, not that the Self rigidly becomes one object among others, now destined for exhaustive intellectual categorization. According to this view, sense contact is not absolutely necessary for an 'object' to be revealed; to become a *viṣaya* it is enough for the 'object' to manifest itself, 'thereby dispelling doubt regarding its existence' (ibid.: 57). The fact that there is a Self is evident by our use of the first-person singular pronoun. That is our starting point and, following the deconstruction of our misplaced predications, our terminus as well. We learn through proper training of our intellect (*adhyāropa*, *anvayavyatireka*), and especially through scripture, to remove our physical ('I am fat', 'I am tall'), mental ('I am happy', 'I am sad') or social ('I am a man', 'I am a Brahmin') ascriptions, purging these as ultimately unreal conditionings of the Self. As Padmapāda concludes:

52 ... *sarvasyātmatāc ca brahmāstitvaprasiddhiḥ / sarvo hy ātmāstitvaṁ pratyeti na nāham asmīti* (BSB 6).

> … the pure consciousness, the *ātman*, is self-established, is the final limit (*avadhi*) of all our aversions and covetings (*hānopādāna*), itself is not an object, fit neither for abandonment nor for possession and, because it is self-luminous (and so always immediately present), is fit to be the substratum of illusory knowledge. (Ibid.: 103–104)

But the representative of Prabhākara's view presses his case, insisting that the outcome of a mechanism of knowledge, *pramiti*, is directly experienced. '*Pramiti* is experience (*anubhava*), self-luminous, and is the result of a *pramāṇa*' (ibid.: 57). Through the instrumentality of *pramiti*, which Prabhākara identifies with *anubhava*, the knower and the known are manifested. It is only through the agency of experience (*anubhava, pramiti*) that we are able to infer the Self: '*Anubhava* is self-luminous and reveals both the object, the cognized, and the knower, the cognizer' (ibid.: 1948: 58).

Such a view raises a worry for Padmapāda – namely, whether there are now two separate events, 'experience' and the Self. He challenges the opponent, asking for clarification concerning Self and *anubhava*. Is the Self conscious and *anubhava* unconscious? Are they both conscious? Or is *anubhava* alone conscious and the Self unconscious? The first alternative is unacceptable for it would result in an unknown, unrevealed world. And if, Padmapāda challenges, one insists that the Self reveals the world and itself through the instrumentality of *anubhava*, two problems result. First, the nature of the Self is consciousness itself, so it is therefore unreasonable to hold that it derives benefit from a separate 'experience' of an object which in turn is both inert and insentient. Moreover, if the Self is said to manifest both the object and itself with the help of experience, an infinite regress develops: 'the act of manifestation will be interminable' (ibid.: 59).

The second view also seems gratuitous. Why should the Self, whose nature is self-luminous (*svaprakāśa*), require 'experience' to reveal itself? If one urges that, despite being of the nature of consciousness, the Self is somehow *not* self-revealing, a reason must be advanced for conceding self-luminosity or immediacy only to experience and not to the Self; but no good reason appears to account for this. Furthermore, it makes no sense to say that the conscious Self is only *mediately* perceptible, but *immediately* perceptible through the help of another; finally, since both the Self and *anubhava* are *cetanarūpa*, they do not require the help of the other (ibid.).

The implications of the third view – holding that only *anubhava* manifests itself as the nature of consciousness while the Self is of the nature of insentience – terminates 'despite one's will' in the conclusion that 'the Self alone is the luminous consciousness'. How so? If *anubhava* is both self-luminous and a quality, as Prabhākara holds, it must be a quality of something; it must have a support or locus, an *āśraya* which then must possess such luminosity. Hence, as Venkataramiah observes, 'if the *ātman* possesses the property of luminosity, it amounts to the *ātman* being self-luminous' (ibid.: 60).

We may summarize several observations based on Padmapāda's comments. *Anubhava* amounts to a different modality of the Self-revealing supreme consciousness. It is the luminous experience of the Self upon the occasion of different mechanisms of knowledge. Through every act of knowledge, the self-revealing Self shines. The Self and *anubhava* are one and the same. The Self, when conditioned by mundane processes of knowledge is *anubhava*, experience. When such adjuncts are 'out of purview', such consciousness is understood as the supreme Self. Such an interpretation has important implications for our consideration of the epistemology of religious experience, particularly when viewed from an internalist perspective. Let us continue with Padmapāda's analysis of experience, now focusing on its principal characteristic, immediacy.

Immediacy of anubhava Our third discussion of *anubhava* in Padmapāda occurs as part of his analysis of everyday perception. We remember that the *sine qua non* for the *vyavahārika* in Śaṅkara and Padmapāda is some unaccountable (*anirvacanīya*), beginningless (*anādi*) process of superimposition (*adhyāsa*). The non-dual consciousness somehow becomes conditioned or transformed or, to put it another way, various 'entities' are transformations (*vivarta*) of the supreme consciousness. Here we are most concerned with the mental transformations of consciousness, and less so with the cosmological speculation. The two, however, are closely related by virtue of their common substrate, consciousness.

With regard to the mental transformations, the *antaḥkaraṇa* itself is both a modification and a manifestation of consciousness. In addition, objects 'out there' are in some sense transformations of consciousness, however 'gross'. Such a view is, of course, hardly self-evident and requires a sophisticated theory to support it. Our project here is less concerned with accounting for this theory than in determining the cognitive implications in the Advaita phenomenology of perception. In traditional Advaita epistemology, a kind of correspondence occurs between the *antaḥkaraṇa* and the external object. Both, we recall, are held to be transformations of consciousness. The same *caitanya* is manifested by two indicators, the mental mode (*vṛtti*) and the object itself. The mental mode is a secondary transformation, this time of the internal organ. It matches or corresponds to the external object (*viṣaya*). The one Self, which is consciousness, therefore thoroughly pervades the act of cognition. When one says 'the jar is cognized by me', consciousness manifests itself both as cognizer and cognized; as Venketaramiah explains, 'the identity relation between the object-limited-consciousness and the internal-sense-limited-consciousness' thus makes possible the perception of the external world (Venketaramiah, 1948: 166).

So the Self in association with the fluid *antaḥkaraṇa* becomes a cognizer. The fruit (*phala*) of this process is immediate perception which thus reveals the object (*viṣayānubhava*). An identity occurs between the result of cognition and its mental mode. When experience and the mental mode have the same object and locus (*jar* and *ātman qua* ego), the ego (*ahamkartā*) 'assumes the role of cognizer both on the strength of its consciousness aspect and of its association with the mental mode (*vṛtti*); as such, we say that the *puruṣa* cognizes the object presented in the intellect' (ibid.: 82).

Although Padmapāda toes the Advaita line and maintains that the Self *per se* does not know or act, he nevertheless places considerable value on the *ahaṃkara* and on mundane perception. The value of each of these mechanisms will pay dividends for us in our conclusions over the epistemic nature of religious experience. For Padmapāda, the *ahaṃkara* 'is the substrate of the power of thought and action; it is the sole basis of agency and enjoyment; it is a light generated by its association with the unchanging intelligence; it is self-luminous; it is immediate perception' (ibid.: 68). Still, 'any power of agency ascribed to *ātman*, owing to its association with the *antaḥkaraṇa*, is illusory, just as the color red is mistakenly ascribed to the crystal when the *japākusuma* flower is placed next to it' (ibid.: 69). The *ahaṃkara* becomes a knot (*granthi*), as it were, 'a tangle of conscious and unconscious elements'. This 'tangle' leads to a valorization of the *ahaṃkara* and to important implications in Padmapāda's theory of perception.

We recall that Padmapāda favours the metaphor of reflection (*pratibimbavāda*) to illustrate the relationship between the *ātman* and the *jīva*. The Self is the 'original' and the *jīva* is the reflection or 'mirror' – that is, consciousness conditioned by mental equipment. Padmapāda's striking nuance is that the reflected image is not distinct from the object (ibid.: 72); instead, what is illusory is 'their appearing as distinct'. As Venketramiah explains, 'the image is real, since it does not differ in essence from its prototype .... Object and image are one and the same' (ibid.: 74). Now, although the object and image possess the same nature (*ekasvabhāva*) and identity (*ekatva*), 'the appearance of the object as distinct is the play of *māyā*; this phenomenon is well-known, for there is nothing incongruous to *māyā*' (ibid.: 76). Such oneness is supported by *śruti* and *smṛti*. The sense of separation from the non-dual real accrues from the *insentient* element being reflected in the mirror; nonetheless, this kind of 'reflection' can recognize its identity with Brahman while the mundane reflection of a face in a mirror cannot. The *jīva*, we are reminded, is sentient, while the body, including its mental equipment, is not. Padmapāda concludes, 'The *jīva*, which may be likened to a reflection, is of the nature of consciousness, and it is not pervaded by the inertness pertaining to the *antaḥkaraṇa*' (ibid.: 77).

The *ahaṃkara*, as a tangle of conscious and unconscious elements, has important implications in mundane observations. First, it means that the supreme consciousness, which is reflected in it, reveals itself in every act of consciousness. Despite this, *śruti* and the threefold process are necessary to remove the 'blinding darkness' of ignorance. This is why I suggest that Padmapāda operates from a 'modest' internalism. The axioms of Advaita and the value that Padmapāda accords to normal cognitive processes suggest that one may access the Self through an introvertive analysis of conscious experience. But, for Padmapāda, this process must be situated in an overall context of text, tradition and teacher (ibid.: 77, 269). In this sense, mere reflection on mundane experience (*anubhava*) is not sufficient either.

Nevertheless, while he insists on the necessary efficacy of *śruti*, the value he gives to the immediacy of experience is significant; indeed, for Padmapāda, immediacy (*aparokṣatā*) is the essential element of experience and extends into supreme *anubhava*. Contrary to Sureśvara, who diminishes mundane experience as flawed, derivative and mediate, Padmapāda sees experience as discreetly revealing the Self, and so it might be considered a 'window' to the supreme. The key to such revelation is immediacy. According to Padmapāda, the immediacy of the Self is the same immediacy in mundane experience; since the experience of all individuals is characterized by immediacy, and since this immediacy is one and the same everywhere, experience itself must be taken to be the self-luminous 'witness' or Self (ibid.: 83).

This is a position that is both promising and problematic. It is promising because it suggests a tantalizing and optimistic evaluation of human experience. Following a proper analysis of experience and consciousness, we may discover, embedded in those very processes, a divine reality. It is problematic because it makes unilateral assumptions about the nature of experience and consciousness. Nevertheless, Padmapāda's valorization of experience, owing to the character of immediacy, appears to favour a modest internalism in his epistemology of religious experience, although, for Padmapāda, as for Śaṅkara and Sureśvara, the economy of liberation requires suitable conditions for a proper analysis of experience – namely, the instruction of a qualified teacher employing acceptable patterns of reasoning. Ultimately, however, such analysis is consummated by the penetrating power of revelation (ibid.: 269). Hence, while mundane experience may be a 'window' to the supreme, it remains a window that must finally be opened by text, tradition and teacher. It is clear, at least in the case of classical Advaita, that the project of liberation cannot be abstracted from its intellectual, cultural, and behavioural conditions. Even the mechanisms of producing knowledge are conditioned by, and indexed to, the goals of such critical thinking. So, as Padmapāda writes, 'the *pramāṇas* have prepared the ground for a deeper inquiry aimed at direct perception of the real' (ibid.: 136).

This section, though much briefer than that on Sureśvara, has reviewed Padmapāda's discussion of experience and focused on an important aspect of Padmapāda's epistemology – namely the notion of immediacy which characterizes mundane and supreme experience. This notion extends Śaṅkara's epistemological reflections in the *adhyāsa bhaṣya* and suggests a modest internalism. It is 'modest' because Padmapāda still indexes introspection and discrimination to the Advaitin culture of liberation. This culture constitutes the 'external circuitry' of Advaita, socially established doxastic mechanisms, and includes various textual (exegetic), doctrinal (reasoning) and traditional (*varṇāśramadharma*, *karma*, *saṃnyāsa*) practices. These practices indicate a strong externalist dimension in Advaita, notwithstanding its incipient internalism. Advaita's externalism may, following William Alston, render *prima facie* justification to claims that follow a particular Advaitin religious experience. However, the stronger its doses of externalism, the less universal is Advaita's soteriology. The reliance on external mechanisms may secure an initial justification of religious claims for Advaita, but at the cost of exclusivity.

For a final look at 'later Advaita' and the analysis of *anubhava* in the economy of liberation, let us examine the *Vivekacūḍāmaṇi*. Of the thinkers examined in this chapter, the author of the *Vivekacūḍāmaṇi* initially seems to represent the strongest agenda for employing personal experience in the programme of salvation. Such an agenda seems most disposed to an internalist epistemology of religious experience, and follows rather closely the 'epistemological logic' of Advaita's principal axioms. This suggests a broader scope to liberation, allowing for a genuine universalism. If this is the case, it is no wonder that *Vivekacūḍāmaṇi* has enjoyed a premier status among twentieth-century apologists for neo-Hinduism. Let us look closely at this text, which has often been ignored by philosophers, if not by devotees, gurus and apologists for Advaita.

The *Vivekacūḍāmaṇi*

The *Vivekacūḍāmaṇi* is a collection of Advaita tenets in fairly straightforward Sanskrit. It has been available throughout most of the twentieth century through the efforts of the Vedanta Society, which has published at least three different editions of the translation by Swami Prabhavānanda and Christopher Isherwood in 1947.[53] The text has often been used by many middle-class Indians, but some Westerners have found it intriguing as well. Thomas Merton, for example, took the text with him on his trip to Asia just before his death in 1968. He apparently found some intellectual or spiritual inspiration from it, for he recorded at least six extended excerpts from it in his *Asian Journal*.[54]

The *Vivekacūḍāmaṇi* is an extended dialogue between a guru and his disciple. More precisely, it represents an ideal encounter between student and teacher. VC 33 clearly indicates this ideal encounter, expanding upon the rather unemotional appeal

---

53 The English editions of Mādhavānanda and Turīyānanda include the *devanāgari* text. Although I consulted their translations, those that follow are mine. Both M. and T. represent standard editions of the *Vivekacūḍāmaṇi* (hereafter, VC), and so in this section I refer only to the verses of the VC; readers may consult either edition for reference.

54 Merton (1975: 37–38, 95–96, 111–12, 117, 267–70). Merton used the 1947 translation of Prabhavānanda and Isherwood.

to discipleship found in Muṇḍaka Upaniṣad 1.2.12;[55] a student, when equipped with the requisite qualifications and finally unbearably provoked by the miseries of existence, *should* beseech (*pṛcchet*) a teacher for instruction. The rest of the VC represents a hypothetical exchange between *jñāni* and the *jijñāsu*. This didactic exchange, absent the martial melodrama of the Mahābhārata, recalls the exchange between Kṛṣṇa and Arjuna in the *Gītā*.[56] *Gītā* 2.7 plainly illustrates the plight of someone whose existential crisis has propelled him to the brink of an emotional and cognitive collapse: 'My mind confused about dharma, I come to you; tell me decisively what's best for me. I am your student. Teach me, your servant!'[57] VC 36 suggests a similar crisis, although such a crisis is by no means an evil thing in Indian philosophy for, painful though it is, it provides a slingshot into new existential horizons replete with cognitive and affective overhaul: 'Save me, your servant, from death, burned by the unbearable fire of the forest of *samsāra*, shaken by the winds of bad luck, numb; I know no other for refuge!'[58]

There are other parallels and references to the *Gītā*. Both are written in verse, primarily *anuṣṭubh* and occasionally *upajāti*, and both share the same proportions of each (VC 2:1). The texts are of similar length (580 verses for the VC, 700 for the *Gītā*), and the authors of each feel free to reinterpret and re-evaluate various traditional categories of Indian thought and practice. This tendency, of course, has been well documented in the case of the *Gītā*,[59] but the author of the VC similarly spins his interpretation and value of traditional categories and practices, such as *prāṇayāma*, the *kośamīmāṃsā*, *bhakti*, and so on. For example, *bhakti*, which is somewhat formally expatiated in *Gītā* 12 (and tenderly evoked in *Gītā* 18), receives a typical Advaitin interpretation in VC 31 and 32: 'Among the means of liberation, *bhakti* itself is supreme; *bhakti*, it is taught, is the investigation into one's nature.'[60]

The author, however, not only adopts the same freewheeling interpretative strategy as the *Gītā*, but also evokes its rhetoric and style. Two examples will serve

55 'Having examined the worlds constituted by works, let a Brahmin arrive at non-attachment ... for the sake of that knowledge let him approach, with fuel in hand, a teacher well-versed in scripture and established in Brahman (*parīkśya lokān karmacitān brāhmaṇo nirvedam āyān … tad vijñānārthaṁ sa gurum evābhigacchet samitpāṇiḥ śrotriyam brahmanniṣṭham*)' (Radhakrishnan, 1992: 678–79). I have slightly modified the translation.

56 There are, of course, many translations of the *Gītā*, the best perhaps being that of Barbara Stoler Miller (1986). The translations of the *Gītā* in this section are mine; the Sanskrit text is taken from Swarupananda (1993).

57 … *pṛchāmi tvāṁ dharmasaṃmūdacetāḥ / yacchreyaḥ syān niścitaṁ brūhi tanme śiṣyaste 'haṁ śādhi māṁ tvāṁ prapannam.*

58 … *durvārasaṃsāradavāgnitaptaṁ dodhūyamānaṁ duradṛṣṭavātaiḥ / bhītaṁ prapanna paripāhi mṛtyoḥ śaraṇyam anyad yad ahaṁ na jāne.*

59 The literature on the *Gītā* is legion. Van Buitenen (1981) helps to contextualize the historical and religious developments suggested in the *Gītā*; the translations of Zaehner (1969) and Radhakrishnan (1976) include notes from the commentaries of Śaṅkara and Rāmānuja. For broader studies of the strategic translations and uses of the *Gītā* see Sharma (1986) and Sharpe (1985).

60 … *mokṣakāraṇasāmagryāṁ bhaktir eva garīyasī / svasvarūpānusandhānaṁ bhaktir ity abhidhīyate.*

to illustrate these evocations. The famous four questions of Arjuna in *Gītā* 2.54 concerning the enlightened one – how does one describe the sage? what does he say? how does he comport himself? how does he walk?[61] – are modulated and nearly doubled in VC 49, a verse which sets out the questions the text aims to answer: what is bondage? how does it happen? how does it remain? how does one get liberated? what is non-Self? what is the Self? how does one discriminate between them?[62] Another parallel recalls one of the most memorized verses in the *Gītā*: '[the Self] never dies, nor is it born (*na jayate mriyate vā kadācit*)'; VC 134 follows the *Gītā* while adding terms which appear elsewhere in the *Gītā* as descriptions of the Self: '[the Self] neither dies, nor is born, nor does it change; it neither grows, nor is destroyed'.[63]

Finally, the *Vivekacūḍāmaṇi* uses terms which recall the *Gītā* as well. For example, according to the VC, one should commence the path to salvation 'having attained the state of yoga (*yogārūḍhatvam āsādya*, VC 9)'. *Yogārūḍha* is a technical term which appears in *Gītā* 6.3 and 6.4, and derives from the root √*āruh*, 'to ascend, mount, undertake, attain, and so on'. Now, owing to its synthetic agenda, the *Gītā*'s various glosses on yoga often have little in common with the technical exposition of yoga found in Patañjali.[64] In a typical *Gītā* developmental strategy, section 6.3a suggests that action is the salvific means for the sage who wishes to attain yoga (*ārurukṣor muneḥ*), but is then followed by the claim that, for the one who has attained yoga, a higher programme, calm (*śama*), is the means.[65] Finally, in *Gītā* 6.4 an equation is established which repeats one of the text's most important themes, namely that yoga is the renunciation of all self-centred ends or desires: 'the one who renounces all intentions is the one who ascends to yoga'.[66] The use of the term *yogārūḍha* by the author of the *Vivekacūḍāmaṇi* serves to borrow the *Gītā*'s theme of ego-detachment, while not, however, moving on to the theme of devotion to Kṛṣṇa. Instead, it is through being devoted or attached to the right view (*samyagdarśananiṣṭhayā*) that the sage climbs to the highest states of yoga. Let us examine the 'right view' that permits this 'ascent'.

61 ... *sthitaprajñasya kā bhāṣā samādhisthasya keśava / sthithadhīḥ kiṁ prabhāṣeta kim āsīta vrajeta kim.*

62 *Ko nāma bandhaḥ katham eṣa āgataḥ kathaṁ pratiṣṭḥāsya kathaṁ vimokṣaḥ / ko 'sau anātmā paramaḥ ka ātmā tayor vivekaḥ katham etad ucyatām.*

63 ... *na jāyate no mriyate na vardhate na kṣīyate no vikaroti.*

64 *Gītā* 6 offers the closest representation of several principal practices described in the Yoga Sūtra. Significant as this representation is, the theist agenda of the *Gītā* surfaces rapidly even here: 'The one who sees me everywhere, and sees all (creatures) in me, I will not lose him, nor will he be lost to me (*yo māṁ paśyati sarvatra ca mayi paśyati / tasyāhaṁ na praṇaśyāmi sa ca me na praṇaśyati*)'.

65 Cf. NS 1.51.

66 ... *sarvasaṁkalpasaṁnāysī yogārūḍhaḥ.* Other repetitions of this theme are found throughout the *Gītā* – for example, 5.12, 5.9, 4.19, 2.46, 2.47 – the most important them, of course, reconfiguring such existential *detachment* into *attachment* to Kṛṣṇa, for example, 12.2, 12.8, 18.55–70.

Principal philosophical issues

The answers to the seven questions mentioned above constitute a complete metaphysic and accompanying soteriology. Both categories are intimately interconnected in any religious world-view; the challenge for us is to determine the primary epistemological modality by which a tradition unifies them. In addition to evaluating the cognitive dimension of religious experience, I will argue that important cultural implications follow from epistemologies of religious experience that are decisively externalist or decisively internalist.

The principal theme of the *Vivekacūḍāmaṇi* is, of course radical non-dualism, versions of which have abounded in India since the sixth century BCE. In the case of the VC, we see familiar Advaita themes: the Self alone is real; what is not the Self is therefore not real. An adaptation of a favourite Advaita maxim appears in VC 20 and is used by the author to gloss the first of Śaṅkara's fourfold criteria for eligibility: 'The firm conviction that Brahman is real and the universe is unreal is designated as discrimination between the eternal and the impermanent.'[67] Unfolding the process of discrimination is the primary agenda of the *Vivekacūḍāmaṇi*, as seen in the title of the text.

While the driving force of the VC is non-dualism, the author nevertheless establishes a division by dichotomy – Self and not-self – in order eventually to deconstruct it. We have seen this strategy in Śaṅkara and Sureśvara, and it seems to be a necessary, or at least reasonable, heuristic: while an esoteric oneness may be the ultimate truth of the universe, everyday experience abounds in pluralities. The author must admit these pluralities but must also reject them as possessing any enduring substantial status. Thus, as in VC 20, Brahman is real and the world is false. This division is even more bluntly dichotomized as Self and not-self in VC 47 and 152, discrimination between which effaces the effects of ignorance and 'produces' liberation: 'This is achieved through proper discrimination between Self and not-self.'[68]

Accepting the dichotomy for the moment, two questions obviously present themselves, and indeed, they are two of the seven questions listed in VC 49: just what is the Self and not-self? The answer is straightforward: the Self is the supreme real; anything that is not the supreme real is therefore not the Self or not-self (*anātman*), and 'when the unreal is eliminated, knowledge of the real Self dawns'.[69] A simple test using the *svarūpalakṣaṇa* of Brahman (*satyam jñānam anantam brahma*) found in the Taittirīya Upaniṣad is sometimes used by Advaitin scholars to illuminate this division by dichotomy. Can a stone, the arm of a body, the body itself, or even the mind be considered the supreme Self? No, since all of these – and

67 ... *brahma satyaṁ jagan mithyety evaṁ rūpo viniścayaḥ / so 'yaṁ nityānityavastuvivekaḥ samudāhṛtaḥ*.

68 ... *tadātmānātmanoḥ samyagvivekenaiva sidhyati* (VC 203).

69 ... *asannivṛttau tu sadātamanāḥ sphuṭam* (VC 205).

all empirical reality – are limited in some fashion. They come into existence and pass out of it; they are insentient; they are finite. Only the supreme bears the marks of the consciousness and existence, and these to a limitless degree. But not even this 'definition' positively denotes Brahman; the theories of implication which we examined when discussing Sureśvara rejected the direct, propositional sense of scriptural texts. Instead, the usual Advaitin view of the Taittirīya definition, beginning with Śaṅkara himself, is that these terms mark the boundaries of that reality which is diametrically opposed to all that is finite, unconscious and unreal. The absurdity of considering anything less than the transcendent Self as the supreme is graphically represented in the author's analysis of the body–mind complex in VC 155–83. The body is inert as a pot (*jaḍaś ca ghaṭavat*), characterized by a unstable nature (*aniyatasvabhāvaḥ*) and fleeting qualities (*kṣaṇaguṇaḥ*); in the end 'only a blockhead has the idea, "I am the body"'.[70]

Despite misgivings over the verbal representation of Brahman, 'positive' characterizations of the Self abound in the *Vivekacūḍāmaṇi*; these are drawn from a stock of such representations found in *śruti* and *smṛti* texts. The *Gītā*, again, is often recalled, for the VC shares much of the *Gītā*'s vocabulary concerning the Self. The Self is self-luminous, indivisible consciousness, ever-existent, one without a second, without form and beyond description (VC 221). This Self is a mass of pure consciousness (*viśuddhavijñānaghana*), spotless (*nirañjana*), calm (*praśanta*), without beginning or end, beyond action, bliss itself (VC 237).

Following the usual upaniṣadic identification of micro and macro cosmoi, the Self is Brahman, the sole real. This means that everything else is false, or unreal in any substantial enduring sense. Indeed, according to the author of the *Vivekacūḍāmaṇi*, all else is mere transformation (VC 213). This rigorous non-dualism follows the same presuppositions and logic of Śaṅkara: the real does not change; the world changes, therefore the world cannot be real. Thus, 'does reality pertain to a superimposed entity? The substrate appears as such through error.'[71] But, as with Śaṅkara, the basis for phenomenal presentations, the *adhiṣṭhāna*, is real. Indeed, in a significant sense even the phenomenal world itself is Brahman for it originates, in a fashion peculiar to Advaita, from the supreme source of the (ultimately illusory) universe.[72] But an important relationship obtains between phenomena and their foundation for 'What is superimposed is not separate from its basis'.[73] So, while 'appearances' cannot be real, their origin and foundation, their *adhiṣṭhāna*, are real; appearances, in effect, possess a borrowed reality. Hence, 'this universe is nothing but Brahman'.[74] Thus, we have the same account of phenomena

70 ... *deho 'ham ityeva jaḍasya buddhiḥ* (VC 160).

71 ... *āropitasyāsti kim arthavattādhiṣṭhāṇam ābhāti tathā bhrameṇa* (VC 235).

72 See BSB 1.1.2, *janmādyasya yataḥ*. Mayeda offers a careful explanation of Śaṅkara's 'early *vivaratavāda*' which avoids Saṅkhya dualism (Mayeda, 1992: 18–26).

73 ... *nādhiṣṭhānād bhinnatāropitasya* (VC 231).

74 ... *etad brahmamātraṁ hi viśvam.*

as we saw in Śaṅkara: appearances 'exist' at least phenomenally; we see them, however fleetingly. While they have no enduring reality as trees, the sun, a chair and so on, the ground out of which they arise, existence, perdures and continues manifesting as other transient entities. 'Brahman, the Real itself, is considered as "this" [universe], but what is superimposed on Brahman is merely a name.'[75] Thus in an important sense, 'The universe does not exist apart from the Supreme Self.'[76]

The universe is 'mere name' (*nāmamātra*), merely superimposed on Brahman. It is ephemeral, insubstantial, imaginary, like a dream (*svapnavat*). The VC then engages in a programme of analysing mundane superimpositions with special appeal to the psycho-physical analysis of the *kośamīmāṃsā*. This inquiry, of course, borrows from the Taittirīya Upaniṣad and has been used frequently in Advaita history as a kind of depth psychology. Through a telescoping process, sheaths of increasing subtlety cover the Self 'as moss covers water' (*paṭalair ivāmbu vāpīstham*, VC 149). Thus the pattern of sheaths first proceeds from the coarse physical body, which is in effect a transformation of food (hence its name *annamayakośa*). The increasingly subtle sheaths which follow are those of vital force (*prāṇamayakośa*), mind (*manomayakośa*), knowledge (*vijñānamayakośa*), and bliss (*ānandamayakośa*). All these sheaths are mere adjuncts or limitations (*upādhi*) of the self-luminous *ātman*. This psychology amounts to a metaphor in Advaita for the importance of the inward journey and requires an examination of the text's method of religious knowing, a programme which eventuates in a transcendent knowing beyond knowledge.

Religious experience

As we have seen before, an intimate relationship obtains between metaphysics, epistemology and soteriology in Advaita and, indeed, in all religious traditions. In foundational Vedānta, we see a dynamism between doctrine, practice and experience. A dynamism also obtains, however, between internalism and externalism in early Advaita. Advaita in 'theory' invites the interpretation of internalism, because of its metaphysic, the privileged access it presupposes and the programme of introspection needed to arrive at supreme truth. Advaita in practice, however, profoundly contextualizes its theory, rendering it local and indexing it to socially established practices that conduce to liberation. This increasing externalism suggests that the doctrines – and the practices intimately related to them – may be *prima facie* justified, as Alston suggests, but that they are locked in their local context. The external circuitry – doctrine, texts, reading and reasoning practices, ethical behaviour – appear to be among the necessary conditions for saving knowledge in the Advaita we have reviewed so far. This has two implications in our analysis of religious experience, one epistemic and one social. The epistemic

---

75 ... *idaṁ tayā brahma sadaiva rūpyate / tv āropitaṁ brahmaṇi nāmamātram* (VC 236).

76 ... *ataḥ pṛtaṅ nāsti jagatparātmanaḥ* (VC 235).

implication is the unsurprising observation that we increasingly cannot evaluate 'religious knowledge' in Advaita apart from the mechanisms that 'produce' and justify it. While this may be unsurprising, it entails considerable work for philosophers of religion both in theory and its application. Philosophers would first need to develop criteria to evaluate causal processes that are considered reliable; the next step would be to apply these criteria to specific traditions in order to determine the range of justification in the religious knowledge which accrues from those processes. All this presumes much philosophical and empirical work, but may yield dividends in our understanding of human 'nature' and reality in its most complete context.

The social implication from our epistemological assessment of Advaita is this: as these externalist mechanisms rise in prominence for Advaita, its universalism is vitiated. In early Advaita, a 'theoretical universalism' – owing to its metaphysic and internalist presumption – is weakened by the apparent necessity of the 'external circuitry' in the economy of liberation. This suggests that the appropriation of Śaṅkara by neo-Hindu apologists is incoherent, at least when they use it to propound Hinduism as a universalist tradition. In Śaṅkara's Advaita, we see a theoretical universalism and a fundamental internalism, but heavy doses of externalism as well. Its metaphysic is deeply implicated in specific knowledges, behaviours and practices, which means recommending it as a universalist faith makes little sense. However, a radical form of Advaita, whose theory is in greater harmony with its practice, and whose internalist epistemology of religious experience follows closely upon its metaphysical assumptions, may be properly universalist. This is my evaluation of the Advaita of Ramaṇa Maharṣi. However, the VC also reveals the tension of internalism and externalism, and this will set the stage for our study of Ramaṇa.

To begin, let us consider the apparent universalism of the *Vivekacūḍāmaṇi*. We see from its premise of non-dualism that Advaita apparently offers some scope for transcending social and cultural boundaries: 'Beyond caste, laws, family, name; free of form, qualification, defects, and beyond time and space (is Brahman).'[77] This at once intimates both a universalist theory of liberation and an internalist epistemology of religious experience. If Brahman is beyond all social and cultural ascriptions, theoretically anyone may realize it; moreover, given Advaita's non-dualism, it would appear that introspection is the best possible method to access the One beyond plurality. Such a programme apparently offers little hope for cognitive satisfaction – at least in the usual sense of the term 'cognitive' – for cognition presumes any number of pluralities, as we have already seen. The author of the text, for example, urges the disciple to 'go beyond the conceptual' (*avikalpaṁ param etya*, VC 70), and reminds him that, in such a state, 'the concept of a witness becomes irrelevant' (*sākṣitvaṁ nopayujyate*, VC 215), because 'there is nothing to be perceived' (*ananubhūtārtha*). Despite these apparently clear themes in the text,

[77] *jātinītikulagotradūragaṁ nāmarūpaguṇadoṣavarjitam / deśakālaviṣayātivarti* (VC 254).

two observations readily become apparent upon a close reading of the *Vivekacūḍāmaṇi*: first, the universalist tendency of the Advaita represented in this text is finally unable to extract itself from its cultural conditions; and, second, a cognitive residue nonetheless remains after liberation – namely that the claim 'There is a knowing beyond knowledge' is *prima facie* justified. We shall explore the first point in the remaining pages of this chapter and argue the second point in Chapter 5 when we consolidate our study.

The *Vivekacūḍāmaṇi* appears to profoundly relativize the value of 'tradition' or culture' on the path to liberation-validating universalist soteriology intimately linked with an internalist epistemology. Such a combination of universalist theory and internalist epistemology has proved to be a potent draw for Western sensibilities, an empirical fact with numerous historical, economic and philosophical antecedents. In the *Vivekacūḍāmaṇi*, for example, no stronger relativizing principle could be urged than in VC 297, which urges the disciple to reject misguided identifications of family, lineage, name, form and stage of life, all of which 'rest in this rotten corpse' (*ardraśavāśriteṣu*), the body. Moreover, the author shows a highly ambivalent attitude towards traditional culture-bound practices, and such apparent openness seems to conduce to a culturally expansive theory of liberation. For example, 'not by yoga, *sāṅkhya*, work, learning, nor by any other means but by the realization of one's identity with Brahman is liberation possible'.[78] VC 59 continues this relativizing process by appearing to diminish the value of scripture: 'When the supreme is unknown, knowledge of scripture is useless; and even when the supreme is known, the scripture is useless.'[79] The final clause of that *śloka* of course recalls similar 'category busters' in BU 4.3.22: among various social deconstructions that occur upon liberation, 'the Vedas are not the Vedas' (*vedāvedāḥ*).[80] VC 61 extends the question concerning the worth of scripture to include all systematic reflection as well; 'for one bitten by the snake of ignorance, without the medicine of the knowledge of Brahman, what good scriptures, *śāstras*, *mantras* or medicines?'[81]

In addition to these relativizing suggestions, the author of the text appears to advocate an internalist mechanism for realization, suggesting something of a do-it-yourself mentality. As with pangs of hunger, the hunger of liberation demands that one feed oneself (VC 52). Moreover, knowledge of reality accrues through oneself alone (*svenaiva*) and not through a scholar (VC 54). This kind of starting point suggests the need for a particular kind of experience (*anubhava*) which is authentic and self-guaranteeing. For example, one is not cured of illness merely by repeating the word 'medicine', but by actually taking the medicine; similarly, 'without the

---

78 ... *na yogena na sāṅkhyena na karmaṇā na vidyayā / brahmātmaikatvabodhena mokṣaḥ sidhyati nānyathā* (VC 56).

79 ... *avijñāte pare tatttve śāstrādhītis tu niṣphalā / vijñāte 'pi pare tattve śāstrādhītis tu niṣphalā.*

80 ... *atra pitāpitā bhavati mātāmātā lokālokāḥ devādevāḥ vedāvedāḥ.*

81 ... *ajñānasarpadaṣṭasya brahmajñānauśadhaṁ vinā / kimu vedaiś ca śāstraiś ca kimu mantraiḥ kim auśadhaiḥ.*

immediate experience of the Self, the mere word "Brahman" does not save'.[82] Indeed, not having experienced the Self, the word 'Brahman' is a 'mere utterance' (*uktimātra*). Instead, one must make every effort (*sarvaprayatnena*) to make this experience one's own, just as a treasure is never uncovered merely by uttering the words 'Come forth!' (VC 65).

One therefore attains this state through one's own experience (*svānubhūtyā*, VC 477). *Anubhūti* is a tricky word to translate, as with *anubhava*, for both mean 'experience' or, perhaps better, 'knowledge through experience'. '*Anu*', of course, is the Sanskrit prefix suggesting 'following' or 'coming after', as in *anumāna*, 'reasoning after' or 'inference'. *Anubhava* and *anubhūti* can also mean 'perception', which affirms the cardinal importance of 'seeing things rightly' or 'right perception' (*samyag anubhūti*). But how we 'see' in Indian philosophy usually depends on how we think. Not only are our mundane perceptions shaped by our mental equipment, but our 'deepest' perceptions – our insight into the way things *really* are – are profoundly conditioned by doctrines about the nature of reality. So, despite the often-heard appeal to the need for experience in the history of Indian religions, experience is always profoundly informed by metaphysical formulations usually expressed in doctrinal teaching. The intimate relationship between doctrine and experience found in Indian soteriologies consistently reveals certain kinds of 'intellectual therapy' which precede affective or emotional transformation; the 'experience' at the heart of liberation is preceded by radical changes in the structure of consciousness, and this in turn requires antecedent cognitive training, the socially established doxastic practices at the core of externalist epistemologies of religious experience. Such a way of construing religious experience of course departs from the perennialist sensibilities that emerged during the Enlightenment and flourished both in the academy and in popular religiosity for much of the twentieth century. But the turn to experience in *classical* Indian soteriologies rarely or never presupposes experience separate from, or uninformed by, a particular way of construing reality. For example, when the Buddha counselled his disciples to be 'lamps' unto themselves, he hardly expected them to discover 'another dharma' in opposition to the one propounded by him. Instead, he enjoined his disciples to confirm, by *their* experience, the truth of the nature of reality to which he bore witness; as Steven Collins has observed, the Buddha is not saying 'Make your own truth', but 'Make the Truth your own' (cited in Gombrich, 1988: 72).

We see something of the same tension in the *Vivekacūḍāmaṇi*, where 'experience' might at first suggest a radically decontextualized or independent programme of liberation. Moreover, in the text, when the term is used in the context of liberation, it has an added nuance of self-authentication, as do states such as pleasure and pain. They are incontestable and self-guaranteeing. The best proof for one's status as a realized one is, again, 'one's own experience' (*svānubhūtiḥ*

82 ... *vinā parokśānubhavaṁ brahmaśabdair na mucyate* (VC 62).

pramāṇam, VC 474). However, these states resist external determination; at best, outsiders can infer, but not unequivocally evaluate, the status of another. Hence the *jīvanmukta* may appear as a fool, a wise one or a king, or he may live in complete anonymity. However he appears, he always roams 'delighted in the Supreme' (*satataparamānandasukhitaḥ*, VC 542).

We are beginning to get a picture of a particular kind of experience internally accessed and apparently free from cultural accretions. Indeed, VC 530 and 531 suggest that such an experience is self-established and transcultural: 'This Self, being evident, ever established, shines. It depends on neither time, place, nor purification.'[83] In addition, according to the author, knowledge depends on the thing itself, a correspondence epistemology with a venerable lineage in the West, although no longer *de rigueur* under the force of twentieth-century analytic and linguistic philosophy. Nevertheless, according to the VC, some propositions, such as 'This is a pot', are self-evident, since what counts as knowledge is whether or not it corresponds to the object *per se*. So, since the Self is self-established, 'what rule is necessary?'[84] The unspoken answer to that question is, of course, 'None'. It seems that introspection might bring one to the transcendent Self, independently of 'time and place' – that is, independently of historical and social context. This permits an elegant entrée to universalism. Theoretically, such introspection would lead to the same experience across cultures. However, as is made clear by the testimony of thinkers and practitioners of various traditions, there is no unanimous agreement on what exactly lies within oneself. Moreover, on closer inspection of the *Vivekacūḍāmaṇi*, such self-evident, independent experience is powerfully shaped, organized and modelled by its teachers and texts. So, neither the relativizing factors mentioned above nor the process of introspection itself is able to extract itself completely from its cultural patterns and organizations.

Before discussing these patterns, mention must be made of the eloquent parallels between the self-guaranteeing sensibility of *anubhava* and the epistemological principle of *svataḥ prāmāṇyavāda* powerfully developed by Mīmāṁsā thinkers, especially Kumārila Bhaṭṭa, and adopted by later Advaitin epistemologists. While consideration of 'mundane' mechanisms of knowing seems far removed from the grand project of liberation, the primary focus of this book precisely considers the possibility of applying, and the extent to which we can apply, these mechanisms to religious knowing. For all Advaitins, consummate experience is itself a blissful knowing beyond knowledge; it is the terminus of all spiritual practice, even if, as with Śaṅkara and Sureśvara, no substantial change or action occurs. But mundane experience can be a 'window' to the real, as we saw in Padmapāda. In later Advaitin epistemology, the cognitive outcomes that follow 'mundane' experience (*anubhava*, *pratyakṣa*) enjoy intrinsic epistemic validity. Cognitions are self-evidently valid

---

83 ... *ayam ātmā nityasiddhaḥ pramāṇe sati bhāsate / na deśaṁ nāpi vā kālaṁ na śuddhiṁ vāpyapekśate.*

84 ... *niyamaḥ ko' nuvekśyate* (VC 530).

until defeated by further experience. This is in contrast to the Nyāya view, which argues that validity is determined by conditions extrinsic to the perceiving process; in this case, truth is a property conferred on cognitions by mediate inferential processes whose basis is experience but includes additional reflective awareness (*anuvyavasāya*) (Chatterjee, 1991: 229). For the Advaitin, however, truth and validity are co-extensive and immediate. We do not wait for justification or confirmation when we note, 'this is a pot' (ibid.). To use Eliot Deutsch's colourful phrase, *svataḥ prāmaṇyavāda* is a 'perverse pragmatism': cognitions are true until proven false (Deutsch, 1969: 87). Their validity is immediate and non-inferential, for otherwise, according to the Advaitin, reasoning to validity lapses into a hopeless regress.

Moreover, cognitions are self-luminous, 'borrowing' or drawing from the one true luminous Self, which thereby implicates the Self in every act of perception. Such a view, clearly recalling Padmapāda, extends far beyond Alston, who argues for the justification of claims that follow *mystical* perception. In this case, *every* act of perception discretely reveals the one true Self as the conscious basis for all experience. The mind, plastic and pliable, in effect 'becomes' the objects of perception. But such a numinous union of mundane and consummate experience is hardly obvious or transparent. Indeed, recalling the Kaṭha Upaniṣad, 'The Self, though hidden in all beings, does not shine forth but can be seen by those subtle seers through their sharp and subtle intelligence'.[85] While this verse implies the importance of the testimony of the saints, it also points to the need for an 'intellectual therapy' meant to decondition egocentric patterns of perception in order to 'see' reality in a highly specific way – namely, to see the Self in all and all in the Self. But to attain such a vision requires a coherent and cohesive culture of liberation – one that draws on the resources of text, teacher and tradition.

The culture of liberation

Despite the rhetoric which relativizes cultural patterns and programmes, a close reading of the *Vivekacūḍāmaṇi* reveals the author's loyalty to traditional social and cultural institutions. Such loyalty is no mere filial devotion, but reveals the author's insistence that liberation occurs only in and through such institutions, despite apparent tendencies in the text towards Advaita's decontextualized universalism. This hedging reveals an ambivalence in the author. On the one hand, its primary doctrine promotes the counterintuitive truth that we are all saved, and that cultural patterns are mere projections (*vikṣepa*) of *avidyā*. Moreover, since categories are mental constructs created by the mind out of ignorance, so too is the category of *jīvanmukta*. In this case, not only are we all already liberated, but those who *really are* liberated, the *jīvanmukta*, cannot be neatly captured by tidy categories of

85 ... *eśa sarveṣu bhūteṣu gūdho'tmā na prakāśate / dṛśyate tvagryayā buddhā sūkṣmayā sūkṣmadarśibhiḥ* (KU 1.3.13).

authentication. He or she may be a royal prince, a wise one or a mad fool, but all these are ultimately constructs, playthings. However, this is too radical for the author, and VC 33 affirms conventional criteria to evaluate the genuine *sādhu* from the fraud; the guru is 'the one well-versed in scripture, sincere, free of passion, who has withdrawn into Brahman, calm, as a fire without fuel, a source of unconditional compassion for the humble'.[86]

So, on the one hand, we hear the rhetoric of universalism, a theory of liberation 'liberated' from its social context. In the end, however, the author unequivocally reaffirms traditional values and cultural programmes of training and transmission which cannot help but profoundly inform much of what the seeker finds on the path of introspection, since it is difficult, to say the least, to live as 'disembodied awareness' in the world. The culture of liberation would appear to be significant in any religious tradition, for very few persons live as decontextualized units in the world. The question is the extent to which the culture of liberation is valued. If this culture is not relativized in significant ways, a more socially circumscribed programme emerges and, consequently, universalism drains away. If these factors are successfully relativized, a universalism, supported by a dominant internalist epistemology of religious experience, flourishes. Let us examine some of these factors in the VC's culture of liberation, primary among which are *śruti* and lineage, despite disclaimers in the text which we highlighted above.

A good place to begin is the VC's *maṅgala* verse. The author offers his salutations to Govinda, the *sadguru*, accessible only through the conclusions of all the Vedānta and inaccessible to the mind and senses. What is curious about this passage is its personalist nuance. The author pays homage to Govinda, an epithet, of course, of Kṛṣṇa, but also the name of Śaṅkara's guru. Moreover, as Mādhavānanda notes, *sadguru* could refer to the supreme, the inner teacher, or it could be a title referring to a particularly qualified preceptor, in which case the *śloka* directly affirms the importance of a teacher in a particular lineage (Mādhavānanda, 1992: 1).

Of course, the structure of the text affirms this as well, for the text is a dialogue between a qualified aspirant and a liberated teacher. Furthermore, the importance of contextualized transmission is emphasized quite clearly. VC 2 speaks to the critical value associated with a human birth, a male birth, and then, finally, birth as a Brahmin. VC 3 extols the rarity of discipleship to a great one (*mahāpuruṣasaṁśrayaḥ*), VC 15 urges a seeker come to a teacher of perfect knowledge (*brahmaviduttamam*), VC 474 reminds us that proof of salvation is demonstrated by the words of a teacher, scripture and reasoning (*śāstraṁ yuktir deśikoktiḥ pramāṇam*). Indeed, while we saw room for an apparently independent path above, VC 81 suggests that success in one's endeavours occurs through one's

86 ... *śrotriyo' vṛjino' akāmahato yo brahmavittamaḥ / brahmaṇyuparataḥ śānto nirindhana ivānalaḥ / ahetukadayāsindhuḥ bandhurānamatām satām*. Recall Śaṅkara's hallmarks of the true guru in the prose section of the *Upadeśasāhasrī* (Mayeda, 1992: 212).

internal resources (*svasya yuktyā*) following the instructions of the kind teacher (*hitasujanagurūktyā*). This clearly means that, while the aspirant is expected to use his own intelligence, it is an intelligence shaped by the organizing instruction and moral example of the teacher.

We saw scripture relativized earlier, yet the VC, in the end, relies on scripture as the ultimate instrument to fashion the transformation of the mind. Indeed, the one who is fortunate enough to obtain a human birth as well as mastery of the scripture (*śrutipāradarśanam*), but who fails to take advantage of these incomparable aids, is a 'suicide' (*ātmahā*), destroying himself by clinging to the unreal (*asadgrahāt*). VC 281 gives equal status to scripture, reasoning and experience as the means to do away with misguided superimposition. Thus scripture reveals the non-dual real, reasoning removes doubts about it, and experience confirms it as true. Thus VC 70: 'Then the disciple must hear the truth of the Self, reflect upon it, and meditate upon it constantly; the sage, attaining the supreme, beyond doubt, enjoys the bliss of *nirvāṇa* here and now.'[87] It is obvious that all three components deeply implicate the 'external circuitry' of Advaita – text, tradition and teacher. Moreover, human relationship, the most important context of all – a teacher, fellow seekers, a society which one renounces, an initiation which one accepts, and so on – is revealed. This is perhaps the broadest and most important context because the reasoning and exegetical practices which remove doubts concerning the non-dual real must be understood partly as discursive analysis and partly as emotional reassurance. For reason cannot arrive at non-dualism with apodictic certainty. In the *Śrībhāṣya*, for example, Rāmānuja astutely criticizes certain aspects of Śaṅkara's thought. However, when a disciple turns to a guru, he looks less for complete intellectual resolution of all philosophical conundrums and more for a reassurance or reinforcing of his world-view. This reassurance includes both cognitive and emotional aspects. Through the words and, better, the example of the good guru, the disciple is encouraged to continue with his particular construction of the world, which in the case of Advaita is so utterly counterintuitive. What is important to note, however, is that the personal experience (*svānubhūti*, *svānubhava*) referred to in the *Vivekacūḍāmaṇi* is not abstracted from its particular social and cultural context; it operates in a complementary relationship with scripture and reasoning.

Śruti is extolled as an important means to salvation in the *Vivekacūḍāmaṇi*, and much of what is found in the text is repackaged from various upaniṣads and *smṛti*. For example: the famous discussion on the nature of love in the Bṛhadāraṇyaka Upaniṣad is repeated in VC 106; the anthropology of the Taittirīya Upaniṣad is found in VC 154–88; the analysis of the states of consciousness found in the Māṇḍūkya Upaniṣad appears in VC 107. The ubiquitous *mahāvākya*, '*tat tvam asi*', is interpreted in VC 241–42, primarily using a method of negation (*apavāda*). Various discussions of the Self are borrowed wholesale from the *Gītā*, as is the

---

87 ... *tataḥ śrutis tanmananaṁ sattvadhyānaṁ ciraṁ nityanirantaraṁ muneḥ / tato'vikalpaṁ parametya vidvān ihaiva nirvāṇasukhaṁ samṛcchati.*

constant *smṛti* worry over untrammelled sensual desire. In the end, 'hundreds of great words speak of the unbroken identity of the Self and Brahman'.[88]

All these supports create a powerful social and mental culture of liberation, one which, far from being an abstract univeralism apparently available to all, is instead deeply embedded in its context, which carries with it a heavy package of primary and ancillary beliefs about reality and the world. These beliefs not only include primary doctrines about the nature of the Self and the world, but important ancillary beliefs, such as the estimate of the human body, sensuality and desire. One may dismiss verses such as vv. 74–88 as a neurotic lecture on the evils of desire and embodiment. But verses such as these – which are hardly unique in Indian literature – serve as an important aid to the intellect, affect and will, for they strengthen a new order of cognitive and emotional values adopted by the seeker. The repeated negative valuations of human space serve to support the movement away from all things transitory and assist the final cathexis to 'the deathless, the immortal'.

So, while knowledge of Brahman is beyond 'time and space', VC 14 nevertheless admits that success in practice is enhanced by 'suitable time, place and circumstances'. These circumstances include the qualifications of the seeker. VC 19 repeats the fourfold treasure which Śaṅkara addresses in BSB 1.1.4: discrimination between the real and the unreal; renunciation of the fruits of action; the various ethical practices; and the intense desire for liberation. At first glance, such requisites seem sufficiently generic to admit anyone, although we saw in the BSB that they contain both doctrinal and social implications: discrimination and renunciation presume heavy doses of beliefs about the nature of the world and the Self – beliefs that can be mediated through persons and communities – and, of course, the privileged community to receive such a package of beliefs were Brahmins. We saw in the BSB that a more explicit privileging of Brahmins occurs in the fourth *adhyāya*. While there is no such explicit reference to Brahmins in the *Vivekacūḍāmaṇi*, certain subtleties reveal it as a text by and for Brahmins. First, it is written in Sanskrit; its form, a dialogue between guru and *śiṣya*, is a largely Brahmin pedagogy. The author, moreover, hopes that those seekers 'who take delight in scripture (*śrutirasikā*)' and whose minds are made pure 'through what is prescribed (*vihita*)' find benefit in the teaching of the *Vivekacūḍāmaṇi*. Brahmins, of course, have traditionally been those most concerned with 'what is prescribed', especially the *nitya* and *naimittika* duties. And of course the access to *śruti* was restricted to twice-born classes; in practice this amounted to a monopoly on the production, control and transmission of scripture by Brahmins.

All of the above suggests that the apparent universalism of the *Vivekacūḍāmaṇi* is nonetheless deeply indexed to its local context. Given such culturally specific modes of eligibility and transmission – the *adhikāra* and *vedānta* – its apologetic use by Isherwood and others makes little sense. But what about a form of Advaita

88 ... *mahāvākyaśatena kathyate brahmātmanor aikyam akhaṇḍabhāvaḥ* (VC 249).

that is unmoored from the traditional *maṭha* system that developed after Śaṅkara – one that successfully relativizes the 'external circuitry' in the programme of liberation? While early Advaita in theory is internalist and universalist, in practice it is externalist and exclusivist. The Advaita of Ramaṇa, on the other hand, is decisively internalist and therefore universalist.

Let me close by referring back to an important distinction that recurs in our discussion of the epistemology of religious experience – namely, how we know 'religiously', and how we know that we know. The former phrase indicates the process by which we know, and the latter indicates the grounds which justify our claims to knowledge. Once again, as in our review of Śaṅkara, we see the interplay of externalism and internalism. Although there are slightly different epistemological emphases in the thought of all our subjects, each nevertheless takes *anubhava* to be the decisive, internally accessed and self-established saving moment for the *mumukṣu*. The process by which we know religiously is profoundly internal for our thinkers, yet it nevertheless comes packed with many kinds of external propaedeutics. These helps set the stage for the final inward turn in Advaita which culminates in liberation; to this end, Advaita's externalism supports the internalism which 'produces' saving knowledge. However, when it comes to the issue of justification, these external elements play a far stronger role. While the question of the justification of beliefs perhaps means little to sages and saints who have actually experienced realization, the claims that follow such experience nevertheless have considerable epistemic import. Given the soundness of the context of liberation – text, tradition, teacher, complete with their sets of coherent intellectual and spiritual practices – the beliefs that follow from Advaitin 'religious' experience – especially the belief that there is a supramundane knowing beyond knowledge – enjoy *prima facie* justification. The implications of such justified beliefs are many and mark critical opportunities for philosophers of religion. Before I address these, let us consider the Advaita of Ramaṇa Maharṣi, who insisted on the truth of 'pure' experience abstracted from cultural accoutrements and whose epistemology is decisively internalist and universalist.

CHAPTER 4

The sage of pure experience: the Advaita of Ramaṇa Maharṣi

Introduction

So far, we have examined religious experience in classical Advaita. In Śaṅkara, Sureśvara and Padmapāda we hear a powerful rhetoric of innate *mokṣa* – no works can fundamentally produce liberation, we come fully equipped for liberation and, indeed, in some relevant sense we already are liberated and so on. However, even though this rhetoric appears to be univocal, admissions of various practices conducive to, though not fundamentally productive of, liberation inevitably leak into the soteriology of Śaṅkara and his disciples. This is easy to understand, for whatever else we may be – the effulgent Brahman or, for that matter, the Body of Christ, or the adamantine essence of the Void – we are also entities packaged in corporal and cultural wrappings. To their credit, early Advaitin thinkers admit this common-sense position.

So, while it may be a truth that we are already liberated, the reality of our existential situation demands that we must, after all, do something to inculcate the virtues, values and cognitive inputs that promote our liberation. In short, while the supreme may be accessed by our introspection, such introspection, according to Śaṅkara, Padmapāda and Sureśvara, cannot do without numerous culturally specific conditions: caste and stage of life, certain programmes of virtue and concentration, the example and teaching of a guru, and above all the Vedas. So, while a universalism seems available in the Advaita of these thinkers, it is a universalism inescapably conditioned by a particular culture and cannot translate well across cultures, unless one radically edits it, as neo-Vedāntins such as Radhakrishnan have done, or ignores it, as nineteenth-century Romantics did.

Still, introspection may appear to be a key to a kind of transcultural awareness of what it is, if anything, that lies within us besides chemicals and amino acids. But, as the editors of a recent anthology in the philosophy of religion warn, introspection may not yield universal insight after all:

> The problem is that the reports people give about what they see when they do look inwardly suggest that there is nothing clear and unambiguous there to be seen: What we see when we look depends in part on what we expect to find, which is itself influenced by our beliefs and by the social setting in which we look. (Kolak and Martin, 1993: 72)

We seem to be returning to Katz and the problem of constructivism: 'our experience of ourselves is not a solid foundation on which to build different views about God and the cosmos, but is itself in part determined by those views' (ibid.).

But what about a modern version of non-dualism, a new edition as it were, one which has no formal affiliations to the *maṭhas* of Śṛngeri, Badrināth, Kāñcī or any other traditional Advaitin institutions? Abstracted from such orthodox, male, renunciant cultures, perhaps the message of pure experience can be accessed by simple introspection after all, with few, if any, cultural accretions. What happens then? What can we know from this experience? Indeed, if Martin et al. modify their above claims with the qualifier 'in part', what happens when that part is minimized? How does such non-dualism translate across cultures? Is this more genuinely universal than its classical predecessor? In this chapter we will examine such a version of Advaita, that of Ramaṇa Maharṣi of Tiruvannamalai in Tamil Nadu.

Indeed, it is probably misguided to identify Ramaṇa as an 'Advaitin' at all, since Advaita represents an entire cultural and institutional matrix which minimally consists of text, tradition and teacher, all of which in turn constitute an 'external circuity' – a complex set of socially established doxastic mechanisms which inform and shape traditional Advaitin programmes of liberation and their subsequent verbal outcomes. Ramaṇa, although a Brahmin, seemed uninterested in traditional patterns of religiosity prior to his transformative experience; following it, he seemed unaffected by the cultural and social distinctions that often paradoxically extend into formal programmes of renunciation in India. In this regard, he deeply internalized the truth of non-dualism which finally renders innocuous all phenomenal differences; moreover, his epistemology of religious experience decisively contributes to this egalitarian universalism as well. Operating from an unambiguous internalism, Ramaṇa minimizes the externalist mechanisms of producing knowledge which, at least traditionally, have implicated exclusivist patterns of social organization and spiritual methodology. While there is no question that the *bhakti* and tantric traditions in India are often properly viewed as a protest against, or critique of, orthodox Hinduism, it is also true that one's soteriological bets are hedged in mainstream Hinduism if one is male, Brahmin and a renunciant. Ramaṇa, by neatly weaving together his metaphysic and internalist epistemology, profoundly relativizes traditional renunciant culture. In effect, he liberates Advaita from its local context; his internalism facilitates the universalism implicit in Advaita's metaphysic.

Of course, there are a number of neo-Advaitins to choose as a representation of a non-*maṭha* version of Advaita. The nineteenth-century Bengali saint Ramakrishna comes to mind, although he also could be considered a devout *śakta* or *vaiṣṇava* as well as an Advaitin.[1] Moreover, an entire monastic system soon developed around

[1] One of the most fascinating recent studies of Ramakrishna has been done by Jeffrey Kripal (1995). Kripal, who is deeply sympathetic to Ramakrishna, offers a close and penetrating analysis of the

him – arguably modelled on Catholic religious orders – with its particular patterns of transmission and training. Śri Aurobindo's verbose evolutionism contain Advaitic elements but represent such novel developments that his 'integral yoga' must be considered as something rather different from original Advaita.[2] Jiddu Krishnamurti is an obvious option as well, although much scholarly work on his life and teachings has already been published, and many of his books are still in print, available in any upmarket bookstore.[3] While he would not describe his teaching as 'Advaita', it was nevertheless a compelling form of non-dualism, free from Sanskrit jargon and traditional Indian systems of training and pedagogy. Indeed, Krishnamurti was something of an iconoclast, which he first demonstrated by his public rejection of theosophical messiahship. Throughout his career as an itinerant teacher, he was highly critical of tradition as a retrograde, stultifying force and urged listeners to be awake, free from all cultural trappings. He also insisted on the importance of personal experience and rejected any possibility of 'second-hand enlightenment'. These are interesting themes that invite further study, although his rejection of tradition might find its logical conclusion in the closing of the Krishnamurti Foundation in Madras. And despite the fact that Krishnamurti probed awareness and mental operations with penetrating insight, his approach was intellectualist, and his appeal was largely to educated classes in India, Europe and America.

Instead, I have selected Ramaṇa Maharṣi as a representation of another penetrating version of modern Advaita for a number of reasons. His life and work are much less known than those of either Aurobindo or Krishnamurti; most of the literature on him remains 'first-generation' in that biographies, collections of his writings, records of his conversations with disciples, and personal reflections on his life have almost all been written by devotees; and little scholarly work on his life and thought has been undertaken, thus meriting a fresh examination. Moreover, like Krishnamurti, Ramaṇa was a South Indian Brahmin who came to his realization through an unusual event, strikingly free from complex theoretical infusions. Like Krishnamurti, he adopted a method of inquiry to enlighten disciples, but with fewer intellectualist digressions. Although less known than Krishnamurti, his appeal was broader and extended beyond the elite and educated classes in India and in the West that were drawn to Krishnamurti. Indeed, as Gavin Flood notes, his teachings have

---

conscious, and perhaps unconscious, expressions of eroticism in the Bengali saint, all of which raise the broader question of the role of sexuality not only in mysticism but in less spectacular, more ordinary forms of spirituality.

2 Aurobindo's rationalism and progressivism reflect his training in England in the early part of the twentieth century, and his philosophical realism is a clear departure from classical Advaita *vivartavāda*. His version of Advaita might be more properly called pantheism, a term often incorrectly applied to Śaṅkara's philosophy.

3 For an eloquent reconstruction of Krishnamurti's life and philosophy see Pupal Jayakaar (1987). A recent unscientific survey at a local bookstore showed ten collections of Krishnamurti's dialogues or writings on the shelves; none of Ramaṇa's books were available (nor for that matter, were any of Aurobindo's).

inspired many other gurus, including the low-caste Bombay *biḍī* maker, Nisargadatta Maharaj (Flood, 1996: 271).

Apart from these reasons for choosing to study Ramaṇa, there is an additional motivation constituted by the reaction to Ramaṇa from the circle of Western scholars who have encountered him. No exposés, no *Karma Colas*, no deconstructions of his life have (yet?) appeared in print. Instead, of the many sincere or fraudulent gurus who have captured the attention of devotees and scholars, Ramaṇa's life and teaching seems to have elicited a similar reaction from many scholars: this person is genuine – admittedly an elusive quality to determine in someone, but a quality we must nevertheless consider and evaluate in reviewing the persuasive force of religious experience. Of course, the fact that many devotees and some scholars have taken Ramaṇa to be genuine does not necessarily mean that he was. Still, their reaction is intriguing and invites a closer look.

A brief survey of some recent and not-so-recent responses to Ramaṇa's life and work highlights the unusually positive reaction to Ramaṇa on the part of contemporary Indologists. Klaus Klostermaier, for example, considers him to be 'among the greatest and deepest spiritual influences coming from India in recent years', and notes that, even after his death, the ashram in which he lived 'is somehow charged with spiritual power, emanating from him' (Klostermaier, 1989: 396). Heinrich Zimmer wrote a study on Ramaṇa in 1944 which included a foreword by C.G. Jung; pared of painful hyperbole ('In India he is the whitest spot in a white space' and so on), Jung writes that Ramaṇa 'is genuine and, in addition to that, something quite phenomenal' (Zimmer, 1944; Maharshi, 1988: ix). While the fact that Jung, a perennialist if ever there was one, was impressed by Ramaṇa is not surprising, a more recent tribute has come from no less than the late Agehānanda Bharati, who, as is clear from his writings, did not suffer fools gladly, and yet agreed that 'Ramaṇa Maharṣi was a mystic of the first order' (Bharati, 1976: 29). And while Ramaṇa has always drawn the positive attention of Indian scholars, leading Western spiritual figures drawn to him have included Thomas Merton (1915–68), Bede Griffiths (1907–93), and Dom Henri Le Saux (1910–73).

Merton's attraction to Ramaṇa is difficult to assess. Only indirect references to Ramaṇa are found in his *Asian Journal*, which nonetheless contains much rich reflection on Śaṅkara, non-dualism, and the *Vivekacūḍāmaṇi*. Still, the fact that Merton mentions locations associated with Ramaṇa and the name of Mouni Sadhu, an early Western disciple of his, suggests that he had more than a superficial knowledge of Ramaṇa's career and impact. Elsewhere, however, Merton spells out his assessment of Ramaṇa's philosophy:

> It is a teaching which recalls Eckart and Tauler, but according to the Maharṣi absolute philosophical monism is beyond doubt. His teaching follows in the pure tradition of Advaita Vedānta. What is important to us above all is the authenticity of the natural contemplative experience of the contemporary 'Desert Father'. (Merton, 1965: 79–80)[4]

[4] 'C'est une doctrine qui rappelle Eckhart et Tauler, mais chez le Maharshi le monisme

Griffiths and Le Saux, Benedictine monks from England and France respectively, were instrumental in establishing the Christian ashram Shantivanam in Tamil Nadu, and both increasingly adopted Advaita paradigms to inform their own spiritual experiences. Griffiths wrote: 'Perhaps the most remarkable example of advaitic experience in modern times is that of Ramana Maharsi' (Griffiths, 1984: 205). He considered Ramaṇa's transformative experience to be 'authentic mystical experience, that is an experience of the Absolute' (ibid.: 206). Using the idiom of Advaita, Ramaṇa was, according to Griffiths, a *jīvanmukta*, one who is liberated while alive. Le Saux concurs, making many noteworthy references to Ramaṇa, all of which affirm the compelling power of his life and experience. Concerning the effect of Ramaṇa's presence at the ashram, he writes:

> Above all there was the presence – that of the Sage who had lived in this very place for so many long years, that of the mystery by which he had been dazzled and which had been so powerfully radiated by him. It was a presence which overarched and enfolded everything, and seemed to penetrate to the core of one's being, causing one to be recollected at the centre of the self, and drawing one irresistibly within. (Abhisiktānanda, 1990: 2)

Le Saux, who eventually took *sannyās* under the name of Abhisiktānanda, detailed Ramaṇa's life in a creative study which synthesized Christian and Advaita mysticism (1974). Significant for our purposes is the fact that he offered a brief account of the mechanism by which realization occurs; it is the 'inward quest', a phrase evoking the internalist epistemology which we have been examining.

Other writers have testified to Ramaṇa's extraordinary life and example, often in the same florid style as Jung. Paul Brunton (1898–1981), the prolific British writer who contributed in no small measure to the Western fascination with the 'mystical East', also met Ramaṇa in his travels and, like many others, was profoundly transformed. He writes, with a certain grandiloquence, 'It is impossible to be in frequent contact with him without becoming lit up, as it were, from a ray from his spiritual orb' (Brunton, 1994: np). But such language – surprising for its emotional force – invites a careful scrutiny of Ramaṇa's life. A more sober, but nonetheless positive, assessment of Ramaṇa is found in recent work of Francis Clooney, who writes: 'People like Ramaṇa testify to the continuing power of the non-dualist conviction there there is only one true self' (Clooney, 1998: 32). In addition to these favourable estimations, Ramaṇa's life and thought have made an impact on contemporary Western gurus as well, such as Andrew Cohen, Andrew Harvey and Master Nome (Flood, 1996: 271; Rawlinson, 1997: 489).

To this litany of praise – or at least positive assessment – of Ramaṇa, let me add my own. In the course of my training in Indian languages and philosophy, I stayed

philosophique absolu ne fait pas de doute. Sa doctrine est dans la plus pure tradition de l'Advaita Védantiste. Ce qui nous importe surtout à nous c'est l'authenticité de l'expérience contemplative naturelle chez ce "Père du Désert" contemporain.'

at the Aikiya Alayam Research Center for Interfaith Dialogue in Madras. While I was there, the late director of the Center, Ignatius Hirudayam, a Jesuit priest, spoke in unqualified praise of the 'Hindu saint' of South India, and soon afterwards I took up his suggestion to visit Ramaṇa's ashram. On my arrival there, I found myself quite moved by the quality of 'presence' that strangely does seem to linger there so many years after his death. After returning to the United States, I chanced on Klostermaier's comment, which of course resonated rather strongly with me. I have found these apparently shared sensibilities intriguing in themselves and, elsewhere, have tried to account for them.[5]

Here, however, I wish to suggest that a fresh examination of Ramaṇa will pay dividends, for many of these Western scholars and spiritual figures consider him to represent the purest form of Advaita in the twentieth century. As such, what Ramaṇa has to say about the nature of experience and the process by which we come to realization has direct relevance to our study for Ramaṇa, I will show, is decidedly internalist in his approach to liberation. In addition, I am concerned with the implications of Ramaṇa's internalism and, more specifically, wish to explore the universalism apparent in his modern expression of Advaita. Ramaṇa not only admits the universalism of Advaita in theory, but clearly accepts it in practice as well, especially in and through his internalist epistemology of religious experience. Finally, I shall consider the merit of two levels of testimony – the testimony of Ramaṇa's life and the testimony of the various scholars, spiritual teachers, gurus, adepts and seekers on Ramaṇa's behalf. What does the often exuberant praise of Ramaṇa mean? What is the merit of such testimony? Does it really tell us anything? Such 'second-order' testimony at the very least drives us to 'first-order' testimony: what does Ramaṇa's life and example reveal, if anything, about the nature of reality or about what it means to be human? At issue here is the quality of human 'presence' and its cognitive implications. The host of outstanding spiritual qualities manifested by Ramaṇa no doubt contributes to his appeal to thinkers and spiritual adepts. Thus an examination of the mechanisms of religious knowing must not only evaluate the verbal claims which follow religious experience but also the epistemic witness of a life which supremely embodies these claims. As such, an epistemology of holiness – an evaluation of the quality of human presence – may promise communion in the face of unresolved philosophical differences: although a 'meeting of the minds' may at times be impossible if one expects a pristine resolution of all conflicting metaphysical claims, a meeting of the heart, which honours all models of holiness, may offer the best hope of realizing what Halbfass called the 'unfulfilled promise' of interfaith dialogue.

The structure of this chapter, then, will be as follows. In the first section I will briefly outline Ramaṇa's life and works. In the second section I will articulate what

[5] See Forsthoefel (2001b). I argue that the internalist sensibility and emphasis on 'experience', hallmarks of the European Enlightenment, consciously and unconsciously predispose thinkers, scholars and adepts to favour internalist epistemologies of religious experience.

I take to be Ramaṇa's principal philosophy, referring both to his writings and to his dialogues with disciples which have been recorded and collected by various editors. The latter must be taken as anecdotal evidence, for, as in the case of the Gospels or the word of the Buddha, the difficulties in determining precisely what Jesus, Buddha or Ramaṇa actually said are legion. Nevertheless, beginning from his years of silence on Arunachala hill, there seems to have been a conscientious effort among his disciples to record faithfully his written responses to questions about the theory and practice of Advaita. Later, when he resumed speaking and lived at the ashram built for him at the base of Arunachala, various disciples wrote down, most often in Tamil, the various exchanges he had with questioners during *satsang*. These in turn have been translated into English under the approving review of the ashram's board of trustees (for example, Venkataramiah, 1994; Mudaliar, 1989; Venkataraman, 1994; Maharṣi, 2000).

At issue in my representation of Ramaṇa's philosophy will be the mechanism of producing saving knowledge and the prospects for a transcultural programme of liberation. In the final section I will demonstrate the manner in which Ramaṇa relativizes or refashions traditional cultures of liberation, thus paving the way for such a universal soteriological programme. The key to such universalism is experience, purged of all cultural accretions, including traditional *paramparā*. Ramaṇa's initial transformative experience becomes a paradigm for a quintessentially modern expression of Advaita, free from traditional patterns of training and transmission. Radhakrishnan recognizes the supreme authority of this experience which allowed Ramaṇa to bypass traditional training: 'Śri Ramaṇa Maharṣi is not a scholar; he has no erudition, but he has the wisdom that comes from direct experience of Reality' (Maharṣi, 2000: np). Such experience – and its method of access – relativizes all cultural patterns and admits the prospects for a genuine universalism. Ramaṇa, who rarely referred to himself in the first person, was once asked by the French Indologist Olivier Lacombe if his teaching followed that of Śaṅkara, to which he responded, 'Bhagavan's teaching is an expression of his own experience and realization. Others find that it tallies with Śaṅkara's' (Osborne, 1993: 9). With this statement he at once distances himself from Śaṅkara and establishes his authority on personal experience. No lineage renders his teaching authoritative, but his own experience does. According to Ramaṇa, this same authoritative experience is available to all, regardless of caste, culture, creed or country.

Ramaṇa Maharṣi: life and works

Ramaṇa's foundational religious experience is fascinating on account of its apparent absence of doctrinal content or religious training. Indeed, one enthusiastic disciple writes: 'His experience was prior to and superior to any scriptures' (Sastri, 1989: i). While this statement surprises with its naiveté, we see it repeated, with greater sophistication, by T.M.P. Mahadevan, an important editor and translator of Advaitin texts. According to Mahadevan, scriptural texts were brought to Ramaṇa's attention *after* his enlightenment; he read and reviewed them in order to dispel the doubts of his disciples. 'But it is quite clear that these citations are offered only as confirmations of the truth discovered by Bhagavan himself in his own experience' (Maharṣi, 1994: iv). Mahadevan's point is that experience came first and words, categories and explanations came later. While Mahadevan perhaps over-minimizes the importance of culture in consciously or unconsciously forming or informing religious experience, his point is clear: Ramaṇa's authority lies not with a battery of texts, nor with a lineage, but with his own direct experience of enlightenment.

Still, although one may be nominally a Catholic, Jew, Hindu or Buddhist, an 'osmosis of the imagination' no doubt allows ideas and symbols of a tradition to filter into the passive awareness of a subject. So, while it may be true that Ramaṇa, born Venkataraman Ayyar, had little or no formal religious training, he was raised in a Brahmin household in India, a land where, after all, it is virtually impossible not to have at least a notional understanding of variant streams of Hindu religiosity. Ramaṇa was born in 1879 to Smārta Brahmins, an orthodox community in south India with a reputation for conservatism. Concerning that tradition, Gavin Flood notes that: 'Although the central Smārta practice was the domestic worship of the five deities, while, of course, abiding by vedic social values and purity rules, there also arose worship of particular deities, especially Viṣṇu and Śiva, who were elevated to a supreme position' (Flood, 1996: 113). The concern for orthodox practice suggests that even nominal Smārta households 'absorb' at least some of the conceptual content of the tradition. Moreover, Bharati notes that for some Śaiva Smārtas, 'monistic Advaita philosophy provides their main ideological framework' (Bharati, 1976: 235).

Ramaṇa's family, which was Śaiva, probably absorbed some of the Smārta conceptual framework; in any case his family engaged in conventional piety, according to B.V. Narasimha Swami, one of his early biographers (Swami, 1993: 11). A family priest occasionally conducted domestic *pūjās*, and his father, Sundaram Ayyar, occasionally visited the local temple and hosted *kālakṣepams*, evenings of spiritual reading (ibid.). Although much of the family religiosity appears conventional, it is important to note that Ramaṇa at least had a notional understanding of traditional Indian religious symbols and categories to which he could refer after his realization at the age of 16.

Venkataraman's childhood years do not reveal any outstanding insight into his destiny. Although endowed with a prodigious memory and a keen intellect, he was apparently indifferent to studies and preferred sports over academic pursuits. Narasimha Swami notes that Venkataraman 'drifted' into conventional Śaiva worship without experiencing any extraordinary emotion or insight (ibid.: 15). What is intriguing, however, is the fact that both the middle school and the high school which he attended were Christian educational institutions. Moreover, at his high school – the American Mission High School in Madurai – he received (Christian) religious instruction. This training, in addition to his cultural Śaivism must also have filtered into his passive awareness, for many years later Ramaṇa himself offered his own interpretation of biblical texts and Christian spirituality.[6] Nevertheless, none of the academic or religious training of Ramaṇa's youth appears to be particularly outstanding – but this all changed forever at the age of 16.

In addition to whatever notional understanding of the supreme Venkataraman may have had, his own emotional and cognitive equipment were brought to bear on a crisis that he experienced in 1896. Gripped by the fear of death, he visualized his death so intensely, as if literally experiencing it, that he expected some kind of annihilation. Instead, he experienced the ubiquity of the transcendent Self and the end of his limited ego. Later he recounted this transformative experience:

> The shock of fear of death made me at once introspective or introverted ... The material body dies, but the spirit transcending it cannot be touched by death. I am therefore deathless spirit. All this was not a mere intellectual process, but flashed before me vividly as living truth, something which I perceived immediately, without any argument. (Swami, 1993: 21)

There are several observations from this passage that I wish to highlight. First, a particular crisis – not unlike that represented in the legend of the Buddha[7] – provoked his search for truth and propelled him *inwards*. This fundamental process of introversion or introspection that ultimately resulted in Ramaṇa's realization becomes the paradigm for future aspirants to liberation. The importance of this representation is underscored by its repetition in virtually every account of his life, either in biographies or as introductions to his writings.[8]

In addition, Ramaṇa represents the knowledge gained from that experience as direct, immediate and alive; for him this experience was an encounter with 'living truth' and no 'mere intellectual process'. This consideration of knowledge as something beyond discursive reasoning is, of course, a common theme in neo-Hindu apologetics, and we have reviewed some of their rhetoric, but Ramaṇa's

---

6 See for example, his comment, '"I am that I am" sums up the whole of the Truth. The method is summarized in "Be still"' (Osborne, 1993: 103). See also his creative interpretation of Christian faith: 'Christ is the ego. The Cross is the body. When the ego is crucified, and it perishes, what survives is the Absolute Being (God), [cf. 'I and my Father are one'] and this glorious survival is called Resurrection' (Venkataramiah, 1994: 86). Ramaṇa also teases an interpretation of the Christian doctrine of the Trinity from a Sanskrit benediction to Dakṣināmurti (ibid.: 87).

7 Indeed, while it is beyond the scope of this study, a future project will highlight the parallels in Ramaṇa's life and thought to the Buddha and to Yogācāra Buddhism; several considerations invite such a study, including Ramaṇa's favourable remarks on Buddhism, his insistence on the ephemerality of all events, and his doctrine of mind.

8 For example, Swami (1993: 21–22); Osborne (1959: i–iii; 1993: 2–3); Godman (1992: 1); Natarajan (1995, i–iii; 1983: i–ii; Om (1990: 4–5). The importance of his account as descriptive and prescriptive is further demonstrated by the fact that it is written in Tamil and in English on a large board in a side chapel at Ramaṇāsramam.

statement is important not because of its neo-Hindu resonance (indeed, while others may have used Ramaṇa as a 'star' of Advaita, Ramaṇa himself seemed rather aloof to all projects in which ego was involved, and this included the Hindu 'church triumphant'), but because he had a direct experience of what he took to be ultimate truth, incontrovertible precisely because he experienced it. He then spent the rest of his life deepening this fundamental experience *and* calling on inquiring disciples to experience it themselves. Moreover, such *felt* knowledge transcended rational categories or circuitous intellectualism. These points – inwardness, direct experience and the transcending of the intellect – are seen repeatedly in Ramaṇa's words and dialogues which we will review in the next section. For young Venkataraman, however, the effects of this transformative experience were immediate. The mundane habits and patterns of conventional life were soon found wanting, and Ramaṇa eventually left his home and travelled to Tiruvannamalai, drawn to Arunachala, a sacred hill in South Arcot district said to be an embodiment of Lord Śiva. After arriving in Tiruvannamalai in 1896, he remained there until his death in 1950.

For over 20 years, he maintained silence, not in obedience to a vow, but to sustain quiet absorption into the Self and deepen his transformative experience. He spent these years in two hermitages on Aruṇāchala itself, Skandāsramam and Virupakṣa cave. By 1915 the 'Brahmin swami' was well known in South India, and a steady stream of devotees began climbing up the hill every day to sit in his presence. Finally, in 1922 he came down the hill and an ashram for the sage and his disciples was constructed at its base. One of his early disciples, the brilliant Sanskrit *paṇḍit* Gaṇapati Śāstri, insisted that the young guru be called Bhagavān Ramaṇa Maharṣi, the name by which he was known for the rest of his life.[9] From his early days on Arunachala until his death in 1950, he fielded questions from disciples, many of whom were non-Indians, and various collections of these dialogues remain in print (Venkataramiah, 1994; Mudaliar, 1989; Maharṣi, 1994). Indeed, Ramaṇa's four most important works, *Nān Yār* (Who Am I?), *Upatēca Untiyār* (Essence of Teaching), *Uḷḷatu Nāṟpatu* (Forty Verses), and *Vicāracaṅkirakam* (Self-Inquiry), were his written answers to his disciples' questions. The style of Ramaṇa's teaching is noteworthy: virtually all his writings were prompted by the persistent requests and questions of his disciples. He himself wrote no systematic treatise, although there is undoubtedly a systematic teaching in his exchanges with disciples. And, although not initially schooled in traditional Advaita, he learned to read and to write in Sanskrit, ostensibly to clear the doubts of disciples and provide a framing mechanism for his own experience.

---

9 Although, in keeping with his fundamental experience, he usually referred to himself in the third person and referred to his body as 'this'. Some translations interject the first-person pronoun where the Tamil uses the interrogative 'who (*yār*)'. Osborne notes: 'For instance, he did not actually say, "I did not know when the sun rose or set" … but "Who knew when the sun rose or set?"' (Osborne, 1954: 96). Once, when a foreign devotee asked for his autograph, he sketched the *devanāgari* symbol for the mantra 'Om'.

Ramaṇa was also a poet, and all but *Nān Yār* and *Vicāracaṅkirakam* are in verse. Much of his poetry represents *nirguṇa bhakti*, an emotional outpouring of faith, but directed to the one supreme real, not to a personal deity with attributes. The closest thing to a 'personal' deity for Ramaṇa is Aruṇāchala hill itself, but this clearly is a symbol for non-dual consciousness and represents the inner 'I' or 'heart', as he preferred to call the Self.[10] Ramaṇa wrote over 40 poems of this type, and his non-dualism rings throughout them. But, for the purposes of this chapter, I will focus on the texts that are more directly philosophical – namely, *Nān Yār*, *Upatēca Untiyār*, *Uḷḷatu Nāṟpatu*, and *Vicāracaṅkirakam*.

In addition to the poetry and philosophical texts, Ramaṇa also translated a number of texts from Sanskrit into Tamil. Six of these are hymns or *prakaraṇa* texts traditionally attributed to Śaṅkara.[11] One of the texts that Ramaṇa translated into Tamil was the *Vivekacūḍāmaṇi*, which afforded him the opportunity to interpret both his experience and the tradition of Advaita; where relevant, I will highlight his Tamil glosses or clarifications that inform his modern expression of non-dualism. Finally, I shall also refer to his responses to questions posed by disciples during *satsang*, for these brief conversations often reveal penetrating analysis and capture the heart of his teaching. Among all these resources we will see a decisive internalist epistemology of religious experience in Ramaṇa's thought and, with it, a universalist Advaita freed from its local context.

Ramaṇa's philosophy

Ramaṇa's teaching is a radical form of non-dualism. There is only the Self; all else is mere illusion. Although his teaching was radical, he nevertheless adapted his teachings to the capacities of his listeners to receive them. So, for example, he occasionally discusses the mechanics of reincarnation, the appropriateness of *saguṇa* Brahman and so on. However, such discussions appear to be concessions to the limitations of his listeners and digress from his fundamental position: the Self alone is. In fact, the core of his teaching can be summarized briefly: individuality is a fiction; the ego, void of substantial reality, is a mere fleeting phenomenon appearing on the association of Self and mind. The single, unchanging, stable, enduring real is blissful consciousness, the supreme Self. This Self is our true nature; that we fail to recognize this is the primary flaw of our condition, and knowledge is the means by which to remedy it.

Ramaṇa uses various terms to indicate this supreme Self: the heart, the centre,

---

10 'Oh Arunachala! in Thee the picture of the universe is formed, has its stay, and is dissolved; this is the sublime truth. Thou art the Inner Self, who dancest in the Heart as "I". "Heart" is Your name. Oh Lord!' 'Five Stanzas to Śrī Arunachala' (v. 2) (Osborne, 1979: 68).

11 See the *Dakṣināmurtistotra*, *Gurustuti*, *Hastamalakastotra*, *Ātmabodha*, *Dṛgdriśyaviveka* and *Vivekacūḍāmaṇi*.

the 'I-I'. This last term serves to indicate the ultimate source of the phenomenal 'I' – that is, the individual identified with body and mind. The use of the term 'I-I' is Ramaṇa's attempt to gloss the uniqueness of the one true Self and to avoid confusion with the phenomenal 'I', the ego associated with a body. Though rarely used by Śaṅkara, for Ramaṇa the term seems to capture the divine source of our transient, phenomenal identities. This source, for him, is none other than pure, unalloyed bliss.

But Ramaṇa's analysis of the human situation and its proper prescription reveals many parallels with Śaṅkara and to later Advaita. Ignorance afflicts humanity: we are seduced by our desires and deluded into thinking that the world and individual selves are real. Such false notions inevitably produce suffering, for emotional attachment to impermanent phenomena invariably yields physical and psychological frustration. Like Śaṅkara, Ramaṇa keenly directed his teaching for soteriological benefits, not intellectual tidiness. And so he was reluctant to spin elaborate cosmologies to account for what we (apparently) see; however, when pressed by devotees who could not grasp his radical non-dualism, he admitted the veiling (*āvaraṇa*) and projective (*vikṣepa*) powers of *māyā* to which Padmapāda and the author of the *Vivekacūḍāmaṇi* also appeal. Philosophically, however, his radical Advaita is more in keeping with the *ajātivāda* of Gauḍapāda and Sureśvara than with gradualist versions of emanationism found in various Advaitin appropriations of Sāṅkhya.

Instead, there is only the Self, and our nature is already complete, already free. In fact, bondage itself is an illusion, because we are already liberated. Right knowledge is the proper prescription to realize this natural freedom, and inquiry, *vicāra*, is the quickest and most effective method. What is interesting here is that inquiry, according to Ramaṇa, is not the *brahmajijñāsa* of Śaṅkara. *Brahmajijñāsa*, we recall, suggests a universal programme of liberation, but Śaṅkara nevertheless restricts the phenomenal process of liberation, the inquiry into Brahman, to those most qualified candidates who conform to the appropriate caste and stage of life.

Ramaṇa's *vicāra*, however, does bear similarity to Śaṅkara's *viveka*. In both cases, the aspirant to liberation engages in a systematic analysis of phenomena in order to arrive at the truth, truth here being defined, as in Śaṅkara, as that which is unchanging, permanent and ultimately blissful. In the *Vivekacūḍāmaṇi*, this analysis peels away non-self in all its configurations – body, mind, *prāṇas*, *kośas* and so on – from the Self. Arriving at the one true real is saving knowledge. But, as we saw, in the *Vivekacūḍāmaṇi* such knowledge is no mere theoretical construct, no mere book learning: 'How can there be liberation merely by saying the word "Brahman"?'[12] Instead, one must realize such knowledge for oneself, and in the *Vivekacūḍāmaṇi* we noted a stylized exchange between a guru and disciple which eventuates in the liberation of the disciple. There are no doubt many reasons why

12 ... *brahmaśabdaiḥ kuto muktir uktimātraphalaiḥ* (VC 63).

Ramaṇa was drawn to the VC; in all likelihood one of these reasons is the text's emphasis on the personal appropriation of saving knowledge. Ramaṇa also insisted, in no uncertain terms, on the need for personal experience to establish and to confirm liberation. This demand, of course, follows on his own experience of realization. In response to a question on the usefulness of reading books on Vedānta, Ramaṇa once said, '... you can go on reading any number [of books] but they can only tell you to realize the Self within you. The Self cannot be found in books. You have to find it for yourself, in yourself' (Osborne, 1993: 95). Elsewhere, he insists, 'Mere book learning is not of any great use. After realization, all intellectual loads are useless burdens and are to be thrown overboard' (Osborne, 1993: 6). In *Nān Yār*, the first brief set of Ramaṇa's written responses to an early disciple's questions, he offers a programme that very clearly evokes the medieval Christian apophatic tradition of entering the 'cloud of forgetting': 'There will come a time when one will have to forget all that one has learned' (Maharṣi, 1995a: 14). The reason for this should be clear: no words, no concepts, no categories can comprehend the limitless Self. It is beyond all name and form. This again is no mere intellectual assent, but an affective knowing. Responding to one questioner, he insists, almost in Ottovian fashion, that *felt* experience is supreme knowledge, not discursive reasoning: 'Thoughts must cease and reason to disappear for the "I-I" to rise up and be felt. Feeling is the main thing, not reason' (Osborne, 1993: 35).

The mind, however, seeks concepts; it craves a 'fixed theory to satisfy itself with' (ibid.: 18). Nevertheless, Ramaṇa, like the Buddha, was highly circumspect about certain intellectual inquiries, such as the precise nature of liberation, and instead pushes the questioner to 'dive within' in order to discover his or her own true nature. He repeatedly warns that mere intellectual disputes are 'vain wrangling', diversions from the project of knowing, by personal experience, the 'living truth' of the Self. Moreover, the mind, by nature, is active, roaming and most often uncontrolled. The ultimate goal, then, is not to fill the mind with theoretical constructs but to calm the mind so that the flash of 'I-I' is possible; this cannot be done with mere book learning. To attain liberation, one must engage in a process of introspection, but this is no academic philosophizing:

> In order to quiet the mind one has only to inquire within oneself what one's Self is; how could this search be done in books? One should know one's Self with one's own eye of wisdom. The Self is within the five sheaths, but books are outside them. Since the Self has to be inquired into by discarding the five sheaths, it is futile to search for it in books. (Maharṣi, 1995a: 14)

What we note here is the introspective, inward turn that Ramaṇa repeatedly recommends, convinced, by virtue of his own experience, that such reflection terminates in ultimate consciousness, the source of all individual mental modifications. This introspection, and the privileged access it presupposes, begin to implicate an internalist epistemology of religious experience, and it follows from

Ramaṇa's radical embrace of Advaitin theory: plurality is external; the one real is internal, therefore, the proper antidote to delusive plurality is 'turning within'.

This insistence on internalism is shown in an endearing exchange between Ramaṇa and Emile Gathier, a Jesuit professor of philosophy at the Sacred Heart College in Shembeganur. The exchange is endearing, because it reveals, on the part of Gathier, a tension found in some scholars who are also persons of faith: one seeks to know God with mind as well as with heart; but complete knowledge, according to some representations of Christian and Buddhist religious experience, let alone Ramaṇa's, may mean the surrender of all conceptualization and controlling intellectualism. The exchange also reveals Ramaṇa's confidence and poetic sensibility as well as his relentless insistence on personal experience as the ultimate confirmation of non-dual philosophy. Gathier first asked Ramaṇa for a summary of his teachings. In response, Ramaṇa directed Gathier to various booklets, especially the short text, 'Who am I?' (*Nān Yār*). But Gathier persisted. The following is an excerpt from their conversation:

Gathier:	But may I have the central point of your teaching from your own lips?
Ramana:	The central point is just the thing.
Gathier:	It is not clear to me what you mean by that.
Ramana:	That you should find the centre.
Gathier:	I come from God. Isn't God distinct from me?
Ramana:	Who asks this question? God does not. You do. So find out who you are and then you may find out whether God is distinct from you.
Gathier:	But God is perfect and I am imperfect. How can I ever know Him fully?
Ramana:	God does not say so. It is you who ask the question. After finding out who you are, you may know what God is.
Gathier:	But you have found your Self. Please let us know if God is distinct from you.
Ramaṇa:	It is a matter of experience. Each one must experience it for himself. (Osborne 1993: 49–50)

The excerpt highlights Ramaṇa's insistence on the 'inward turn' to discover one's Self, and in doing so one attains 'plenary experience', to use Mahadevan's favourite phrase. One encounters, experiences and realizes the God within: 'When perception of name and form ceases, there is the vision of the Self. This is also the vision of God, for God and the Self are the same' (Maharṣi, 1995b: 25).

The simplest, most direct method to discover the Self within is through penetrating inquiry, *vicāra*. In *Nān Yār* and elsewhere, Ramaṇa offers a description of this inquiry. Using the simple question, 'Who am I?', the aspirant penetrates all phenomena and discovers that the body, organs, vital airs and mind are all finally inert and insentient, a method not dissimilar from the *ātmānātmaviveka* of Śaṅkara and the *Vivekacūḍāmaṇi*. With this analytic tool the aspirant seeks to discover the source of the phenomenal 'I' – that is, the individual ego.

Here we must spell out in greater detail two senses of 'I', the limited 'I' or 'I thought' and the ultimate source of identity, 'I-I'. The 'I-thought' is a furtive appropriation, as it were, of consciousness by the mind. The individual 'I' is a product of the mind and is constructed by endless identifications: I am a man, child, student, Indian, Brahmin, scholar and so on. However, all these are fundamentally unreal and insubstantial – something like characters in a drama, mere temporary identifications. All these 'I am not'. So, to ask the question 'Who am I?' implies an awareness of the subject of the question. 'Thereupon if one inquires "Who am I?" the mind will go back to its source, and the thought that arose will become quiescent' (Maharṣi, 1995a: 8). The mind resolves into the Self; dualities and all false identification fade away and one realizes the source of all consciousness, the supreme Self.

This process is internal and reflective: 'one must dive into himself and find whence the "I" emerges' (Maharṣi, 1992: 31). Ramaṇa repeats this call to inward reflection frequently. For example, he enjoins one questioner, 'You must find true consciousness internally. Therefore you are directed inward' (Osborne, 1993: 32). In Gaṇapati Śāstri's Sanskrit text, *Ramaṇa Gītā*, a collection of over 300 *ślokas* constructed as a dialogue between Gaṇapati Śāstri and Ramaṇa, Ramaṇa contributed but one verse, his so-called *Eka Śloki*, which is found in chapter two of Śāstri's text. Many devotees consider this verse as the 'quintessence' of his teaching:

> Brahman alone immediately shines as the Self, the 'I-I' in the cave of the heart. Enter the heart diving with questioning mind or through breath control, and be established in the Self.[13]

This inwardness is illustrated elsewhere:

> Not letting the mind go out, but retaining it in the Heart is what is called 'inwardness' (*antar-mukha*). Letting the mind go out of the Heart is known as 'externalization' (*bahir-mukha*). Thus, when the mind stays in the Heart, the "I", which is the source of all thoughts, will go and the Self which ever exists will shine. (Maharṣi, 1995a: 8)

So Ramaṇa, convinced of the supreme Self by virtue of his own experience, repeatedly challenged his questioners to discover their deepest self in their own experience. When disciples were afraid, he would ask, 'Who is afraid?'; when worried, 'Who worries?'; when one was concerned about what happens after death, his response rarely involved the metaphysics of transmigration, but rather the direct simple question, 'Who dies?', or, as in the exchange with Gathier, 'Who asks the question?' concerning the nature of the soul and God. The answers to all these

---

[13] ... *hṛdayakuhara madhye kevalaṁ brahmamātraṁ hy aham aham iti sākṣātmarūpeṇa bhāti / hṛdi viśa manasā svaṁ cinvatā majjatā va pavana calana rodhāt ātmaniṣṭhe bhava tvam* (Maharṣi, 1988: 1)

questions are the same: it is the individual person who is afraid, worried, wonders about death and speculates about metaphysics. More specifically, it is the ego, the 'I' defined by external circumstances such as health, body, mind, profession, social status and so on that is fearful and anxious. Why? The individual 'I' generates a complex of identifications, but these are inherently unstable and invariably passing. Nevertheless the ego invests itself in such identifications and is desperate to maintain them. Fear, worry, grief and speculation all reflect attachment to the complex of identifications and represent something like a survival strategy on the part of the ego or individual personality. But the ego lives only in borrowed forms; it is a 'formless ghost which feeds on any form it holds, which when sought for, takes to flight' (Maharṣi, 1992: 28). Who is afraid, resistant, worried and so on? It must not be the Self, for the Self is ever free from any suffering; it is blissful. Instead, inquiry seeks to eliminate the ego:

> Internally posing the question, 'Who am I,' one reaches the heart and the ego sinks crest-fallen, and immediately reality manifests itself spontaneously as 'I-I'. Revealing itself in this manner, it is not the ego, but perfect being, the absolute Self. (Maharṣi, 1992: 32–33)

So, concerning the mechanics of birth, death and rebirth, Ramaṇa would first challenge the questioner 'Are you born now?', in order to drive home the ubiquity of the Self and to raise one's self-awareness beyond localized manifestations; indeed, '*Mokṣa* is to know that you were not born' (Venkataramiah, 1994: 115). With regard to the cycle of *samsāra*, he modulates traditional teaching on rebirth, which often contains detailed description of subtle bodies and their suitcases of *karma*; instead, 'the birth of the I-thought is a person's birth, and its death is his death. After the I-thought arises, wrong identification with the body arises ... What is it to you who dies or is lost? Die yourself and be lost, becoming one with the Self of all' (Osborne, 1993: 30–31).

Ramaṇa holds that the persistent question, 'Who am I?', is the 'principal means for the removal of all misery and the attainment of supreme bliss' (Maharṣi, 1994: 12). Ultimately, it is the only question necessary for realization and terminates in a 'wordless illumination of the form "I-I"' (ibid.: 12). This question is the direct means for 'destroying the mind', a process of resolving all mental chatter and ego identifications into the one true Self. Thus, he urges the aspirant to quiet the mind, with its many mental protests, with the 'inward turning' of inquiry. The goal of this process is to experience the divine Self within, to *know*, but not to *think*.

Revalorizing the culture of liberation

Ramaṇa's fidelity to a non-dualistic metaphysic and his internalist epistemology opens space for a universalism freed of traditional patterns of training and transmission. Our main concern here will be to highlight his appropriation – and relativization – of traditional religious practices and institutions, which in part distinguishes his version of Advaita from long-standing programmes of renunciation in India. By relativizing socially established patterns of transmission and instead emphasizing an internalist epistemology, Ramaṇa ushers in a universalism that is in harmony with the premises of Advaita.

Yoga

First, like Śaṅkara, Ramaṇa holds that Brahman is neither seen nor known in any conventional sense. Brahman is not one object among others to be grasped by the intellect (Maharṣi, 1992: 33; Osborne, 1993: 47). Indeed, the project of liberation involves 'lulling the mind' (*manolaya*) – that is, calming the chatter of the mind through breath control and meditation. Ultimately, however, Ramaṇa advocates the 'destruction of the mind' (*manonāśam*); such a state does not indicate a catatonic torpor or schizophrenic shock, but the final elimination of all identifications generated by the mind. In the terms of yoga philosophy, one finally dissociates from natural constitutions and associates, or realizes, spirit – in this case, one's true Self.

In Ramaṇa's introduction to his Tamil translation of the *Vivekacūḍāmaṇi*, he recognizes, drawing from traditional yoga pyschology, that the former tendencies of the mind (*pūrva vācanaikaḷ*) constitute the principal obstruction (*taṭai*) to liberation. Meditation (*nididhyāsana*) amounts to resolving the mind in the heart until these forces are destroyed. This process is called by various cognate terms such as *ātmānusandhānam*, *bhakti*, yoga, or *dhyāna*. Ramaṇa's first gloss on *nididhyāsana*, *ātmānusandhānam*, includes both analytical and affective overtones. The Sanskrit verb *anusandhā* means 'to inquire into', 'to search', 'to examine' and so on, but its semantic range additionally includes 'to calm', 'to quiet' and 'to compose'. One might then interpret Ramaṇa's use of the term *ātmānusandhānam* as the 'calm that emerges through inquiry'. To convey the importance of such extended contemplation, Ramaṇa borrows a metaphor from many traditions of meditation; he suggests that unswerving concentration on the Self, constant like the unbroken flow of oil, produces *nirvikalpa samādhi*: 'This readily and spontaneously yields that direct, immediate, unobstructed, and universal perception of Brahman, which is at once knowledge and experience and which transcends time and space.'[14]

To help the disciple access the reality beyond subject and object, Ramaṇa highlights the importance of singleminded concentration necessary to eliminate mental chatter and to prepare for the flash of 'I-I' – what he calls the *aham-sphurti*. In his other works, as well as in his translation of the *Vivekacūḍāmaṇi*, he frequently uses the Tamil term *nikṣṭai* (meditation) to convey this sense of heightened

[14] … *cahaja nirvikaṟpa camātiyil pirayattaṉamiṉṟiyē puṟam eṅkum ellā kālamum ēkamāy pirakācikkum appiratipanta aparōkṣa pirahma cākṣātkāra jñāṉāṉupavam sittiy ākum* (Maharṣi, 1987: 113).

concentration. However, he borrows terms from early and later yoga traditions to gloss absorption in the Self, in effect redefining them according to his principles. For example, in his introduction to the *Vivekacūḍāmaṇi*, he speaks of *nirvikalpa samādhi*, his term for *asamprajñāta samādhi* in the yoga tradition. But the *Vivekacūḍāmaṇi* rarely uses these terms, and certainly not in the highly technical programme of psychological transformation found in the Yoga Sūtra. In fact, there is no reference to '*nirvikalpa samādhi*' in the Yoga Sūtra. The four *samāpattis* of Yoga Sūtra 1.41 refer to heightened states of awareness 'with cognition' (*samprajñāta*). These four states are 'argumentative' (*savitarka*), 'non-argumentative' (*nirvitarka*), 'reflective' (*savicāra*), and 'super-reflective' (*nirvicāra*) (Eliade, 1990: 80). These technical terms refer to an intense training of the mind, a gradual penetration of an object of meditation with an all-absorbing single-pointed attention until one obtains a state in which subject and object disappear, and being and knowing become fused. At this point in the Yoga system, one is prepared to 'enter' an even more refined state in which consciousness may now receive a direct revelation of the Self (*puruṣa*) (Eliade, 1990: 83).

But this hyper-intense programme of psychology is hardly Ramaṇa's agenda, nor, for that matter, that of the *Vivekacūḍāmaṇi*; Ramaṇa nowhere recommends the arduous psychological programme of yoga as ultimately effective because it implies a process of becoming – something which both Ramaṇa and Śaṅkara considered antithetical to the truth. With regard to the famous maxim in the Muṇḍaka Upaniṣad, 'He who knows Brahman becomes Brahman',[15] Ramaṇa is blunt: 'It is not a matter of becoming but being' (Mudaliar, 1989: 232). 'Is it not ludicrous? To know him and become him? The sage is Brahman – that is all' (Venkataramiah, 1994: 173).

While Ramaṇa does concede some temporary benefit to breath control, penetrating inquiry remains his preferred mechanism for revealing one's true Self. Still, he typically appeals to *nirvikalpa samādhi*, a non-discursive realization of the Self void of all conceptualization (*vikalpa*) (Maharṣi, 1987: 113, 123, 157). Occasionally, he adds a further gloss on the term, speaking of *sahaja nirvikalpa samādhi*, a term which also does not appear in the Yoga Sūtra and often suggests tantric overtones. For example, in his review of yoga traditions, Eliade also examined medieval schools of tantra and suggested the following; 'Like the Brahman of the Upaniṣads and Vedānta, and the *nirvāṇa* of the *Mahāyānists*, the state of *sahaja* is indefinable; it cannot be known dialectically, it can only be apprehended through actual experience .... One realizes the state of *sahaja* by transcending the dualities ...' (Eliade, 1990: 268–69). While Ramaṇa is hardly concerned with the more *outré* methods of tantra, he is concerned with the innate (*sahaja*) quality of liberation. His appropriation of various technical terms in yoga illustrates his use of them for his own particular purposes. Less concerned with a careful progression of enstatic states according to classical yoga and more

---

15 ... *brahma veda brahmaiva bhavati* (MuU 3.2.9).

concerned with a particular kind of innate state (*sahaja sthiti*) that transcends all concepts and dualities, Ramaṇa clearly knew what he was doing in his creative departure from the yoga school:

> In yoga the term *samadhi* refers to some kind of trance and there are various kinds of *samadhi*. But the *samadhi* I speak of is different. It is *sahaja samadhi*. From here you have *samadhana* (steadiness) and you remain calm and composed even while you are active. You realize that you are moved by the deeper real Self within. You have no worries, no anxieties, no cares, for you come to realize that there is nothing belonging to you. You know that everything is done by something with which you are in conscious union. (Godman, 1992: 150–51)

This conscious union is *sahaja samādhi*. Indeed, as we saw earlier, Ramaṇa uses various terms to indicate the supreme, non-dual real: God, the Self, the Heart, the 'I-I'; *sahaja* may be included among these synonyms of the divine to indicate that one's Self is the real, natural state of one's being. When a questioner worried over the transience of states of *samādhi*, Ramaṇa replied with the same poetic sensibility which he typically used when glossing traditional terms, 'What is *samadhi*? *Samadhi* is one's essential nature. How then can it come and go?' (Venkataramiah, 1994: 552).

Concerning traditional practices associated with yoga, Ramaṇa frequently appropriates them for a quick reinterpretation. For example, what really constitutes the three phases of *prāṇāyāma*? 'Completely giving up the identification with the body alone is exhalation (*recaka*); merging within through the inquiry "Who am I?" alone is inhalation (*puraka*); abiding as the one reality "I am that" alone is retention (*kumbhaka*). This is the real *praṇayama*' (Godman, 1992: 140). Indeed, while breath control offers propaedeutic benefits, a more advanced aspirant 'will naturally go to control of mind without wasting his time in practicing control of breath' (Godman, 1992: 140). An extended reconstruction of Patañjali's *aṣṭāṅga* yoga occurs in the *Vicārasaṅgraham*, and Ramaṇa self-consciously recognizes his project: 'The eight limbs (in this case, of knowledge) are those which have been already mentioned, viz., *yama*, *niyama*, etc., but differently defined.' The guiding principle in his reconstruction is a profound inward turning to resolve the mind in the heart. Indeed, even the preliminary virtues of *yama* and *niyama* are decidedly focused on mental discipline corresponding to his method of inquiry, rather than strictly ethical or physical preparations (Maharṣi, 1994: 33–35).

Similarly *āsana* and *jāpa* are reconfigured according to Ramaṇa's philosophical and poetic sensibilities. According to Ramaṇa, yogic postures, *āsanas*, are designed to make the adept remain firm, but 'Where and how can he remain firm except in his own real state? This is the real *asana*' (Godman, 1992: 143). In the same manner he reconfigures *jāpa* and *pūjā*, allowing such practices for their propaedeutic benefits but making sure that a broader point about the nature of realization is made. *Jāpa* and *pūjā* will lead into inquiry, but '*japa* is our real nature. When we realize the Self, then *japa* goes on without effort. What is the means at one stage becomes the goal at another. When effortless, constant *japa* goes on; it is realization' (Mudaliar, 1989: 210).

Ramaṇa insisted that inquiry into one's nature was all that was finally necessary for liberation. The chanting of mantras and various rituals were of minimal use, and even breath control (*prāṇāyāma*) was only modestly helpful in the programme of liberation. However, while Ramaṇa did not actively promote traditional Indian practices, he occasionally gave discreet encouragement to certain practices, such as listening to Vedic recitation or silently chanting mantras (worthwhile, according to Ramaṇa, only if one is properly initiated). These ancillary practices are helpful only as means to calm the mind (*manolaya*) and minimize its *rajāsic* tendency. As with Śaṅkara and Sureśvara, such practices purify the mind; but purification here has less to do with moral or ritual purity than with minimizing mental chatter and inducing calm. States of calm induced by these methods, however, are only temporary; a permanent state of identification emerges through repeated and deepened inquiry.

The guru

Both Śaṅkara and Ramaṇa hold that ignorance of one's true nature and destiny is the fundamental flaw of humanity. Ramaṇa, however, often emphasizes a different nuance, holding that forgetfulness is the basic problem. 'Forgetting', of course, suggests that, at some point, we already *knew* the answer to our problem situation, but that it has receded from our active apprehension due to our habitual mental tendencies and behavioural patterns. Recollection, the necessary antidote to forgetfulness, suggests a platonic role of the guru, who in this case serves as the midwife to the birth of innate knowledge rather than transmitting cosmic *śakti* through the touch of a peacock feather.[16] We are the Self already. We know this in some relevant sense although, owing to misplaced, habituated identifications, it has escaped our active attention. Through the gentle exchange with a realized teacher we can recall and deepen this truth: 'We have forgotten the Self and imagine that the body or the mind is the Self' (Osborne, 1993: 31). The prescription for this? 'Remember who you are' (ibid.: 89). In the *Vicārasaṅgraham*, Ramaṇa modulates his interpretation of traditional *mārgas*: 'Never forgetting one's plenary self-experience is real *bhakti*, *yoga*, *jñāna*, and all other austerities' (Maharṣi, 1994: 12).

While Ramaṇa relativized and reinterpreted numerous traditional Indian practices and institutions, one that he does not relativize is the role of the guru. But, for Ramaṇa, who always maintains a harmony between Advaita theory and practice, guru, grace, God and Self are all identical terms. Nevertheless, a tension can be seen

16 Although, arguably the two are not mutually exclusive. Muktānanda was reputed to use the peacock feather in his initiations. William Barnard offered an intriguing account of such transmission and then framed it in the debate over constructivism in a paper delivered at the American Academy of Religion Annual Meeting, 1994, in Chicago.

in what he says about grace and the guru. On the one hand, release, as with early representations of Buddhism, is an individual effort: 'God and the Guru will only show the way to release; they will not by themselves take the soul to the state of release' (Maharṣi, 1995a: 13). On the other hand, the guru's grace appears to be irresistible: '... just as the prey which has fallen into the jaws of the tiger has no escape, so those who have come within the ambit of the guru's gracious look will be saved and not be lost; yet each one should by his own effort pursue the path shown by God or guru and gain release' (ibid.). In the end, grace penetrates the disciple's effort, setting the stage for his or her realization: 'We cannot attain realization of the Self by our own mind, unaided by God's grace' (Osborne, 1993: 82). In Ramaṇa's *Gītāsāra*, a collection of 42 *ślokas* of the *Gītā* which Ramaṇa took to be the text's most important verses, at least six of them indicate the dynamic between individual effort and divine grace (10.10, 10.11, 9.22, 7.17, 12.15, 18.62). The last verse in Ramaṇa's collection, 18.62, may be taken as his last word on the matter of individual response and divine care: 'Go to him alone for refuge, O Bhārata; through his grace you shall obtain supreme peace, the eternal abode.'[17]

Grace, however, should not be construed as something external to the subject. Instead, it is the divine operating within and outside the individual soul to usher in ultimate self-revelation. In fact, in keeping with the premise of non-dualism, there is no gracious act *per se*, for there is *only* grace; 'Grace always is, and is not given' (Venkataramiah, 1994: 119). In a response to another petitioner, Ramaṇa explained, 'Grace is there all along. Grace is the Self. It is not something to be acquired. All that is necessary is to know its existence' (Osborne, 1993: 83). The appropriate response to the incessant presence of grace is surrender, a term which Ramaṇa repeats frequently.

As grace is there all along, so is the guru; however, the guru here is not so much the physical form of a human, but the divine reality already dwelling within us: 'The Guru is both inner and outer. From the outside he gives a push to the mind to turn inward, while from the inside he pulls the mind toward the Self and helps in quieting it. That is the grace of the Guru. There is no difference between God, Guru, and Self' (ibid.: 115).

The physical guru, however, is important, for he teaches both by word and, perhaps more importantly, by example. And while Ramaṇa certainly taught in his dialogues with disciples, part of the charm of his teaching is his eloquent silence. The old adage seems to hold up in his case: action (or in this case a highly focused, intentional 'inaction') speaks louder than words. When asked why he did not go forth and preach, Ramaṇa replied, 'How do you know I don't? Does preaching consist in mounting a platform and haranguing the people? Preaching is simple communication of knowledge and can be done in silence too' (ibid.: 105). Moreover, verbal words are at least two steps removed from their original source –

---

17 ... *tam eva śaraṇaṁ gacca sarvabhāveṇa bhārata /tatprasādāt parāṁ śāntiṁ sthānaṁ prāpsyasi śāśvatam.*

the nameless, the infinite – and silence in fact more effectively transmits the truth. Indeed, 'The highest form of grace is silence. It is also the highest spiritual instruction .... All other modes of instruction are derived from silence and are therefore secondary. Silence is the primary form. If the Guru is silent, the seeker's mind gets purified by itself' (ibid.: 125). Silence, reflecting and modelling an inner surrender to the Self, finally carries more persuasive power than verbose elocution. The importance of the *guru–śiṣya* relationship quite probably accounts for part of the appeal of the *Vivekacūḍāmaṇi* for Ramaṇa, since the text includes a model of that relationship and highlights the inestimable moral authority of an enlightened teacher. Better to associate with him (*satsang*) and thereby benefit in numerous ways: doubts cleared, passions calmed, perspective reordered. In short, the guru models a way of 'being' in the world; but this is no mere vocational disposition, as, say, an artist models a bohemian lifestyle, a scholar models a life of study, and a professional athlete models a life of training and discipline. Instead, as Ramaṇa concluded from the Muṇḍaka verse, the realized guru *is* being. Thus, as a result of conscious union (*sahaja samādhi*) with the Self, the *jīvanmukta* emanates compassion, wisdom, and grace, bearing witness in his or her life to the truth which words only approximate.

The presence of the guru also stimulates faith (*śraddhā*). Ramaṇa closely follows the *Vivekacūḍāmaṇi's* gloss on *śraddhā*, emphasizing in his Tamil version, as in the Sanskrit, a co-equal importance of *śruti* and guru in the constellation of faith: 'faith is the certainty which accepts both the truth of the words of Vedāntic scriptures and the words of a guru'.[18] However, he adds that faith "is the cause of direct awareness of Brahman' (*cākṣātkarattiṟ kētuvāṉa cirattai*), which slightly nuances the Sanskrit text which says 'faith is that by which the real is perceived' (*sā yayā vastu upalabhyate*). Both versions seem to give pride of place to faith in the causal matrix leading to liberation. This is at first perplexing if one operates out of a typical theistic understanding of faith.

But faith here is not the devotionalism of theistic Vedānta whereby one recognizes one's difference from the divine and surrenders to the supreme in humble submission, even in servitude (*kaiṅkarya*). God and surrender are indeed often referred to in Ramaṇa's comments with disciples; however, he had little patience for the dualistic presuppositions of some forms of Vaiṣṇavism, 'So God cannot get along without their services? On the contrary, God asks: "Who are you to do service to Me?"; He is always saying: "I am within you; who are you?" One must try to realize that and not speak of service' (Mudaliar, 1989: 227). Nevertheless, surrender – meaning the giving up of private plans and particular agenda, all of which are marked by will and pleasure – is an important psychological moment in the life of the disciple. Surrender is the letting go of a constricted identity, the ego, in favour of the unlimited Self.

---

18 ... *vēdāntasāstiramum kuruvākkiyamum cattiyam eṉakkoḷḷum nicciyam* (Maharṣi, 1987: 117).

So the importance of faith as part of the causal matrix for realization should be clear. Faith allows for a restructuring of mind and affect to receive and deepen Vedāntic truth. One's mind is refashioned according to the truth of non-dualism. But while faith hardly amounts here to popular devotionalism, it still suggests, at least initially, a cognitive assent and affective resolution perhaps best seen in popular devotional movements. This is why the author of the *Vivekacūḍāmaṇi* adds that 'among the mechanisms which produce liberation, *bhakti* indeed is supreme'.[19] Ramaṇa concurs in his Tamil translation: 'among the means which result in the attaining of liberation, *bhakti* alone enjoys highest prestige' (... *bhaktiyē mikavum cirōkṣṭam*). The reason for the high prestige of devotion in the process of liberation is the same as that of faith. Devotion, like faith, consists of a mental and volitional energy whose outcome is the refashioning of heart and mind. This energy, in Ramaṇa's philosophy and that of the *Vivekacūḍāmaṇi*, springs from the same source: the ineffable Self; the energy of concentration which focuses on this source is the same, however it is termed. This is why Ramaṇa says, in his introduction to the *Vivekacūḍāmaṇi*, that '*nididhyāsana* which is constancy in the self (*ātmāṉucantanam*) is otherwise called *bhakti*, yoga, *dhyāna*' (Maharṣi, 1987: 113).

Śruti

Ramaṇa is ambivalent about the importance of *śruti* and other expressions of conventional piety. Owing to his method of inquiry, these mechanisms are finally minimized in his epistemology of religious experience. For example, one questioner asked if there was any efficacy in bathing in the Ganges, to which Ramaṇa replied, 'The Ganges is within you. Bathe in this Ganges; it will not make you shiver with cold' (Osborne, 1993: 63). And yet, when the questioner then asked if disciples should read the *Gītā*, perhaps the most important scripture of all, Ramaṇa replied without hesitation, 'Always'. But elsewhere, he minimizes the worth of scriptures: at best they point to the existence of the Self; 'apart from that, they are useless' (ibid.: 8). Nevertheless, he does accord value to *śruti*; after all, he chooses to translate the *Vivekacūḍāmaṇi*, a text which also relativizes scripture but in the end concedes its importance in the economy of liberation (VC 241–45). In his translation, Ramaṇa clearly affirms the *Vivekacūḍāmaṇi*'s insistence on internalizing the (non-dual) truth of scripture as part of the process of liberation. And elsewhere Ramaṇa repeats the *Vivekacūḍāmaṇi*'s emphasis on the need for scripture; one example illustrates both the theory of innate *mokṣa* and the witness value of scripture: 'Precisely *being* the partless Brahman is liberation: this itself is the esoteric conclusion of the entire Vedānta to which *śruti* testifies.'[20]

But his ambivalence to the ultimate value of scripture can be seen in other

---

19 ... *mokṣakāraṇasāmagrahyāṁ bhaktir eva garīyasī* (VC 31).

20 ... *cahala vēdānta cittānthattiṉ rahasyam ithuvē accurutikaḷēy itiṟ piramāṇam* (Maharṣi, 1987: 169).

glosses in his Tamil translation, not to mention in other conversations with disciples. For example, Ramaṇa offers a rather literal translation of VC 59, which poetically dismisses the ultimate importance of scripture: 'If one is ignorant of the nature of the ultimate, reading scripture is ineffective, and indeed after one knows the supreme, reading scripture is completely unnecessary.'[21] Indeed, according to the Sanskrit and Ramaṇa's Tamil version, one must 'cross the great forest of *śāstras* which dupe the mind' and rely, with the help of a realized teacher, on a particular kind of experiential knowledge of the Self to be liberated.[22]

In VC 479, Ramaṇa follows the Sanskrit, which in this case actually makes no reference to 'inner experience', but instead emphasizes one's own reasoning powers (*taṉ yuktiyālum*), scripture (*curuti pramāṇattālum*) and the clarifying words of the guru (*uraitta kuruvacanattālum*) as the means by which the disciple knows the Self (*ātmatattuvam aṟintu*). Still, all this generates the direct experience of the non-dual Self, and indeed, following the disciple's brief (*koñca kālam*) experience of heightened absorption in the Self, the disciple offers his salutations to the guru, honouring him with the epithet, 'O one of consummate experience!' (*makāṉubhavā*). Such a title reveals both the method and the goal of Ramaṇa's project for ultimate awareness: a particular kind of experience which is both revelatory and self-guaranteeing. And yet it is an extraordinary, special kind of experience. Concerning this unique experience Ramaṇa once explained, 'What is *anubhava*? It is only going beyond the pairs of opposites or the *triputi* (of knower, known, and knowledge)' (Mudaliar, 1989: 216).

So we have here the common Advaitin claim for a knowledge that transcends discursive thought, a non-dual knowing beyond knowledge. The experience of the Self is a particular kind of knowledge which should not imply a localized knower – someone who *has* knowledge of the Self – for, in keeping with the premise of Advaita, there is nothing separate from the Self that can be known. Knowledge, on this interpretation, is a direct awareness of the one real in which the duality of subject and object has ceased to exist. Concerning the *tripuṭī*, Ramaṇa is quite clear: 'There is a reality beyond these three. These appear and disappear, whereas the truth is eternal' (Venkataramiah. 1994: 342). Ramaṇa does not engage here in debate or persuade with incontrovertible logic; instead he authoritatively issues a comprehensive statement about the nature of reality. The implicit source of the authority is no scriptural canon or canons of logic but the truth of Ramaṇa's own experience.

Ramaṇa asserts the soteriological value of scripture while at the same time minimizing its importance. Although affirming the non-dual truth of *śruti*, Ramaṇa hardly ascribes a magical potency to scripture, say, in the manner of Sureśvara.

---

21 … *parattuvattaiy aṟiyāviṭṭāl cāstiraṅkaḷ paṭittal palaṅ koṭāmaiyiṉ niṣpalam; parattvattaiy aṟinta piṉṉar cāstiraṅkaḷ paṭittal vēṟu payaṉiṉmaiyiṉ niṣpalamē* (Maharṣi, 1987: 121–22).

22 … *maṉamayakkattiṟ kētuvāna sāstira jāla makāraṇyattai kaṭantu tattuva jñāniy ākiṟa kuruvāl ātmatattuvattaiy anupavamāy aṟiya vēṇṭum* (Maharṣi, 1987: 122).

Moreover, he finds no ultimate worth in traditional meditations on the *mahāvākyas* which in effect construct yet another identification. In the end, Ramaṇa's *vicāra* method rejects all positive identifications, even the apparently supremely positive identification with Brahman. His method is an inward movement to the source of consciousness, not a rarefied intellectual process. In a sense it is a 'downward movement' to discover the source of intellect, not a heady, 'upward' movement of increasing analysis and abstraction. This means that his single, persistent question, 'Who am I?', cannot be construed either as a mantra itself – that is, as a device for concentration, nor is it an intellectual tool used to arrive at positive identifications, 'I am Brahman', 'I am That', 'I am Śiva' and so on. Such statements are subjective affirmations once removed from the source. Three *satsang* responses indicate his estimate of such methods:

> Even to repeat *aham Brahmasmi*, or think of it, a doer is necessary. Who is it? It is 'I'. Be that 'I'. It is the direct method (Godman, 1992: 71).

> The text is not meant for thinking, 'I am Brahman'. *Aham* [I] is known to every one. Brahman abides as *aham* in everyone. Find out the 'I'. The 'I' is already Brahman. You need not think so. Simply find out the 'I'. (Ibid.: 70)

> ... the bonds of birth and death will not cease merely by doing many repetitions of *mahavakyas* such as 'I am Siva'. Instead of wandering about repeating 'I am the supreme', abide as the supreme yourself. The misery of birth and death will not cease by vocally repeating countless times 'I am that', but only by abiding as that. (Ibid.: 125)

Vivekacūḍāmaṇi 65 carries this agenda further by interpolating a *mahāvākya* to indicate the ultimate ineffectiveness of 'mere words' and all positive identifications. Moreover, in his translation we again see the importance of the guru and the failure of strictly intellectualist methods of analysis:

> Without destroying the perceived world, and without experiential knowledge of the Self, the mere phrase, '*Brahmaivāham*' will not produce liberation, which consists of merely *being* Brahman ... so, one hears a realized teacher's exegesis and considers it; but without direct experiential knowledge and constant meditation, attaining the Self, which is hidden by *māyā*, is impossible by reasoning and argument.[23]

A summary of the sequence of the path to liberation (*mokṣa cātaṉa kiramam*) is suggested in VC 69 and 70 and includes virtues held in esteem by all traditions of

---

23 ... *ātmatattuvattaiy aṉupavamāy aṟiyāmalum 'pirahmaivāham' eṉṉum vākku māttirattāl pirahma māttiramāy irrukkum muktiy aṭaiya māṭṭaṉ. ... pirahmattaiy aṟinta kuruviṉ iṭattil corūpa lakṣaṇattai ciravaṇañ ceytu, atanai maṉaṉam paṇṇi, nirantaran tiyāṉipatāl uṇṭāhum aparōkṣa aṉupava jñāṉattāl aṭaiyal ākum allāmal, māyaiyāl maṟaipaṭṭuḷḷa svasvarūpattaikku tarka yuktikaḷāl aṭaiya kūṭātu* (Maharṣi, 1987: 122).

Vedānta: detachment (*vairāgya*), tranquillity (*śama*), self-control (*dama*), and forbearance (*titikṣa*); these are important because they contribute to the refashioning of will and affect necessary for the revelation of the Self. One simply cannot experience infinite awareness if one is obsessively preoccupied with temporal satisfactions, so a particular culture is necessary to assist in the shaping of affect and will. These virtues, when embodied in the lives of teachers and saints, bear witness to the metaphysical claims made by these very teachers. The holiness of the saints reveals a moral coherence that supports, lends credibility or contributes warrant to broader doctrinal and metaphysical claims. While not incontrovertibly or logically demonstrating the truth of these claims, their lives instead offer a 'logic of holiness' which demonstrates a life lived in truth. Such lives unify in striking, stellar ways the movements of body, mind and heart, thus becoming 'windows to the real' or 'rumours of angels', to borrow Peter Berger's phrase. Minimally, they strengthen the credibility of the claims about the nature of reality made by teachers such as Ramaṇa; maximally, these examples allow us to peer into the heart of reality and in some peculiar way discover our own.

These virtues both prepare for, and follow from, the formative experience of liberation. With VC 70 we see yet another appeal of the *Vivekacūḍāmaṇi* for Ramaṇa: following the traditional sequence of the practice of virtues, hearing and reflecting, and meditation, the author of the VC writes, 'then the wise one, having attained the immutable Supreme, experiences, here and now, the bliss of *nirvāṇa*'.[24] The key here is realization here and now (*ihaiva*), a theme that Ramaṇa repeatedly insisted upon, showing his fidelity to the long-standing Advaitin doctrine of the *jīvanmukta*. This doctrine is, of course, accepted not because of intellectual coherence but because of the lived, felt experience in Ramaṇa's own life. Ramaṇa modulates the phrasing of the verse somewhat, using words that carry extended implications for him. He writes:

> The discriminating one experiences the unending bliss of liberation right here and now, through the immediate and direct awareness of Brahman; this emerges through *nirvikalpa samādhi*, in turn produced by incessant meditation.[25]

There are several things to note here. First, Ramaṇa adds much, both by words and emphasis. He underscores the importance of liberation in one's lifetime by adding a double emphatic suffix (*iṭattilēyē*), which suggests absolute certainty that this is the case. Second, he adds terms that are not present in the verse: 'immediate' (Tam. *cākṣātkāra*; Skt *sākṣātkāra*), 'direct' (Tam. *aparōkṣa*; Skt *aparokṣa*), and 'absorption without conceptualization' (*nirvikalpa samādhi*). Again, the addition of the qualifiers is of no grave consequence, for it accords with traditional glosses of

24 ... *tato avikalpaṁ param etya vidvān ihaiva nirvāṇasukhaṁ samṛcchati.*

25 ... *annirantara tiyāṉattāl uṇṭākum nirvikaṟpa samādhiyaṟ peṟappaṭṭa aparōkṣa pirahma cākṣātkāra ñaṉa palattāl vivēki ivvilattilēyē mōkṣāṉantattaiy aṉupavikkiṉṟaṉ* (Maharṣi, 1987: 123).

the experience of liberation, and we saw earlier how Ramaṇa appeals to *nirvikalpa samādhi* in a manner different from the schools of Yoga. But his inclusion of this meditative state interjects an epistemological truth, where the Sanskrit suggests one of ontology. In the latter, the Supreme is unchanging (*avikalpa*) nature. But Ramaṇa suggests that the ultimate state is void of thought, void of imagination. And, unlike some of his more pithy *satsang* statements, here he does suggest an extended process of liberation: constant meditation (*camātinikṣṭanātal*) leads to *nirvikalpa samādhi*, which in turn is 'the cause for the blissful pleasure of non-duality'.[26]

What I wish to stress among these additions to the Sanskrit is the non-cognitive (at least in the traditional sense of the term) dimension of realization. We saw earlier that Ramaṇa's project rejects all mental identifications, including those stimulated by *śruti*. Indeed, his project rejects the mind altogether, inviting one to leave the mind and return to its source. The question is, can one *use* the mind to get beyond the mind? If one is optimistic about the mind's usefulness for liberation, one might employ either a positive or negative approach in versions of Advaita *sādhana*. Earlier we saw that Ramaṇa rejects all positive identifications outright, even supreme identifications such as 'I am Brahman' or 'I am Śiva'. Additionally, however, he rejects the negative way – *neti-neti vāda* – of classical Advaita, because it too is an intellectual process. The assumption in the traditional practice is that, by peeling away all identifications, the real 'I' may be experienced; indeed, this is a driving theme in the *Vivekacūḍāmaṇi*. However, Ramaṇa repeatedly warned of the intellectualism of the practice, saying that it was a mental activity that could not finally take one beyond the mind. Such acts of discrimination sustain, in a residual and subtle manner, the 'I-thought'; although discrimination intends to eliminate mind and body, the very act of discrimination retains residual 'I-thought' and cannot eliminate itself (Godman, 1992: 68). So, in short, programmes which suggest affirmation ('I am Brahman') or negation (*neti-neti*) share a belief that the Self can be discovered by the mind; but to these approaches and to those listeners who were prepared to grasp it, Ramaṇa was uncompromising. The goal is to destroy the mind, *not* to employ it service of the Self. Concerning *neti-neti* meditation, Ramaṇa once said the following;

> No – that is not meditation. Find the source. You must reach the source. The false 'I' will disappear and the real 'I' will be realized. The former cannot exist without the latter. There is now wrong identification of the Self with the body, senses, etc. You proceed to discard these, and this is *neti*. This can only be done by holding onto the one which cannot be discard. That is *iti* [that which is]. (Godman, 1992: 70)

---

26 ... *atvaitāṉanta racāṉupavattiṟ kētuvāṉa nirvikaṟpacamāti* (Maharṣi, 1987, 157). Interestingly, Ramaṇa recognizes that one can lose the 'grace' of *samādhi* and return to the ego-driven dilemmas of duality. While the *jñani* may not return to bondage (ibid.: 143), warnings nevertheless abound elsewhere over the tenuousness of liberation (ibid.: 153). The remedy for the unmoored ego here, and in his talks elsewhere, is relentless inward inquiry.

What is the real 'I' and how does one reach it without the mind? How do the nuances of Ramaṇa's philosophy square with the VC? After all, discrimination is the premier virtue in the text, and many verses are dedicated to show precisely what the Self is not. Moreover, protests notwithstanding, Ramaṇa himself must admit at least a provisional use of the mind; one must, after all, start somewhere. Indeed, this is the case in his translation of the *Vivekacūḍāmaṇi*. For example, his record of the requisites for Advaita *sādhana* again slightly modulates the Sanskrit: Ramaṇa writes: 'Who is fit for inquiry into the Self? The intelligent one, who, besides the other qualities cited in scripture, is characterized by a forceful ability to pick out the unessential and grasp the essential.'[27] Mental capacity and mental function are clearly implied here as some process of elimination is necessary to pick out the 'essential and unessential'. Indeed, Ramaṇa later interpolates the term *neti-neti* as a requirement for the *kośamīmāṁsā* that begins in VC 151, writing that one must 'remove, with sharp intellect, the objective five sheaths from the Self, saying, "not this, not this"'.[28] By this 'process of removal' (*taḷḷum apavātattāl*) one comes to realize that the effulgent Self is 'distinct from all forms, such as body, etc., as a stalk of grass in its sheaths of leaf'.[29] The importance of the intellect is once again shown in Ramaṇa's translation of VC 136; moreover, this verse is important because it is the only Sanskrit construction which parallels Ramaṇa's peculiar term for the inner Self, the 'I-I'. Although there is actually no other Sanskrit use of the term 'I-I', Ramaṇa interpolates it frequently in his translation, trying to draw attention to the source of consciousness from which the local 'I' emerges; he did, of course, use this term frequently in his other works and in his *satsang* conversations as well. The following is Sanskrit VC 135 and Ramaṇa's translation, which partially includes VC 136; notice the single Sanskrit use of 'I-I', Ramaṇa's use of the term, and, Ramaṇa's protests elsewhere notwithstanding, the importance of the mind:

> The supreme Self directly shines in the three states of consciousness as witness of the mind, the 'I-I'.[30]
>
> As the witness to the mind (in all three states of consciousness), know through experience 'This I is Brahman;' through a one-pointed mind know the supreme Self which shines immediately and ever present as 'I-I'.[31]

So we do need the mind to get beyond the mind. Indeed, 'Without experiencing

---

27 ... *metāviyāy cārattai kirakittu acārattai taḷḷa kūṭiya cāmārttiyavānāy cāstiraṅkaḷiṟ kūṟiyuḷḷa lakṣaṇaṅkaḷ yāvūm taṉpālamaiya peṟṟōṉ ātma vicārattil atikāri yāvaṉ* (Maharṣi, 1987: 116).

28 ... *cūkṣmaputtiyāl ātmāviṉiṉṟum tiruciya pañcakōcaṅkaḷai nēti, nēti (italla) eṉavē pirittu* (Maharṣi, 1987: 134).

29 ... *muñcum pulliṉ mattiyil ikṣīkai (tuṇṭu) pōla anta tēhāti tiruciyavarkkaṅkaṭku vilakṣaṇamāy* (Maharṣi, 1987: 134).

30 ... *vilasati paramātma jāgrādiṣv avasthāsu ahamaham iti sākṣāt sākṣirūpeṇa buddheḥ*.

31 ... *jākrāti avastaihaḷil puttikku cākṣiyāy iruntu 'aham, aham' eṉavē nittiyāparōkṣamāy pirakācikkum paramātmāvai ēkākkira cittattāl 'inta nāṉ pirahman' eṉṟu aṉupavamāy aṟi* (Maharṣi, 1987: 132).

Brahman through the single, subtle, mental mode of *samādhi*, by those of subtle intellect, saving knowledge is impossible by any gross outward manner.'[32] In this state, 'the *jñāni* experiences in the heart the true "I", the single totality of Brahman ....'[33] This 'I-I' is the seat of consciousness, independent of all mental functions and modifications, yet it illumines all mental operations. The value Ramaṇa places on this term is seen in his Tamil benedictory verse. This verse is premier not only because it is textually prior to the translation, but also in the sense of value and prestige, and so highlights the central dynamic in Ramaṇa's thought. In a clever play on words, he interchanges the Tamil word '*akam*' ('inner', 'internal', 'within') with its Sanskrit homophone '*aham*' ('I') without adopting Sanskrit orthography (because the intervocalic 'k' in Tamil is pronounced as an 'h'). So, 'the Self shines within (*akam oḷira ātma*) as "I-I (*akam akam*)", which in turn removes the primal ignorance of "I" (*akam eṉum mūlavittaiy akaṉṟila akam akam*)'.

In this play of words, we see a condensed form of Ramaṇa's philosophy. The true Self, the 'I-I', already *is*, 'embedded', as it were, within us. It already shines within us; in some sense we know this source because we operate from it in our mundane inflections of the first-person singular pronoun. So the 'I-I' is the hidden source of the 'I', the ego, which in turn is the fulcrum for of all identifications and the locus of ignorance. However, since this source (*akam akam*) is within (*akam*), we must dive inward to discover it. We must merge our mind into the source. In far more numerous places than in the Sanksrit *Vivekacūḍāmaṇi* Ramaṇa interjects the term 'I-I', using it as a verbal symbol for non-verbal pure experience.

The 'I-I', in one sense, could be considered yet another term for the many poetic glosses on one's real nature: *ātman*, Brahman, *jāpa*, *dhyāna*, *mouna* and so on. Yet, Ramaṇa prefers the term 'I-I' as a verbal expression for the ultimate, wordless reality. To grasp or to realize the 'I-I' does presume mental operation and fitness of intellect: 'The Self makes itself known as being, consciousness, bliss and is self-effulgent in the heart as "I-I". Through your subtle intellect, know this eternal blissful awareness to be the Self or the true 'I', which always shines as 'I-I' in the heart.'[34]

Āśrama *and* adhikāra

Ramaṇa revalorizes other traditional customs or practices as well. For example, he reconstructs the worth of the *āśrama* system, rejecting the notion that the *saṃnyāsi*

---

[32] ... *camātiyāl aticūkṣmamāṉa viruttiyoṉṟāl avv aticūkṣma prahmam, atitcūkṣma puttimāṉkaḷāl aṉupavamāy aṟiya paṭumē allāmal stūlatirukṣṭiyāl aṟivataṟ kevarālum cakkiyamākātu* (Maharṣi, 1987: 157).

[33] ... *ēkaparipūraṇa prahmattai ñāniyum camātiyiṉkaṇ hirutayattil 'akam' eṉavēy aparōkṣamāy aṉupavipatāl* ... (Maharṣi 1987, 163).

[34] ... *hirutayattil 'aham, aham' eṉṟu satā tāṉ ākavē jvalittu koṇdirukkum nittiya ñānānanta ātmāvai aticūkṣma puttiyāl 'aham' (nāṉ) eṉṟa aṟivāyāka* (Maharṣi, 1987: 142).

is superior or, in the traditional sense, even necessary. Instead, '*Sannyāsa* is only the renunciation of the I thought, not the rejection of external objects' (Maharṣi, 1994: 14). Ramaṇa astutely recognizes the psychological insight that external circumstances often have little to do with mental clarity. We bring our package of mental habits and behavioural patterns to any locale: 'Wherever you go, even if you fly up into the air, will your mind not go with you?' (Osborne, 1993: 91). Elsewhere, he writes, 'Change of environment is no help. The one obstacle is the mind, and this must be overcome whether in the home or in the forest. If you can do it in the forest, why not in the home?' (ibid.: 87). Rather than a social state or religious institution, *saṃnyāsa* is a primarily a mental state; it means 'renouncing one's individuality, not shaving one's head and putting on ochre robes' (ibid.: 91). So while, according to Śaṅkara, in theory all are qualified for liberation in virtue of the ultimate truth of non-duality, in practice, one needed to abide by the social states; indeed, *saṃnyāsis* themselves are established in a hierarchy according to *Upadeśasāhasrī* 2.1.2. Ramaṇa, however, takes as absolute the premise that we all are already liberated; realization is not only our destiny, it is who we are here and now. So to the question whether one should remain at home (*gṛhastāśrama*), Ramaṇa replies with a typical rejoinder, 'You are to remain in your true state' (ibid.: 96). But can married persons realize the Self? Ramaṇa responds as follows:

> Certainly. It is a question of fitness of mind. Married or unmarried a man can realize the Self, because the Self is here and now. If it were not, but were obtainable by some effort at some future time, if it were something new to be acquired, it would not be worth seeking, because what is not natural cannot be permanent. What I say is that the Self is here and now and that IT alone is. (Ibid.: 90–91)

The above quote raises the question of eligibility. Was eligibility for 'inquiry' limited to Brahmin male renunciants? Clearly the above suggests fitness is a mental state, involving discipline and intention, not a happenstance of birth. We can further answer the question of eligibility by reviewing the theory and practice of Ramaṇa's method of inquiry. Indeed, Ramaṇa applied the same strategy of asking 'who' it is who is married or is concerned with the merits of celibacy: 'First find out who the wife and husband are. Then the question will not arise' (ibid.). Indeed, he offers his own gloss on chastity or celibacy, *brahmacārya*, '*Brahmacārya* means living in Brahman; it has no connection with celibacy as commonly understood. A real Brahmachari is one who lives in Brahman and finds bliss in Brahman which is the same as the Self' (ibid.). Presumably, 'dwelling in Brahman' need not be indexed to sexual identity.

According to Ramaṇa, there is only the one, true Self; all else are mere temporary, ultimately unreal modifications, and these include caste and gender specifications. Mudaliar reports that a family once asked permission to receive Ramaṇa's *darśan* at *Skandāsramam*; when he asked why they had asked permission, the father replied, 'We are untouchables'. Mudaliar then started to go to

Ramaṇa when it occurred to him that 'even to ask Bhagavan would be an injustice to him, so I told the man that caste had no meaning with Bhagavan and that they would be welcome' (Mudaliar, 1989: 214).

Mudaliar's intuition reflects Ramaṇa's programme of raising one's awareness beyond any temporary identification, including caste. Sexual identifications as 'male' or 'female' must also be transcended in the programme of liberation. So the eligibility for saving inquiry is determined by mental state, not by sexuality. The practical application of this truth is seen in the fact that women were among Ramaṇa's many disciples and often petitioned him in *satsang*. Perhaps the most telling example of Ramaṇa's attitude towards women is his attention to his mother, Alagammal, especially upon her death. By this time, Alagammal had become a disciple, long abandoning her maternal instinct to bring the young swami home and have him resume a 'normal life'. As she was dying, Ramaṇa stayed with her, keeping his right hand on her heart and her left hand on her forehead. He did this for some time even after she died, to the consternation of Brahmin disciples who were concerned about ritual purity. Finally, he returned to the group of disciples and announced, 'come along, there is no pollution', the implication being that Alagammal was 'absorbed' and therefore did not require the usual purificatory rites (Osborne, 1954: 78). This event compares with the death of one of his early disciples, Palaniswami; Ramaṇa performed the same ministry to his devoted friend, but apparently without success. Nonetheless, although Palanaswami apparently did not become a *videhamukta*, the manner of his death promised a rebirth conducive to eventual liberation (ibid.). These examples reveal the practical dimensions of Ramaṇa's more expanded notion of *adhikāra*; eligibility here is not dictated by culture or gender, but by one's repeated renunciation of ego and attachment. With regard to whether or not to cremate the Alagammal's body, Ramaṇa was never directly asked what to do, but his disciples recalled that he once responded to precisely this question put to him years earlier by Gaṇapati Śāstri; he affirmed that holy women were to be buried, 'Since *Gnana* and *Mukti* do not differ with the difference of sex, the body of a woman Saint also need not be burnt. Her body also is the abode of God' (ibid.).

Universalism

Finally, let us consider the universalism of Ramaṇa's philosophy, which emerges from a radical application of the Advaita metaphysic and a decisive internalist epistemology of religious experience. Accordingly, all people are already liberated, and can access that liberation through introspection. Ramaṇa's epistemology of religious experience privileges this inward dimension and at the same time relativizes traditional Indian practices such as purifications and *saṃnyāsa* and admitting all seekers to the path of inquiry, regardless of gender, caste or stage of life. Some of these practices, such as *saṃnyāsa*, were taken by Śaṅkara to be a necessary condition for the possibility of liberation, and *saṃnāysa* itself was restricted to Brahmins.

Ramaṇa's universalism, however, shows up in other ways as well. First, numerous Westerners found considerable strength and peace in Ramaṇa's presence; these persons, by no means traditional *adhikārins*, nevertheless received the verbal and silent *upadeśa* of Ramaṇa. Some of these Westerners have compiled their own collections of Ramaṇa's wisdom or their own reflections on his life. These include books by Arthur Osborne, Paul Brunton, Mouni Sadhu, S.S. Cohen, Major Chadwick, and others.[35] The fact that Westerners were encouraged in the introspective path of inquiry reinforces the universal application of Ramaṇa's non-dualism. Venkataramiah records a conversation with an unidentified American engineer, who asked several questions concerning the mind, the Self and grace, and finally said, 'You are Hindu, we are American. Does it make any difference?' Ramaṇa replied simply, 'No' (Venkataramiah, 1994: 114). Ramaṇa's openness to all seekers reinforces in practice the universalism present in Advaita's theory. A similar universalism can be seen in the thought of Swami Vivekānanda, the brilliant disciple of the nineteenth-century Bengali mystic, Ramakrisha. In theory, we are all the supreme Self; therefore anyone, not just Brahmins or Indians, may access that reality. This again differs from Śaṅkara, although, to be fair, he did not have European and American seekers beseeching him for wisdom. Nevertheless, while Śaṅkara admitted a theoretical universalism, in practice he was an exclusivist: you must be a (male) (Brahmin) renunciant to attain liberation.

This openness and universalism in Ramaṇa is not merely demonstrated by the throng of visitors seeking his presence, but also by what he said. One disciple raised what seems to be a contemporary question in the study of religion: 'One speaks in terms of Christianity, another of Islam, a third of Buddhism, etc. Is that due to their upbringing?' Ramaṇa replied: 'Whatever may be their upbringing, their expression is the same. Only the modes of expression differ according to circumstances' (Osborne, 1993: 67). Elsewhere he adds, concerning distinctions of 'East' and 'West', 'All go to the same goal' (Venkataramiah, 1994: 114). Ramaṇa's perspectivalism here is hardly in vogue, at least among contemporary scholars of religion in the West, but it is entirely in keeping with his fundamental metaphysic: we are the Self; differences are only circumstantial modifications. In the end, 'the highest state is the same and the experience is the same' (Osborne, 1993: 67). Again, he allowed his universalism to include practical inclusivity. All seekers, whether Indian or not, were encouraged to know the Self through the method of inquiry. As a universal programme, the Self could be (internally) accessed by persons of all

---

[35] Osborne was an English disciple of Ramaṇa who spent the last 20 years of his life at Ramanāsramam and died in 1971. He wrote several other books in addition to those cited in this study, and he edited the ashram journal, *The Mountain Path*, as well. Brunton (1994) refers to his encounter with Ramaṇa in his travels through India. Mouni Sādhu (1957) was a German who also lived for many years at the ashram and wrote of his experiences with Ramaṇa. S.S. Cohen (1993) translated some of Ramaṇa's Tamil works and wrote of his own encounter with him, as did Chadwick under the name Sadhu Arunachala (1994).

religious traditions as well. However, according to Osborne, 'Bhagavan had many followers who were not Hindus – Christians, Muslims, Parsis – and none was ever recommended to change his religion' (Osborne, 1993: 62–63).

What we see is a genuine universalism that follows from a harmony of Advaitin theory and practice: the theory is the metaphysic of non-dualism, and the practice is a decisive internalist epistemology of religious experience. The result is a form of Advaita that transcends the social and cultural settings of South Asia. What I wish to insist on is that Ramaṇa pushes Advaita to its natural conclusion whereas Śaṅkara does not. While Śaṅkara's epistemology of religious experience fluctuates between the poles of internalism and externalism, in significant ways it is externalist. This limits Advaita to a local culture. Ramaṇa, on the other hand, operates much less ambiguously from an internalist epistemology, which renders his Advaita universal, a characteristic that seems to be in keeping with the fundamental premise of Advaita in any case.

For Ramaṇa all external mechanisms are highly relativized by this method, and thus his internalism opens space for a universal programme of liberation – one that successfully transcends culture and its various doxastic mechanisms. In a sense, Ramaṇa's internalism, following upon his non-dual metaphysic, 'liberates' Advaita from the culture of liberation which was established, in important ways, by Śaṅkara. I will now evaluate the cognitive and social implications that follow from our internalist, apophatic traditions as well as the externalist, cataphatic tradition that emerges in a systematic way with Rāmānuja, one of Śaṅkara's most important Vedāntin critics.

CHAPTER 5

The cognitive and social implications of the epistemology of religious experience

Cognitive implications

This study has been concerned with the vexing problem of 'religious experience' – terms which one scholar once described as twofold 'weasel words'. Our central question is stated simply: what, if anything, do we know from religious experience? A related question immediately follows: how do we know it? But in our attempt to answer these questions, we discovered certain social implications concerning the epistemologies of religious experience which dominate versions of Advaita. This chapter will review our work and spell out the cognitive and social implications of religious experience.

In Chapter 1 we reviewed the historical and philosophical issues surrounding recent Western discussion of religious experience and concluded with a discussion of two epistemological models, internalism and externalism. These epistemological models attempt to explain how we know anything at all, let alone how we might know something from religious experience. Indeed, it was the purpose of this study to apply these models to relevant Indian soteriologies and arrive at some conclusions concerning the cognitive dimension of religious experience.

Although the models of internalism and externalism have their broadest scope when they are used to account for how we know anything at all, typically discussion of internalism and externalism is more precisely limited to theories of epistemic justification. Indeed, if one expects to find, in epistemology, discussion of the nature of knowledge *per se*, one quickly discovers that the emphasis in epistemology is often justification or warrant. Rather than discuss *what* knowledge is, discussion involves *how* knowledge comes about and, further, how such knowledge is justified.

The term 'justification' suggests some sort of evaluation or conclusion concerning one's repertoire of beliefs: one who holds a justified (or warranted) true belief is in good 'epistemic shape', at least concerning that particular belief. There are good grounds for the belief, and it seems reasonable, on the part of the believer, to hold it. Moreover, the term suggests degrees: one can be more or less justified in holding a certain belief. How one arrives at justification or warrant, and so finds oneself in good epistemic shape, is one of the central concerns of internalism and externalism. In addition to addressing concerns of justification, these theories can be extended into broader accounts of the mechanisms of knowledge, a principal focus of this book.

Although epistemologists have not used the terms 'externalism' and 'internalism' unambiguously, a generalization can nevertheless be made which applies to justification and the account of knowledge. Externalism suggests that at least some of the justifying factors in the process of knowing need not be internally accessible; they may be external to the agent, and they may be contingent as well. Frequently, externalism is associated with causal theories and reliabilism. In other words, among the significant factors which justify a belief is an 'appropriate causal ancestry' of that belief. Sometimes this is understood as a doxastic practice whose process and outcome are measured in terms of reliability, and indeed one of the most important versions of externalism is reliabilism. In this case, one of the important justifying factors is a 'reliable process' in which the cognitive outcomes of such a process are likely to be true. And so reliabilism is a subset, perhaps the most dominant subset, of externalism. We saw that Plantinga recognized the value of reliabilism but added further constraints on externalism by insisting on the 'proper function' of cognitive faculties in an appropriate cognitive environment. Under these conditions, the outputs of such mechanisms enjoy warrant. Examples of such cognitive mechanisms which, when functioning properly in an appropriate environment produce knowledge, are perception, testimony and memory.

These three are, of course, 'mundane' mechanisms, and the adjudication of the claims which follow from them need careful scrutiny to determine the range of justification which might accrue. But these same mechanisms can be carefully extended into the realm of sacred perception, sacred testimony and sacred memory. As mundane, 'rational' mechanisms, these practices themselves are socially established and operate, as 'knowledge-producers', in a broad cultural dynamic that contains explicit or implicit assumptions of what counts for knowing and knowledge. The *a priori* dismissal of 'religious knowing' ignores the circular and self-referential nexus of socially established ideas which privileges one pattern of knowing while rejecting another. In other words, if the 'religious knower' is somehow at fault for living in a 'bubble', an atmosphere replete with metaphysical and epistemological assumptions, so also at fault for the same reason is the rationalist, empiricist or materialist who dismisses religious knowing as impossible or unverifiable. Such imperial dismissal more often demonstrates the exercise of power, which sets the terms and method of discourse, rather than any lucid reasoning practices. A critique that 'sacred perception' is invalid either because it is radically unverifiable or non-probative or that the conditions of such knowing function in their own particular cultural matrix fails to note its own self-referential and imperialist matrix. Instead of everyone living in their own little bubbles, or as 'frogs in the well', it behoves us to stretch our cultural matrices as far as possible and extend our patterns of knowing; the fruit of this enterprise is a greater self-understanding and a greater understanding of reality in its most complete context. These two objectives are, of course, closely related, and in Advaita they are coextensive. One way to begin to realize them has been demonstrated in this book – namely, to examine how we know anything at all and then to extend it, as far as possible, into the realm of religious knowing. This has the benefit of drawing upon standard methods of knowing while not holding to the positivist assumptions so often latent in them.

For example, let us take one mundane externalist mechanism of producing knowledge, testimony – in this case, the testimony of a person learned in any discipline, whether car mechanic, doctor or astrophysicist. Most people have neither the time, skills, nor training to understand the inner workings of a car, the human body or the universe and instead must rely on the testimony of someone skilled in these matters. Externalism presumes that relevant socially established doxastic mechanisms, functioning properly in an appropriate environment, confer justification on the beliefs produced by the testimony of a properly qualified person: for example, there is an appropriate causal ancestry to the belief 'The gaskets in my car engine are blown', because I have taken my car to a mechanic who has diagnosed a problem of leaking oil. This is not to say, however, that the testimony is absolutely free from error. In the case of my car, I may learn a painful lesson of the failure of testimony; I may come to know that the gaskets in my engine were not blown (and so did not need the repairs), but that the Jiffy Lube mechanic failed to tighten the oil filter properly. Everyday life bears witness to the limitations of testimony: the diagnoses of doctors and mechanics are unfortunately wrong on occasion, sometimes with disastrous or costly consequences. And, of course, the history of science shows that new knowledge replaces the conscientious work of thinkers and scientists from previous generations. This is not to suggest that one can know something false, but to emphasize the fact that what counts as knowledge is somehow vulnerable: when the mechanisms which produce knowledge are properly functioning, they may produce beliefs that are strongly warranted. However, the beliefs may lose their warrant upon the challenge of overriders and defeators. And this, of course, also applies to the beliefs that follow from the testimony of the saints.

As an externalist mechanism, the testimony of the saints should be viewed on a par with the testimony of 'eye witnesses', expert witnesses or experts in a specific field. Each has a specific knowledge, gained by quite specific patterns of experience (study, training, practice), and is thereby equipped to say something credible in certain contexts. The testimony of experts carries considerable merit or warrant – it is not indubitable, and it may be overturned in the face of new information, but it nonetheless is justified, at least on a *prima facie* basis. And we ought not to dismiss or minimize the value of such justification on account of its being 'merely' *prima facie*. *Prima facie* justification makes possible a whole host of decisions – intellectual and moral – allowing for movement, process and growth. In a courtroom trial the *prima facie* justification of claims made by an expert witness may be the impetus needed to break a deadlocked jury and move the trial to an efficacious end. Most of us, in fact, live our lives on the basis of *prima facie* justifications, not on apodictic proofs that yield undefeatable certainty. We gather evidence, assess data and make tentative claims which in turn are further justified or are overturned in the face of new data.

Similarly, the religious sage or adept is a particular kind of expert whose testimony, by virtue of his or her training and experience, is substantive, weighty and carries warrant. To categorically reject this on account of scientism or some latter-day positivism reveals an epistemological imperialism that flies in the face of lived experience, which includes any number of 'immaterial' events, such as time, consciousness and love. Moreover, such rejection would require creating *ex nihilo* whole hosts of 'knowledges' rather than building upon the scientific and philosophical contributions of others, a project that is both manifestly impractical and absurd. Instead, the testimony of the saints is *prima facie* justified and invites close scrutiny. Hence, there are epistemological implications to 'holiness', which should be construed as a certain kind of embodiment, a way of being, that itself is an outcome of training and experience. For example, a supremely skilled mechanic or surgeon moves effortlessly and confidently, first embodying his knowledge in action, then following it with verbal formulations in the form of diagnoses; these carry considerable weight – they are justified – precisely by virtue of that person's training and experience. Similarly, the sage, embodying his or her knowledge in action and skilfully offering it to others, bears witness to the coherence – and excellence – of his or her training and experience. His or her verbal formulations carry considerable weight; they are justified. In both cases, their testimony may be overturned, but not before the review of further evidence. To dismiss the testimony of the saints in an *a priori* manner asserts an imperialism that must in turn cancel itself out. The fact that there are conflicting verbal (metaphysical) claims of saints should be no more a worry than the conflicting testimony of 'worldly' experts. To adjudicate such claims, a careful assessment of all the data, including training and experience, is required. The conflicting metaphysical claims of saints can mean only that we need to examine them and consider their coherence at every level – intellectual, moral, empirical – and then make a decision, just as the jury must make a decision based on the witness of an expert skilled in a certain field.

Prima facie justification implies movement and examination. And it is precisely the role of philosophy of religion to facilitate this process. Movement and examination in turn imply a constructive role in philosophy of religion, one which builds on the knowledge of past thinkers, integrates new data into broader patterns of experience, and arrives at 'new' knowledge, or at least new claims that enjoy *prima facie* justification. In our case, the knowledge of thinkers includes the wisdom literature in the East and in the West, the testimony of saints and adepts and a current global reality in which the interpenetration of ideas and cultures – the delicate stretching our cultural matrices – is increasingly self-evident. Philosophy of religion, here stimulated by an important externalist mechanism, testimony, has the goal of increasing our knowledge, specifically the knowledge of reality in its most complete context. But to succeed in this, it must draw upon the epistemological services of both externalism and internalism.

Internalism proposes that individuals are equipped with the relevant mechanisms to arrive at justification and the account of knowledge. These mechanisms are internal to the subject, and the justifying factors in the account of knowledge are somehow directly and cognitively available to a subject. What is it that is 'internal'? Relevant beliefs, beliefs about perceptual states, and even the perceptual states themselves are likely candidates. All three, of course, have been implicated in our discussion of Advaita, and each supports a *prima facie* justification of the claims that follow Advaitin religious experience. Because internalism sometimes looks (introspectively) to the foundations of knowledge, it is sometimes associated with 'foundationalism', the theory that certain beliefs – 'basic' beliefs – require no justification. The problem here, of course, is determining what count as criteria for basic beliefs and how one accounts for moving from basic beliefs to more complex beliefs. For some, perceptual beliefs or perceptual states have been taken to be properly basic – that is, they require no further justification. This of course is Alston's strategy in *Perceiving God*. There is no non-circular way to justify beliefs which follow sensory experience without relating them to the sensory experience, or what he calls 'experiential presentation'. We take that person to be at least *prima facie* justified in holding to his or her perceptual belief. Similarly, according to Alston, there is no non-circular way to justify the beliefs which follow religious experience without referring to the experience itself. We may therefore take the subject to be at least *prima facie* justified in holding that belief.

While Alston obviously focused on Christian mystical perception, *anubhava*, in Advaita, is also a kind of mystical perception, cognitively available to everyone; indeed, according to Advaita, *anubhava* constitutes our deepest selves and the deepest truth of reality. Owing to a profoundly internalist methodology, the verbal claims following a saving experience may be *prima facie* justified. However, *anubhava* is also the outcome of externalist doxastic practices that include text, tradition and teacher. Whether gained, as in the case of Ramaṇa, by a strict process of introspection or by deeply patterned externalist practices, *anubhava* is a quite specific kind of experience – a self-guaranteeing event, coextensive with a knowing beyond knowledge. And such non-dual knowing is a kind of transcendent genius – it is a super-knowledge that is also a supra-knowledge – which ranges far beyond the scope of discursive reasoning.

Can we say anything about this knowing, other than that it seems, from this plane, to be impossible? I think we can. Because of the contributions of both internalism and externalism, which include the analysis of mundane experience, the verbal outcomes following a saving experience, the coherent intellectual and ethical practices 'surrounding' experience, and perhaps above all the testimony of saints and sages, we can say that the claim, 'There is a knowing beyond knowledge' *is prima facie* justified. And to say that it is *prima facie* justified indicates movement and invites examination. It moves us away from dogmatic or imperialistic *a priori* dismissals, and it moves us to careful study of the claims themselves. *Prima facie* justification thus becomes a stimulus to assess and to evaluate the methods and claims of religious knowing and, in so doing, incrementally increases the broadest scope of our knowledge.

We have applied internalist and externalist epistemologies as an heuristic to examine classical and modern Advaita thinkers and saints. I have argued that, owing to its metaphysic, internalism is the presumptive operating epistemological mechanism concerning 'religious' experience in Advaita. It is presumptive because internalism follows from Advaita's metaphysic, the privileged access it presupposes and its methods of introspection. This kind of internalism operates in all our Advaitin subjects: we are the Self and liberation is a matter of realizing who we are; this is done by turning within and discovering this truth, rather like someone, looking for a favourite necklace, discovers it around his or her neck. The Self is inward, immediate, self-established, self-evident and self-luminous. Given these axioms of Advaita, internalism offers the best interpretation of the epistemology of Advaitin religious experience; however, its strength, in the versions we studied, ranges from weak or modest (early Advaita) to strong (Ramaṇa Maharṣi). We should stress, however, that the internalism of Advaita is more concerned with 'truth' than with a formal theory of justification. It is the externalist dimension of Advaita that fulfils the latter function, for Advaita's repertoire of teachings, transmissions and normative practices all contribute to the 'appropriate causal ancestry' that issues in reliable beliefs.

Although the most relevant epistemological model for interpreting religious experience in these thinkers is internalism, we noted heavy doses of externalist constraints in our subjects, especially in Śaṅkara and Sureśvara. Śaṅkara helps to establish a dominant and essential culture of liberation, despite his arguments over the futility of action in the economy of liberation. And Sureśvara develops a sophisticated theory of exegesis which establishes the fundamental Advaitin method of proper reading, defining various intrepretative strategies which are used even today. 'Text, tradition and teacher' has been our alliterative shorthand to indicate a complex network of exegetical, ritual and institutional practices which work to transform the heart and mind of the candidate and prepare him for liberation. These external mechanisms are decisively indexed to the programme of liberation for our early Advaitin protagonists with concomitant social and theoretical implications.

Social implications

To begin with the theoretical implication. Observing the dynamic tension between internalism and externalism in Advaitin thinkers, especially vivid in our classical subjects, I will suggest the following: although in a given epistemological framework internalism may be dominant, it is in the end insufficient in itself. Put another way, no matter how relativized the external mechanisms may be, internalism cannot function without them. This assertion may be viewed as too strong, given my interpretation of Ramaṇa's soteriology; however, Ramaṇa himself benefited, at least in an inchoate way, from the social and religious context of Smārta Brahminism. There is no doubt that Ramaṇa privileges internalism in the programme of liberation, and that he appropriated traditional categories and defined (or relativized) them according to his experience. Nevertheless, he did accord provisional value to some doxastic practices, such as reading the *Gītā* and practising breath control; prophylactics such as these helped to calm one's mental chatter. Indeed, to conduce to this end, he encouraged public recitation of the Veda, a practice that is still maintained at Ramanāśramam. I would suggest then, noting the oscillation in Advaita internalism, that in religious epistemologies there is no (ultimately successful) internalism without externalism. However, to prove this as it applies to religion would require a broader empirical study of the epistemologies of religious experience in other religions. To prove this on a purely conceptual level would require first demonstrating the failure of a host of versions of internalism and externalism to explain adequately how we come to know; then, owing to these failures, demonstrate the success of the hybrid. John Pollock (1986) takes this approach in advocating his version of externalism, as does Plantinga in his own extended study (1993a, 1993b, 2000); Plantinga's *siddhānta*, so to speak, is a stronger form of externalism than either Pollock's or Alston's.

My aim here has been to use the categories of internalism and externalism as heuristics to understand the process of religious knowing in specific Indian soteriologies and, by extension, the process of religious knowing in general. Admittedly, generalizations are often dangerous, but the following seems indisputable: based on my study of Advaita, perhaps the closest thing to internalism one could hope to find, it is my contention that *all* religious programmes will involve both internal and external mechanisms for producing what counts as knowledge in the relevant traditions. An electric relationship thus exists between these models and one or the other may dominate, although still derive benefit or influence from the other. We observed in Chapter 1 that the 'bleeding of the boundaries' of internalism and externalism has been recognized by Western epistemologists, and Alston's position itself represents features from both theoretical frameworks (Fumerton, 1988; Alston, 1989; Swain, 1988). My contention here is that programmes of religious knowing cannot properly be understood without the theoretical services of both externalism and internalism.

A second observation can be made. When the dominant epistemology of religious experience is internalism, we can expect a universalist thrust in the religious movement. Conversely, when the externalist mechanisms are minimized and internalism is emphasized, one can expect a universalism in the particular religious movement. This partly explains the early success of Advaita in the West and the powerful inroads of various forms of Buddhism in American religiosity. Take, for example, Klaus Klostermaier's assessment of Advaita *sādhana*. Noting the manner in which Śaṅkara refashioned *saṃnyāsa* in terms of study and self-consciousness, rather than yoga, he writes, 'with its emphasis on introspection and unperturbed serenity of mind, it has created a prototype of universal appeal free from sectarian fervor and masochistic self-torture' (Klostermaier, 1989: 334). While this idealized assessment overlooks the polemical battles between camps of Vedānta as well as political struggles within the Daśanāmi *maṭhas*,[1] the potential for universalism is nevertheless strong in Advaita: however, I wish to suggest that it was not merely the rhetoric of Vedāntins that captivated the imagination of Westerners; it was also the appeal of an epistemological model that serves its fundamental metaphysic particularly well. This appeal, of course, is intuitive and non-analytical; few persons unschooled in philosophy are familiar with the term 'epistemology', let alone with the terms 'externalism' or 'internalism'. But the promise and programme of Advaita is compelling; to be constituted by liberation and to access that truth apparently by means of simple inwardness is a powerful draw to many persons disenfranchised by powerful religious institutions in the West which, for many, too often transmit oppressive rules as well as truth. The apparent simplicity of this programme is suggested by Sarah Grant, one of the great pioneers of interfaith dialogue in India; in her foreword to Abhiṣiktānanda's *Hindu–Christian Meeting Point* (1990) she writes:

> This Advaitic experience is first of all an experience of interiority ... It draws man back continually to what is most inward in himself, to the 'cave of the heart' as the upaniṣads call it, where God dwells, not as in a tabernacle, within and yet separated from man, but as the living source of his being, of his very 'I'. (Grant, 1990: viii)

And a contemporary Western guru in the lineage of Paramahaṁsa Yogānanda, Kriyānanda, has written, 'surely the answers lay *within* man, not in a continual search for happiness "somewhere else", or even "somewhere out there"' (Krīyānanda, 1973: 84). As we have seen, what is 'within' in Advaita is the one true real, the source of all consciousness and existence. John Grimes makes the same point as Krīyānanda but with a stronger theoretical analysis:

> Any approach to an 'other' concerns a search 'elsewhere' – and all the difficulties inherent in such a search. If the so-called incomprehensible absolute is grounded within each individual's own personal experience – not as an object, but self-luminously evident, not in a theoretical concept or abstract idea, but in fact – then the Absolute is an indubitable fact of everyone's experience and coincidentally eminently practical. (Grimes, 1992: 198)

This 'radical empiricism', as Grimes calls it, has a polemical conclusion. In a related article, he argues that 'a non-anthropomorphic absolute is more consistent and logical than a theistic deity and can be empirically anchored as well' (Grimes, 1990b: 337). This is a challenging position and is directly related to our work in this study. Once again, we see the overlapping boundaries of epistemology and metaphysics, as well as the constructive potential of philosophy of religion. This last concern develops around the issue of doctrinal claims that both fuel and follow the

---

1 For an account of some of these historical developments, see Cenkner (1983).

religious experience; the critical examination of doctrines is a necessary part of the process of determining the range of justification which claims enjoy. In addition to this analytical task, creative, constructive philosophical efforts build upon such justified claims, incrementally extending our knowledge of humanity in its most complete context. 'In its most complete context' of course implies metaphysics, and metaphysics, in some traditions, implies God, and, in others, an impersonal Absolute. Epistemology therefore envelops metaphysics, and metaphysics unfolds with epistemology; done in tandem, creatively and cautiously, they contribute to religious knowing. And if this knowing paradoxically involves a 'knowing beyond knowledge' or a rather specific 'knowledge of God', then it is the charge of the philosopher of religion to examine the doctrinal and experiential claims of such knowing and their range of epistemic merit. This is what I hope I have accomplished in this book.

I have specifically examined the process by which Advaitins arrive at a 'knowing beyond knowledge', paying close attention to the context, conditions and cognitive outcomes of religious experience. Grimes's words here are a clear expression of the Advaita position, and one can especially hear in them the echoes of Śaṅkara, Padmapāda, and, if we add slight nuances, Ramaṇa. Through an examination of experience *per se*, we discover the substrate of all individual conscious acts. This process is internal and self-justifying. Although Grimes overminimizes the externalist dimension in Advaita – especially *śruti* and guru – it is precisely because of the dominant internalism in Advaita that we can expect a universalism that comes across occasionally in a none-too-subtle fashion; upon returning from the 1993 Parliament of the World's Religions in Chicago, one enthusiastic presenter wrote: 'One reassures oneself that humankind is one, and that Vedāntic philosophy too will soon unite mankind' (Ganguly, 1995: 16). A less triumphant conclusion suggests that, given the metaphysical premise of Advaita and its internalism, we can expect a religious programme that translates particularly well across cultures. Since saving knowledge reveals self-established (and ubiquitous) consciousness, it is apparently spared the dilemma of being indexed to particular cultural manifestations – for example, Viṣṇu lying on his sofa in *paramapada*. Such 'highly ramified' accounts of the Supreme may be less credible to outsiders, although, given the epistemological process by which the subject arrives at such descriptions, they may nonetheless be justified (cf. Smart, 1962; Alston, 1991).

Before I consider one such 'highly ramified' account, let me say that Advaita is not alone in the universalism that follows from its presumptive internalism. The appeal of various popular representations of Buddhism in America can be at least partly explained by a dominant internalist epistemology of religious experience. There is, of course, no supreme Self to be discovered upon introspection: indeed, the absence of unanimity in our 'introspective turn' is perhaps the most serious flaw of internalism and is the first plank in the argument that builds toward a synthesis of the two epistemologies. In addition, it suggests the need to carefully examine the metaphysical doctrines that both fuel and follow the religious experience. In any case, according to certain popular representations of Buddhism, we come equipped with the mechanisms to observe our habits, addictions and dispositions; observing the mind, without engaging in defences or dramas, can lead to peace. The problem of such popular representations of Buddhism is that, while they do capture important elements of Buddhist theory and practice, they still oversimplify the context and culture of traditional Buddhist paths and therefore minimize the broader set of doxastic practices – the intellectual, ethical, meditative, and ritual elements of various Buddhisms – all of which, taken together, constitute an important externalist element in these traditions. In other words, these elements constitute belief-forming mechanisms that are coherent and consistent within the tradition itself; indeed, 'experience' tends to confirm the doctrine that is taught. And although early Buddhist debate worried over the relative importance of these socially established practices – especially when they suggested that *nirvāṇa* was somehow caused – these practices nevertheless feature in important ways in various forms of Buddhism and thus represent a significant contribution of externalism in Buddhist epistemologies of religious experience.

But, as some representations of Buddhism suggest, if the mind itself is the object of concentration, one can theoretically engage in a spiritual programme apparently pared of excessive cultural baggage; one can 'Be a lamp unto oneself', as a recent exhortation declared in an advertisement for audiotapes and books on Buddhist spirituality. A view such as this is easily seen in many of the popular and currently readily available contemporary books on Buddhist spirituality and endorses a private, isolated kind of do-it-yourself spirituality. Even highly trained and skilled teachers, such as Jack Kornfield (1995, 2001) and Pema Chodron (1997, 2001), seem to diminish the externalist dimension of Buddhist soteriology in their books, preferring radical honesty, openness and compassion in the present moment to arrive at peace.[2] Spiritual advice such as this is, of course, often helpful and praiseworthy: indeed, Kornfield's and Chodron's books show remarkable compassion. My point is that the internalism which they assume reveals a universalism as well.

The reverse seems to be true for traditions that might be interpreted as primarily externalist in producing knowledge. Here one might say that traditions such as Shinto or shamanism are less universalist in their appeal not just because of an absence of a sweeping global principle but because their epistemologies of religious experience rely more heavily on external mechanisms, particularly various forms of ritual, for producing knowledge. And these external mechanisms are local, particular and culture-bound. This is not to say that persons cannot penetrate these traditions and acculturate to them, but it is to say that traditions such as these do not

2 Both were trained in traditional Buddhist methods. Chodron was trained by Chogyam Trungpa, the abbess of Gampo Abbey in Nova Scotia, and makes extensive use of Tibetan Buddhist categories to analyse emotional states. Yet, none of this appears as *sine qua non*; what is necessary is to observe the mind.

migrate well, although one does occasionally note workshops on shamanism and 'psychic navigation' in New Age Centres in large metropolitan areas. It might be a good idea to carry out empirical study to determine and compare the number of Buddhist meditation centres, self-help groups, and study centres with the number and availability of shamanism workshops. It is my suggestion that Buddhism partly owes its growing appeal in North America and Europe not only to its universalist metaphysic, but to a dominant internalist epistemology of religious experience – at least one that has been represented on a popular level; the inward, introspective turn that popular Buddhism represents accords well with Enlightenment epistemological sensibilities.

This is not the place to engage in an extended discussion of the many kinds of Buddhism already available in America, their varied histories and philosophies, and all the reasons behind their increasing popularity among North Americans. Some writers have already made inroads into this kind of study, perhaps the most fascinating being that of Rick Fields (1992) and Charles Prebish (1979). My suggestion is that it is not only various universalist principles ('all is suffering', 'we are all Buddhas') that account for its appeal but also the internalist mechanism of accessing the saving experience, especially as it has been represented by Western teachers.

The problem of internalism, however, shows itself in the case of Advaita and Buddhism. What we discover when we go 'within' is not entirely obvious; there is a world of difference between the substantial, immutable, one, true Self and the doctrine of the emptiness that is central to most versions of Buddhism. Indeed, the notion of Self, according to early Buddhism, was the determinate cause of desire, which in turn is the primary cause of suffering. 'Cessation of desire' is one gloss of *nirvāṇa*, as is emptiness itself. But, as John Fenton (1981) has shown, *pace* the perennial philosophy, the wisdoms which Śaṅkara and Nāgārjuna intend, despite their use of similar apophatic language, are not the same. The failure of 'pure internalism' to deliver an incontrovertible metaphysical verdict suggests the need for external mechanisms of religious knowing in the programme of salvation. When these external mechanisms involve doctrine, as they surely will, part of the process of checks and balances will be the evaluation of doctrinal claims that both inform and follow the religious experience. This suggests a critical role for the philosophy of religion. Let me use the traditions of Vedānta to explore further the implications of religious epistemologies.

We have already seen that the dominant internalism of Advaita suggests the possibility of a universalist programme – a programme which has been borne out in practice in the twentieth century, with many ashrams springing up in America more or less loosely based on Advaitic principles. These include the Vedānta centres established by the Ramakrishna Mission, the Vedānta centres in New York and San Francisco based on the teaching of Brahmānanda Sarasvati (Dr Ramamurthy Mishra), Yoga centres based on the teachings of Śivānanda, the ashrams of Dayānanda, and Advaita retreat centres in North Carolina and California based on the teaching of Ramaṇa Maharṣi. But a competing form of Vedānta is worth looking at. Rāmānuja's Viśiṣṭādvaita is a far more localized and conservative project. There are no Viśiṣṭādvaita ashrams in America or Europe and, while there are important swamis, gurus and *ācāryas* representing this lineage in India, only one, Swami Nārāyaṇa Jeer, toured briefly in America in 1995.

There are many reasons for the dominance of Advaita over Viśiṣṭādvaita in American understanding of things Indian, including the early appropriation of Advaita by European Romantics and American Transcendentalists and an aggressive marketing of Advaita as the premier version of Indian spirituality by twentieth-century Indian apologists. In addition to these reasons, however, one must include the implications of Advaita's epistemology of religious experience. As suggested above, Advaita's presumptive internalism allows for a greater, universal appeal. Rāmānuja's operating epistemology relies more heavily on externalism, and therefore Viśiṣṭādvaita is more decisively indexed to its culture. This does not mean that persons from non-Indian cultures cannot penetrate that tradition in an affective, spiritual manner. Indeed, Francis Clooney's important book, *Seeing Through Texts* (1996), illustrates such an empathetic engagement with the religious poetry of Nammaḷvār and later Śrīvaiṣṇava theologians. Nor does it mean to imply that Viśiṣṭādvaita has no purchase on truth. It merely suggests that Viśiṣṭādvaita does not migrate well as a universalist movement. The reason for this, I suggest, is a heavier externalist dimension in its religious epistemology.

How and what we know in Rāmānuja's soteriology

Noting the attention Rāmānuja gives to the cosmogonies of the Viṣṇu Purāṇa, Sarvepalli Radhakrishnan, who was otherwise a sympathetic supporter of Rāmānuja, once lamented that 'Rāmānuja's beautiful stories of the other world, which he narrates with the confidence of one who had personally assisted at the origination of the world, carry no conviction' (Radhakrishnan, 1989: 720). Although Radhakrishnan's distress is perhaps understandable – we will see rather vivid descriptions of the divine and the divine realm shortly – it reveals a severe underestimation of the mechanism for generating 'religious' knowledge for Rāmānuja: scripture. As van Buitenen correctly observes, if Rāmānuja 'ever indulges in wondrous stories, he is forced to do so by his texts. This is exactly the point: he takes texts seriously' (van Buitenen, 1956: 36).

This tradition is highly shaped by a rather literal approach to scripture. Here we have a primary mechanism for generating knowledge, *śruti*, the approach to which must be to recognize the authority of all texts, and not to privilege a select few, as Śaṅkara does in his analysis of the upaniṣads. Rāmānuja severely criticizes Śaṅkara for arbitrarily establishing a twofold hermeneutic: first, according to Rāmānuja, Śaṅkara inappropriately privileges certain Vedānta texts – the relatively few *mahāvākyas* that establish the *paramārthajñāna* – while at the same time devaluing the greater number of texts which describe the absolute in anthropomorphic terms and so illustrate the *vyavahārika* (ibid.: 57; de Smet, 1954). All scriptural texts, according to Rāmānuja, are equally authoritative, and it is incumbent on the preceptor to reconcile apparently conflicting *śruti*. Rāmānuja does this in the *Vedārthasaṅgraha* which, in some ways, is an unusual text, since its structure does not follow the traditional pattern of upaniṣadic commentary. Rather than compose a verse-by-verse commentary, Rāmānuja attempts to represent a total vision of the upaniṣads, discussing controversial texts in a relevant, coherent manner (Raghavachar, 1978: i). He does this by analysing texts according to the Viśiṣṭādavaita metaphysic: '*bheda*' passages indicate the real differences between *cit*, *acit*, and *īsvara*; '*ghataka*' passages (so-called mediating texts) affirm Brahman as the inner self of all, the *antaryāmin*; and '*abheda*' texts affirm the unity of the world with Brahman. All texts, then, have equal value and, moreover, none is divested of its primary significance.

Rāmānuja's estimate of upaniṣadic texts is a direct response to and an indirect criticism of Śaṅkara's use of *lakṣaṇā*, 'implication'. According to Rāmānuja, this is the second serious flaw in Śaṅkara's method of interpretation, for it is all too arbitrary. Van Buitenen notes that Śaṅkara's references to *lakṣanā* are discreet and, in some cases, must themselves be implied, and Halbfass observes that Śaṅkara's references to *anvayavyatireka* are less common and obvious than those of Sureśvara (van Buitenen 1956: 57; Halbfass, 1983: 56). Indeed, we saw that Sureśvara's extended discussion of exegesis constituted one of Sureśvara's important contributions to Advaita.

Although Śaṅkara does not unpack these hermeneutical terms as precisely as Sureśvara, he is clear concerning his approach to texts: the exegete is justified in some cases to appeal to a secondary use of scriptural terms. The most famous example of this of course is the *mahāvākya*, '*tat tvam asi*'. The use of *lakṣaṇā* and/or *anvayavyatireka* allows for the common-sense rejection of individual corporal–mental units as the Supreme Brahman. This method removes what is incompatible between the two terms, affirming the relevant continuity that obtains between them, namely consciousness. However, using another grammatical term, *sāmānādhikaraṇya* (coordinate predication), Rāmānuja argues that the identity of a subject should not be established by the rejection of the primary and natural significance of coordinate terms. The identical import of terms in their usual signification should be always be sustained, otherwise the danger of caprice follows. Applied to the *mahāvākya*, one unity, Brahman, is affirmed, with the Self as his body. Thus, the natural identity of 'that' and 'you' is upheld: 'you (*tvam*)' signifies Brahman (*tat*) – in other words, Brahman = Brahman. The two terms, *tat* and *tvam*, refer to the same reality, just as, in the stock example, 'blue lotus' represents two terms that refer to the same entity. According to Rāmānuja, Brahman is indicated in the *mahāvākya* as the Supreme Reality (*para Brahman, tat*) and as the Supreme Indweller (*antaryāmin*, *tvam*) of the individual soul. The soul, then, is both substantially and accidentally divine. It is real, sharing the same essential nature of Viṣṇu, knowledge, but in a relevant sense different from the divine; while sharing the same nature as the Supreme, it nevertheless exists in a dependent relationship with it. The soul in some sense is an attribute or mode of the divine and, with the entire insentient universe, constitutes the body of God.

One can see the implications of this theory of scripture and one hears echoes in some fundamentalist Bible classes: scripture means what it says and says what it means. Applied to Rāmānuja, this means that a rather amazing content of the divine is revealed through *śruti*, and the whole of this is wrapped in a faith and confidence in the vision of scripture: 'Even as the supreme Person is eternal, the system of words embodying the knowledge concerning him, his worship and the fruits accruing therefrom, is eternal' (Raghavachar 1978: 180). Before we even commence the following examination of the cognitive content that accrues from an experience shaped by scripture, a fundamentally external mechanism for producing knowledge, we can see potential problems looming: different scriptures, different experiences, different knowledges.

We see that Rāmānuja has rather decisive things to say about the nature of God and what one might expect when one encounters him in love. Far from Advaita *arūpatva* of Brahman, Nārāyaṇa possesses the most auspicious and sublime form, 'at once worthy and pleasing to him' (ibid.: 176). Those devotees, purified by devotion and ritual practices, may indeed perceive the divine form:

> His luster is that of a fine mountain of molten gold. He has the splendor of a hundred thousand suns. His pure eyes have the beauty of the petals of a lotus .... His brows and forehead and nose are charming. His coral-like lips radiate a pure smile. His cheeks are tender and radiant. His neck is lovely like a conch. His exquisitely tender ear-lobes are almost touching his high shoulders .... (Ibid.: 172–73)

Such a graphic description of God may strike some Westerners, who are far removed from the cultural edifices that support it, as bizarre. Rāmānuja even extends his account, adding descriptions not only of the beautiful form of Nārāyaṇa, but of his auspicious ornaments as well, including the *kuṇḍala*, *kaustabha*, conch, discus, mace and sword. The key element to note, however, is not the reader's reaction to such descriptions, but the epistemological process by which Rāmānuja arrived at them. That Nārāyaṇa has such a form is true, because *śruti* and *smṛti* affirm it as such. But Ramaṇa Maharṣi once made an oblique reference to Viśiṣṭādvaita in criticizing such supersensuous visions, for they all, in the end, betray the truth of the non-dual real:

> What is realization? Is it to see God with four hands, bearing a conch, a wheel, club, etc.? Even if God should appear in that form, how is the disciple's ignorance wiped out? The truth must be eternal realization. The direct perception is ever-present Experience. God Himself is known when He is directly perceived. It does not mean that He appears before the devotee in some particular form. Unless the Realization is eternal it cannot serve any useful

> purpose. Can the appearance with four hands be eternal realization? It is phenomenal and illusory. There must be a seer. The seer alone is real and eternal. (Venkataramiah, 1994: 442)

Two issues emerge from these passages, one which adverts to externalism, the other to internalism. On the one hand, we see Rāmānuja's absolute dependence on scripture for shaping his concept of God. At the same time, we see the mutual reinforcing of his *viśiṣṭādvaita* metaphysic and hermeneutic, for the same *śruti*, of course, has quite a different purport according to Śaṅkara (not to mention Madhva and other *dvaitavādins*). This mutually reinforcing pattern of belief formation – doctrine and scripture – constitutes external doxastic practices with their own sets of checks and balances: a linguistic theory that supports the metaphysic, exegetical, ritual, meditative practices and so on. These external mechanisms, coherent and organized, are indexed to their cultural context and in some sense contingent. But what about an uncontingent experience, a direct perception of the divine that nullifies all temporary designations? Such immediate awareness (*sākṣātkāra*) is central to the internalism of the various Advaitin masters we have studied; but 'direct perception' or immediacy is a pivotal epistemic moment for Rāmānuja as well, one which, far from delivering a knowing beyond knowledge, instead decisively yields knowledge of God.

Such knowledge begins with scripture, an external medium, sets of timeless verbal formulas that reveal the insight and vision of ancient seers. As transmitted in the lineage of Rāmānuja, the *śruti*'s purport indicates a divine that is at once the inner dweller of all individual souls as well as the supreme Brahman with form. In an important sense, Brahman can be perceived by those of purified faculties. In the *Vedārthasaṅgraha*, he again quotes, approvingly, of an earlier Viśiṣṭādvaitin theologian, Dramiḍācārya, called the Bhāṣyakāra:

> The Bhāṣyakāra (Dramiḍācārya) comments as follows: 'Inherent and natural is the form of the creator. But it is not perceptible to the eye. It is perceptible only to the purified mind, equipped with other spiritual means. The Vedic text lays down, "He is not apprehended through the eye. He is not within the reach of speech. But he is apprehended through a pure mind".' (MuU 3.8)

In a sense, such divine perception is also admitted, but only in a provisional way, by Ramaṇa Maharṣi. A disciple once asked, 'Do we not see God in concrete form?' Ramaṇa answered, 'Yes', but with an immediate qualification: 'The form and appearance of God-manifestation are determined by the mind of the devotee. But it is not the finality. There is a sense of duality' (Venkataramiah, 1994: 207).

But an objection very similar to this was raised by Rāmānuja in his *Vedārthasaṅgraha*. Here, he comments on the words of another earlier theologian, Taṅka, who apparently wrote a commentary on the Brahma Sūtra (no longer extant). Concerning the *śruti* text, 'The Puruṣa of the golden form is seen', the *pūrvapakṣa* might conclude that 'the form (of God) may be artificial, being assumed to favor the individual self, as it is possible for the omnipotent Lord to assume such forms' (ibid.: 174). This suggests an awareness on the part of Rāmānuja of a competing theory of divinity, one which admits that how we 'see' or understand God depends on the perspective of the devotee. And, naturally, 'perspective' is shaped by all sorts of intellectual and cultural supports. Were he to accept this position, Rāmānuja might actually represent the 'perennial philosophy' far earlier than Aldous Huxley and Huston Smith! For such a position actually moves the theory of divine perception into a universalist mode: there is indeed one, ultimately imperceptible divine, which manifests itself according to the conceptual and cultural predilections of the disciple. But Rāmānuja would have none of this. Again, quoting Taṅka, he insists: 'But His form is real and supersensuous, because śrutis state that it is perceptible to the inner eye' (ibid.). There is a 'look', it seems, to God. The phenomenal content of this look is real and is corroborated by scripture.

So what do we have here? Clearly we have the possibility of perceiving God in this tradition. But to 'see' God in Rāmānuja's theology requires abundant cognitive, conative, and affective training. The cognitive input includes a notional understanding of God as creator, sustainer, a being somehow both transcendent and immanent to the physical universe. In Rāmānuja's tradition, the supreme Brahman is the inner soul of sentient and insentient universe. Notional understanding is transmitted through external doxastic mechanisms – in this case, primarily through scripture but also through a vast array of cultural programmes such as teaching, ritual, pilgrimage, myth and so on. These formative mechanisms also include the Nālāyira Tiviya Pirapantam, the 'Sacred Collect' of songs by the *āḻvārs* – saints whose experience of God poured forth in poetic and spiritual inspiration. For Śrīvaiṣṇavas, the Tiviya Pirapantam attained sacrosanct status as Tamil canon; indeed, they regard the four works of Nammāḻvār, often considered the most important *āḻvār*, as the 'Tamil Veda'. Vasudha Narayanan has skilfully articulated parallels between the Sanskrit *śruti* and Nammāḻvār's most famous work, the *Tiruvāymoḻi*, and the rhetoric used by Śrīvaiṣṇava theologians to establish the Tamil songs as authoritative canon (Narayanan, 1994: ch. 2). What is important for our purposes is to recognize the epistemic and cultural implications here; by establishing a Tamil canon Śrīvaiṣṇavism at once creates powerful sets of doxastic mechanisms while indexing itself to a local culture. However beautiful Tamil is, it remains primarily a regional language; Sanskrit, after all, is a pan-Indian language. Note, for example, the presumed universalism in the words of the Śaṅkarācarya of Dwaraka: 'Sanskrit is India and India is Sanskrit' (Cenkner, 1983: 129). There are, of course, important ideological overtones to 'Sanskritization' which invite fruitful investigation. Here, however, I wish to highlight the empirical observation that Sanskrit has been represented as a linguistic medium that transcends culture and regional specifications. Indeed, Friedhelm Hardy has argued that while Tamil *bhakti* was probably a source for other *bhakti* movements in India, its emotionalism was transmitted, in Sanskrit, through the Bhāgavata Purāṇa (Hardy, 1983).

The songs of the Tamil saints express their sacred experience, often with themes of ecstatic union, separation, anguish and joyful reunion. Their experience, poured forth in sacred song, is considered paradigmatic *bhakti* – a model and ideal for the community of Śrīvaiṣṇavas. And while the saints expressed their *anubhava* in song, later commentators expressed their own 'spiritual experience' or 'enjoyment' as they studied and commented on the songs; hence the commentaries are sometimes called *anubhavagrantha* (Venkatachari, 1978: 94). So, here we have an ideal experience of the saints, their expression of it in sacred song, and the exegetical reflection on their 'songs of experience' all of which represent, in Śrīvaiṣṇavism, external mechanisms which, when interiorized, conduce to the salutary religious experience of the laity. Clooney, Carman and Narayanan have analysed some of these songs as well as the comments on them by Śrīvaiṣṇava theologians (Clooney, 1996; Carman and Narayanan, 1989; Narayanan, 1994). Indeed, Narayanan's study of communal recitation suggests a 'transitive' opportunity for attaining the vision of God: by participating in the public recitation of the songs of Nammāḻvār, the community too may 'see' God (Narayanan, 1994: 133, 145). Clooney has also illustrated the formative process of reading texts and commentaries on Nammāḻvār's songs in the Śrīvaiṣṇava tradition, an integrated process which shapes the subjectivity of members of the community. All these doxastic practices – poetic, textual, exegetical and ritual – inform the mind; they propose a way of understanding, and permit access to, the divine. But they are decisively externalist mechanisms. And, in this tradition, God, it seems, allows himself to be rendered as a 'content', something to be understood, to be known, to be seen. But such 'knowledge of God' appears to be tentative, elusive, even in a great saint such as Nammāḻvār:

> Now I understand him. Do I understand him? The one whom I understand is beyond understanding. No one can comprehend his nature: Is it this? Is it that? When we are on the verge of understanding him he goes beyond our vision and remains the incomprehensible one. (TVM 8.8.5) (Kaylor and Venkatachari, 1981: 18)

But to hope to 'see' God, mental content must not only be informed by the doctrine of the tradition; it must also be informed by love. The inner faculty – call it mind or heart – must be informed by love. As R.D. Kaylor and K.K.A. Venkatachari note in their study of the *Tiruvāymoḻi*, the very first stanza of Nammāḻvār's poem 'makes clear his view that apart from an attitude of reverence and worship one cannot even begin to comprehend God' (ibid.). Nammāḻvār addresses his mind and exhorts it to surrender to God:

> O my mind! to him who is supreme, to him who contains within himself all that is, to him who gives pure knowledge without confusion, to him who is the Lord of the ever-wakeful devas, to him who is the remover of all miseries, bow down and offer your worship. (TVM 1.1.1) (Ibid.)

To perceive God in this tradition presumes a profound cultivation of heart and mind. This cultivation is completely transformative and affects all dimensions of the human person, including cognitive, affective and conative dimensions. This comprehensive existential stance is called *bhakti* and holds pride of place in Rāmānuja's soteriology. The promise of *bhakti* is a direct perception of the divine, *sākṣātkāra*. *Bhakti* reveals the dominant externalism of Rāmānuja's method of religious knowing, although it is complemented by a critical internal dimension.

Bhakti *in Rāmānuja*

In the *Śrībhāṣya*, Rāmānuja expends considerable energy arguing that *bhakti* is the direct means of salvation. But while *bhakti* involves the affect here, the way in which Rāmānuja uses the term in its technical sense hardly suggests the emotionalism of the *ālvārs*. Instead, *bhakti* indicates a careful training of the intellect and the will in addition to affective cultivation. In this, Rāmānuja follows his predecessor, Yamuna, whose *Gītārthasaṁgraha* establishes the foundation on which Rāmānuja builds his theory of salvation. Yamuna writes:

> It is the doctrine expounded by the Bhagavadgītā that Nārāyaṇa, who is the Supreme Brahman, can only be attained by means of bhakti, which is brought about by observance of one's dharma, the acquisition of knowledge and the renunciation of passion.[3]

Notice that *bhakti* here is a kind of state that is 'brought about'. It is generated by very important intellectual, cultural and moral supports which in turn constitute sets of significant belief-forming mechanisms, doxastic practices, which shape the subjectivity of the *bhakta* and his religious experience. However, this subjectivity is best characterized as 'being in relationship' with the divine, for the divine is 'other' and the method to access it is, in a significant way, externalist. For example, the intellectual support, *jñāna*, represents both the elementary content of the Vedānta tradition (we are not constituted by materiality, we have a soul, there is a supreme Brahman, ignorance and demerit trap the soul in cycles of birth and so on) and the more specific content of Viśiṣṭādvaita (the soul is both constituted by and possesses knowledge, the individual souls and the insentient universe constitute the body of God, God is the inner soul of all souls and so on). The cultural supports include the *varnāśrama* dharma: note the use of the term '*svadharma*' in footnote 3; *svadharma*, as the *Gītā* makes abundantly clear, is no universal ethical principle, but 'duty' carefully delimited by caste and stage of life. Rāmānuja himself is quite clear on the importance of the *varnāśrama* system, as his emphasis on eligibility indicates

3 *svadharmajñānavairāysādhyabhaktyekagocaraḥ / nārāyanaḥ paraṁ brahma gītāsāstre samīritaḥ* (*Gītārthasaṁgraha* 1; reprinted in van Buitenen, 1968: 177).

in ŚB 1.1.1 and his comments elsewhere show as well (for example, ŚB 3.3.39). These external cultural supports, mandated by scripture, are crucial in developing the culture of *bhakti* because they create the context in which the *mumukṣu* begins his process of transformation. Finally, the moral and ritual supports include the cultivation of specific virtues and religious practices. Rāmānuja lists 15 ethical and devotional practices that all contribute to shaping the subjectivity of the *bhakta*. These serve, in his programme, to eradicate the effects of ignorance and sin and prepare the mind and heart for higher stages of *bhakti*.

So *bhakti* represents a kind of energy that engages the heart, mind and will – a comprehensive existential stance which recalls Paul Tillich's contemporary analysis of faith. It implicates a more 'holistic' knowing, one that accesses the full range of human resources, including, or perhaps especially, love. It recalls the Christian scholastic tradition which made intimate associations between love and knowledge, and certainly the cognitive dimension of love (that is, emotion) has been effectively demonstrated by Proudfoot (1985) and Macquarrie (1992). Indeed, Rāmānuja makes clear that the highest form of *bhakti*, *para bhakti*, is a 'particular kind of knowledge' (*parabhaktirūpajñānaviśesa*). This particular cognitive state, what might be called an 'affective knowing', is preceded by 'lower forms' of *bhakti* which include ritual acts and the fundamental knowledge of the Vedānta.

Rāmānuja is careful to distinguish what precisely he means by saving knowledge. Knowledge is not mere sentential understanding of *śruti*, although such understanding is the intellectual support and antecedent of saving knowledge. However, because of the cumulative effects of congenital ignorance, the Vedānta texts aim at inculcating a knowledge other than the 'mere knowledge' of the meaning of sentences. 'Real' knowledge, so to speak, is *upāsana*, meditation, and Rāmānuja establishes *nididhyāsana* as what he precisely means by meditation. Liberating knowledge is the nature of meditation, and meditation 'has the form of constant recollection, unbroken like the flow of oil'.[4] This theme is repeated in the *Vedārthasaṅgraha*: 'by the term *vidyā* is meant meditation that has developed into *bhakti*.' So we see an increasing identification of terms: *vidyā–nididhyāsana–upāsana–bhakti*. But this affective knowing, employing both the mind and the heart, is by no means a mere intellectual construct: 'Only meditation of the form of *bhakti* leads to the attainment of Brahman and the efficacy of mere meditation is denied by the phrase, "not by the exercise of intelligence"' (Raghavachar, 1978: 101). It is not a strictly intellectual kind of knowing, nor is it 'mere' feeling; it is a knowing which is informed by textual, doctrinal, cultural and affective supports.

Such knowing both informs, and is informed by, particular kinds of religious experience, which here must be inclusive of an entire pattern of life for the *bhakta*. In short, the *bhakta* allows for a refashioning of heart and mind according to the socially established doxastic practices of Śrīvaiṣṇava culture. *Bhakti*, as shaped by

[4] ... *dhyānaṁ ca tailadhārāvat avacinnasmṛtisantāna rūpam* (ŚB: 56).

these cognitive inputs, is clearly a 'particular kind of knowledge'. Moreover, it is valued for its own sake (because its object is of maximal value), and it seems to stimulate the grace of God: 'The supreme Person, who is overflowing with compassion, being pleased with such love, showers his grace on the aspirant, which destroys all his inner darkness' (ibid.: 98). Indeed, the inherent value of *bhakti* is clear: such a state, according to Rāmānuja, 'is an absolute delight in itself; [it is a state] in which meditation has taken on the character of the most vivid and immediate presentation'. We note that a necessary condition for such presentation is *smṛti*, recollection or memory.

Memory, of course, is a mental faculty that both shapes, and is shaped by, experience. Memory is shaped *by* experience in the sense that experience – here inclusive of one's environment and personality – establishes the conditions that make a particular event memorable. Memories are created out of the experience of the subject, and this includes the entire cognitive and affective package of the subject. The subject brings herself to an event – her disposition, temperament, conceptual reflections, habits, tendencies, physical state and so on – but the remembered event in turn continues to shape the personality of the subject. This is perhaps most obvious in cases of personal trauma, but is also readily apparent in 'good' memories, special moments of resolution, healing and peace. In either case, a disposition to view the world or other persons in a certain way may either be created or reinforced. That memory continues to shape a person's subjectivity is fundamental to contemporary psychology – a fact long recognized in Indian psychology as well.

But memory in many Indian traditions, both *āstika* and *nāstika*, is a major problem; shaped by 'subliminal activators', it creates kinds of identifications and projections that ensnare the individual more tightly in the net of *samsāra*. It is precisely the goal of classical yoga to wear away, through focused concentration, the residual effects of memory and so gain a transparent awareness of pure consciousness. But Rāmānuja, while recognizing the negative intellectual and psychological effects of *vāsanas*, nevertheless holds for a particularly efficacious kind of memory or recollection, although, as Clooney notes, he does not elaborate much on his comments (Clooney, 1996: 129). Nevertheless, Rāmānuja makes an intriguing claim: 'That recollection has the same character as seeing'[5] and, by way of explanation, 'recollection has the character of seeing due to the intensity of mental conception'.[6] 'Intensity of mental conception' of course is the same energy that allows for yogic perception; what privileges *upāsana* over the *pratyakṣa* of the yogi is the object of concentration. The object of *upāsana* is the most real, sublime, beautiful Nārāyaṇa, who deigns to be accessed, physically (*ārcā*) and mentally

5 ... *sa ca smṛtir darśanasamānākara* (ŚB: 56).

6 ... *bhavati ca smṛteh bhāvanāprakarśāt darśanarūpatā* (ŚB: 59). The conjuction *ca* has an emphatic force – for example, 'it is indeed the case'. M. Narasimhachari takes it as Rāmānuja speaking of himself (personal conversation).

(*sākṣātkāra*). Concerning the latter, among the many 'descents' (*avatar*) of God, one might include the descent of divine 'content'. God is a real being, who allows itself to be perceived, seen and even apprehended conceptually, as it were; crucial to this knowing is a motivated appropriation of texts and increasing internal clarification. This 'divine emptying' at once suggests the monumental humility of God and an utterly optimistic appraisal of the human powers of understanding.

Through sustained recollection and the intensity of mental conception, initiated by a culture of virtues and especially training in scripture, we are able to grasp God, understand God, love God. Indeed, we may even see God. Elsewhere Rāmānuja explains, 'having the character of seeing means having the character of direct perception'. So 'recollection', according to Rāmānuja, is exalted to *darśana*, 'seeing' or 'perception', and the character of perception means obtaining the state of immediate presentation (*pratyakṣatāpattiḥ*). But the very givenness of this experience and its social context return us to the work of William Alston and the importance of a constructive role for the philosophy of religion.

Conclusions

The discussion of Rāmānuja's mystical perception is appropriate, since an important part of Alston's project demonstrated the structural continuities between sense perception and mystical perception. This is not to say that the frequency of mystical perception or the number of persons who experience it is identical with that of sense perception, but it is to say that there are structural similarities, the most significant of which is that something is 'given' or presented to consciousness. A critic might reply that whatever is given may be a mere hallucination or a dream, but we recall that Alston worked at great length to debunk a kind of epistemic imperialism: the refusal to accept the claim 'God is loving me now' as justified on the basis of religious experience. The grounds for refusal is the circular nature of the justification. In a 'here's-mud-in-your-eye' strategic rejoinder, Alston argued that the rejection of the claims that follow sense perception could be argued for the same reason as the rejection of mystical beliefs: there is no non-circular way to justify the belief 'I see an oak tree' except on the basis of sense presentation. Instead, we accept the claim on the basis of sense presentation and require no further justification. The claim is justified, at least until further notice. If, on closer inspection, we discover that the tree is not an oak but an elm, we are willing to discount what was formerly held to be knowledge in the face of new information, and sometimes this information is itself based on new, or closer, or more detailed presentations.

Similarly, argues Alston, the claims that follow religious experience are based on mystical presentation; since, as in sense presentation, there is no non-circular way to justify the claims that follow religious experience, these claims are also justified, at least until further notice. They are granted *prima facie* justification. This is no small victory and signals movement and examination, a genuine call for critical, constructive work in the philosophy of religion. But to grant even this tentative epistemic victory, we recall that a number of limiting conditions must first be in place, including self-support and external checks.

Not all claims based on religious experience are justified, according to Alston. These must emerge out of coherent doxastic practices, with considerable self-support, and internal and external checks as well as an absence of overriders and defeators. And, even so, the claim is awarded only *prima facie* justification. Notice the number of limitations embedded in this process. First, we see Alston's externalism: a certain kind of perception emerges from doxastic practices. These are limited to cultural patterns of learning and practice with their own coherent checks and balances, which in turn ensure that the subjectivity of the experiencer is normatively informed by intellectual and affective cultivation. This suggests, for example, that absent these conditions, the claims following certain experiences are not justified. For example, a soldier suffering from post-traumatic shock who says he has seen Jesus may well have seen Jesus, but his claim to that effect is not justified. But the claim of a monk, long accustomed to prayer and silence, to feel and know the presence of Christ may be justified.

Applying this to Viśiṣṭādvaita, we recall that the premier doxastic practice for Rāmānuja is the study and recitation of the Veda, but this practice itself is set in a context that includes considerable ritual and moral expectations; additionally, Śrīvaiṣṇavism includes the singing of the sacred songs of the *āḻvārs* as critical formative mechanisms as well. The two streams of Vedānta, the Sanskrit and Tamil traditions, together constitute a powerful doxastic mechanism with considerable self-support. 'Self-support' suggests a reinforcing process; in addition, it suggests that practices and teachings not sanctioned by the *ubhāya vedānta* tradition are rejected. We see here that one's vision is being fundamentally shaped by the same kinds of mechanisms that we reviewed in Advaita: text, tradition and teaching.

There are two points that I wish to make about this in reference to Viśiṣṭādvaita, one cultural and one epistemic. We will see that these points are related to one another by Viśiṣṭādvaita's primary metaphysic and externalist epistemology of religious experience. While there is a critical internal element to religious knowing in Viśiṣṭādvaita – as there must be, I think, in all soteriological systems – the causal epistemological processes that inform religious experience and justify its claims are more heavily externalist in Viśiṣṭādvaita than in Advaita. It is for this reason that I claimed earlier that Viśiṣṭādvaita succeeds less well as a *universalist* movement. This is not to disparage any of the poetic or intellectual treasures of Viśiṣṭādvaita; in many ways, its poetry is unparalleled and its philosophy is profound. However, its externalist epistemology of religious experience renders it local and less universalist; this tradition is decisively indexed to Tamil culture and does not migrate well as a universalist movement. This explains, in part, why few Westerners who are not scholars are drawn to it as part of their 'spiritual quest' as so many have been drawn to Advaita. Viśiṣṭādvaita also relies more heavily on external causal processes – the entire constellation of Vaiṣṇava *sādhana*, including all intellectual, affective, and conative training implied by *bhakti* – to 'create a memory': that is, to establish Vaiṣṇava conditions which make Vaiṣṇava religious experience possible. This 'memory' in turn 'funds' or shapes subsequent religious experience. The conditions for such 'memory' and the 'memory' itself are, of course, conceptually loaded, informed by *śruti* and songs, doctrine and exegesis, passion and emotion. These last two, which indicate the will and the heart, seem to be an 'odd couple' in a series identifying 'conceptually loaded' instruments, but we recall that both emotion and will are 'conceptual' in the sense of needing to pick out the feeling or the focus of will and to identify its source. All these formative mechanisms conduce to a particular kind of religious experience in Śrīvaiṣṇavism. And so it is no surprise, given these mechanisms and Viśiṣṭādvaita's primary metaphysic, that Rāmānuja's theology is boldly cataphatic. But the processes to create a memory and to draw from that memory in faith and devotion are self-referential and mutually reinforcing; and in the end these processes establish a framework for normative religious experience for the Śrīvaiṣṇava community.

But these processes do not appear to have an 'escape clause', as it were; they are not relativized in Viśiṣṭādvaita as they are in Advaita, and therefore Viśiṣṭādvaita has difficulty extending its scope beyond Tamil culture[7] – not that this is of any concern to most Śrīvaiṣṇavas.[8] This does not mean, of course, that Viśiṣṭādvaita does not have a universalist metaphysic or 'theology of religions'; its 'qualified non-dualism' captures the whole of sentient and insentient reality and, in the *Vedārthasaṅgraha*, Rāmānuja articulates a kind of 'anonymous Vaiṣṇava' theology of religions which interprets 'religious pluralism' in terms of its primary metaphysic: all deities, even those (erroneously) presumed to be the ultimate reality, in fact derive their very power and authority from Viṣṇu himself.[9] Although Śaiva *bhaktas* think they are worshipping Śiva, they are actually worshipping the Lord Viṣṇu himself, the *antaryāmin* of Śiva.

Nevertheless, the realism and particularism of Viśiṣṭādvaita valorize the entire

7 A 'market indicator': books on Advaita spirituality vastly outnumber those of Viśiṣṭādvaita – although of course, the 'market' indicates consumer appeal, not necessarily 'truth'. Norman Cutler (personal conversation) once noted that A.K. Ramanujan's translation of Nammāḻvār's poems, *Hymns for the Drowning*, immediately went out of print after it was published in 1981 (an Indian reprint was published in 1993), but his *Speaking of Siva* has never gone out of print since it was first published in 1973. Cutler suggested that the heavy cultural components in Nammāḻvār's poetry were lost on most Americans, while the 'anti-structure', *nirguṇa* inspiration, and, I might add, its call to 'unmediated experience' have a perennial appeal for many Westerners.

8 Although M. Narasimhachari, former chair of the Vaiṣṇava department at the University of Madras, seemed to lament the lack of international exposure of Śrīvaiṣṇavism and the lack of prominent Viśiṣṭādvaita teachers with 'star quality', especially compared with non-dualist luminaries such as Ramaṇa, Ramakrishna, and Aurobindo (personal conversation). In 2000, he himself gave numerous lectures on Śrīvaiṣṇavism to colleges and communities in the United States; and in 2000 and 2001, he was invited to teach at the newly established Oxford Centre for Vaiṣṇava and Hindu Studies.

9 'Religious pluralism' here means specifically the plurality of *āstika* deities; the *nāstika* are quite beyond the pale for Rāmānuja.

aggregate of Tamil culture which in turn establishes the justifying conditions of religious experience. Indeed, its metaphysic can be construed socially to validate and affirm mundane reality as divinely 'given': all differences, including social distinctions, are real and substantial and are preserved in a unified whole as the body of God. No *paramārthika* nullifies or cancels social or metaphysical realities. We saw that Śaṅkara's Advaita theoretically cancels distinctions, but in practice he tended to preserve them – a reason why he is sometimes called the 'champion of orthodoxy' among *āstika* traditions. Ramaṇa's Advaita, however, took seriously the social implications of the Advaita metaphysic. All persons were equal in his eyes, not by virtue of 'human rights' but because of something far more fundamental: all persons *are* the luminous Self, pure consciousness; distinctions and particulars are not real. So all persons were welcome at his ashram, including women, non-Brahmins and non-Indians. Rāmānuja's realism and particularism, on the other hand, preserve all distinctions – social as well as metaphysical – in a unified, sacred whole. In a sense, this particularism 'divinizes' Śrīvaiṣṇava culture but at the same time locks it into a regionalism that sometimes issues in sectarian rivalry.

By comparison I draw attention again to the universalism implied by Advaita's presumptive internalism. The Self, beyond form and particularization, effulgent and blissful, is our deepest truth, and we need only to go inward and access it. The experience of the inward self is self-justifying and confirms the truth. The late H.W.L. Poonja, an Advaitin guru based in Lucknow, was transformed by his encounter with Ramaṇa Maharṣi in 1944; his recollection of Ramaṇa's words suggests both the inward and universal dimension of Advaita; Ramaṇa urged Poonja to 'return to formlessness, which is your own Self; this advice I will give you will be available anywhere, any part of the world; just keep quiet' (Wisdom Video, 1997). 'Keeping quiet' suggests the inward turn to discover and experience the source of phenomenal consciousness. But, if we combine this internalist epistemology with Advaita's primary metaphysic, we are reminded that culture is contingent, not ultimately real. And this allows Advaita to transcend culture, to generate a universalism initiated by the twin programmes of metaphysics and the epistemology of religious experience. Douglas Harding, a contemporary spiritual teacher whose own method of introspection in some ways parallels Ramaṇa's method of inquiry, has commented on the broad appeal of Ramaṇa's spirituality: 'Ramaṇa speaks to us in the West according to what is universal, neither East nor West. The valuable part of Ramaṇa Maharṣi to me is what is not Indian but universal' (ibid.). On the other hand, Viśiṣṭādvaita's realism and particularism, which reinforces, and is reinforced by, its externalism, valorizes all forms, especially forms of divine expression and, above all, the form of God.

The second point I wish to make is epistemic and related to the cultural point. We saw the particularism of Viśiṣṭādvaita shape its localism; it also impacts its epistemology of religious experience, especially 'direct perception' (*sākṣātkāra*) of God. The entire set of doxastic practices – ritual, study, doctrine, poetry – set the stage for an emergent 'memory' in the individual and communal experience of

Śrīvaiṣṇavas. A 'memory' is created out of these practices – a way of understanding God through heart, mind and will – and this memory establishes the conditions which make possible a particularly intense experience of God, a direct or immediate perception of God. But this perception is particularist, according to doctrine and training of Viśiṣṭādvaita. We see God who is other than us, and who is endowed with form 'suitable to him'. But the belief that issues from such religious experience is justified, according to Alston's theory, for it meets all the relevant tests which he establishes.

We see an important challenge in Alston's theory. How can we account for diverse religious beliefs which issue from rather different sets of doxastic practices? Alston's work focuses on Christian mystical practice, but we can easily substitute Vaiṣṇava mystical practice, and conclude with the following: Nammāḻvār's claim of union with Kaṇṇaṉ is *prima facie* justified, for it emerges in the context of doxastic practices which are socially coherent and free of overriders and defeators. We see the difficulties that loom, for such processes will yield competing and conflicting claims which may nonetheless be *prima facie* justified. Such an outcome seems much less a philosophical victory than a confusing burden. Nevertheless such justified claims, however tentative, are opportunities for further critical, constructive work which slowly, carefully, contributes to a more complete understanding of ourselves and the nature of reality. And such *prima facie* justification is of considerable importance to those of us not privy to the kind of ecstatic experience of Nammāḻvār and who wonder whether there is something divine 'out there' (or 'in there', as the case may be) and whether reality in its broadest scope comprehends more than mere physical existence. Moreover, the cumulative weight of such accounts offers powerful testimony to a divine reality, and testimony itself, as a significant epistemic mechanism, offers powerful witness to the prospects and possibilities of knowing religiously.

But testimony to what? To a blue Viṣṇu? To Mary, appearing in a blue dress before the visionaries of Medjugorje? Ninian Smart argued that the cumulative weight of 'minimally ramified' testimonies argues favourably for the fact that 'something is out there', but what *that* is remains inconclusive. The 'more highly ramified the account', the less likely it is to be true. On this take, the report that 'I see Viṣṇu before me lying on his sofa' is not likely to be true. But Alston's analysis suggests something stronger. Nammāḻvār is *prima facie* justified in his claim of union with the divine, based on the experience itself.

In considering any mystic's experience, it is important to remember that we are assessing the justification of the claims which follow the experience. We are not dismissing the account, nor are we offering mere naturalistic explanations. In a sense, we take them literally in order to evaluate the warrant of the claim that follows the experience. It is obvious that, in an important sense, we cannot invalidate anyone's experience. Any experience 'is what it is' to the subject, but the claims that follow from experience can and ought to be evaluated – they bear scrutiny. There is nothing fundamentally wrong with this process; indeed, in informal ways we do this every day, and most of the work of trial lawyers is to critically examine the claims of witnesses and defendants. The pay-offs from such a scrutiny in the philosophy of religion are promising – nothing less than increased self-knowledge and knowledge of our enviroment in its broadest possible scope.

We see once again the relationship of epistemology and metaphysics and the pivotal role of philosophy of religion, for it is precisely the bailiwick of philosophy of religion to examine the rationality of metaphysical claims, the experiential conditions for knowledge and the coherence of doctrine. This last point is significant because externalism presumes the coherence of doxastic practices, and doctrine, of course, constitutes an important part of belief-forming mechanisms. Thus philosophy of religion, as a critical, cross-cultural, and constructive programme, gradually, asymptotically and conceptually makes inroads into the deepest truths of reality, even when, as in the case of Advaita, such truths culminate in a non-conceptual, non-dual knowing beyond knowledge.

Is there a way of escaping the dilemma of competing and conflicting *prima facie* justified claims? The answer lies in the question, by boldly affirming the invitation implicit in the term '*prima facie* justified claims'. Rather than wringing our hands and worrying that such claims are conflicting and merely tentative, we need to recognize their liberating potential; given the (justifying) conditions out of which these claims arise, we may say that Nammāḻvār is justified in his claims of intimacy with Kaṇṇaṉ, St Teresa is justified in her claims of passionate union with the Divine Lover and al-Junaid is justified in his ecstatic claim, 'In wondrous and ecstatic Grace, I feel Thee touch my inmost ground' (Arberry, 1990: 59). Less elegantly, the claim that 'There is a knowing beyond knowledge' is also justified. Each of these claims is *prima facie* justified, and each may or may not be overturned on receipt of new information. But *prima facie* justification appears to be more patient and tolerant of apparent contradictions than dogma and ideology. How 'God' is reported to be in the claims of mystics *may* be how God *is*, but their reports, their words and their claims may be overturned upon new information, as claims following perception are sometimes overturned upon closer inspection. Similarly 'what' is God or the Supreme is imperfectly known, tentative and certainly invites closer inspection. And the cumulative testimony of saints and seers suggests that there *is* a divine reality, although what that is demands close examination of the religious experience of the saints, the claims that follow it and the conditions under which it arose. This in turn makes necessary a study of the socially established mechanisms which 'produce' religious experience in order to evaluate those claims and determine their justification.

Thus we see two epistemological opportunities implied in the use of the term '*prima facie* justification'. The first is the invitation to weed out, from claims that follow religious experience, the incredible and insubstantial, the justified from the unjustified. By focusing on 'justified' and 'unjustified', the negative tension that persistently follows terms such as 'false' and 'true' is eliminated. Evaluation concerns the epistemic status of a belief, and not a value or moral judgement.

The second opportunity implied by use of the term '*prima facie* justification' concerns the potentially large universe of such claims. By examining the mechanisms which produce 'religious knowing' and justify it, we rapidly observe a large set of apparently conflicting metaphysical claims. These apparently conflicting claims, the people who hold them, and perhaps the thinkers who think about them, can live in the positive tension of the term '*prima facie*'. This means that these claims, our tentative knowledge, may be revised upon new information and new experiences. And, as our starting point for this study and these insights, we have the testimony of the saints and sages. Their glimpses of the Supreme offer invitation and promise to thinkers and seekers. By examining the conditions and mechanisms of religious knowing and paying close (epistemic) attention to the context and claims of religious experience, we may learn something about reality and, perhaps more importantly, may ourselves be transformed by it.

Bibliography

Abhisiktānanda [Henri Le Saux] (1974), *Saccidānanda: A Christian Approach to Advaitic Experience*. Delhi: ISPCK.

Abhisiktānanda [Henri Le Saux] (1990), *Hindu–Christian Meeting Point*, Delhi: ISPCK.

Alston, A.J. (1959), *The Realization of the Absolute: The Naiṣkarmya Siddhi of Śrī Sureśvara*, London: Shanti Sadan; reprint 1971.

Alston, A.J. (1987), *Śaṅkara on the Absolute*, London: Shanti Sadan.

Alston, A.J. (1989a), *Śaṅkara on Discipleship*, London: Shanti Sadan.

Alston, A.J. (1989b), *Śaṅkara on Enlightenment*, London: Shanti Sadan.

Alston, William P. (1986), 'Perceiving God', *Journal of Philosophy*, **83**, 655–64.

Alston, William P. (1989), *Epistemic Justification: Essays in the Theory of Knowledge*, Ithaca, NY: Cornell University Press.

Alston, William P. (1991), *Perceiving God: The Epistemology of Religious Experience*, Ithaca, NY: Cornell University Press.

Alston, William P. (1992a), 'The Autonomy of Religious Experience', *Philosophy of Religion*, **31**, 67–87.

Alston, William P. (1992b), 'Literal and Nonliteral in Reports of Mystical Experience', in Steven T. Katz (ed.), *Mysticism and Language*, New York and Oxford: Oxford University Press, 80–102.

Arberry, A.J. (1990), *Sufism: An Account of the Mystics of Islam*, London: George Allen & Unwin.

Arunachala, Sadhu [A.W. Chadwick] (1994; 1st edn 1961), *A Sadhu's Reminiscences of Ramana Maharshi*, Tiruvannamalai: Sri Ramanasramam.

Babb, Lawrence (1981), 'Glancing: Visual Interaction in Hinduism', *Journal of Anthropological Research*, **37**, 387–401.

Bader, Jonathan (1990), *Meditation in Śaṅkara's Vedānta*, New Delhi: Aditya Prakashan.

Bagger, Matthew C. (1999), *Religious Experience, Justification, and History*, Cambridge: Cambridge University Press.

Balasubramanian, R. (1978), *Some Problems in the Epistemology and Metaphysics of Rāmānuja*, Madras: University of Madras.

Balasubramanian, R. (1983), *A Study of the Brahmasiddhi of Maṇḍana Miśra*, Varanasi: Chaukambha Amarabharati Prakashan.

Balasubramanian, R. (1984), *The Taittirīyopaniṣad Bhāṣya-Vārtika of Sureśvara*, Madras: University of Madras.

Balasubramanian, R. (1988), *The Naiṣkarmyasiddhi of Sureśvara*, Madras: University of Madras.

Balasubramanian, R. (1990), 'Advaita Vedānta: Its Unity with Other Systems and its Contemporary Relevance', in *Indian Philosophical Systems*, Calcutta: Ramakrishna Mission Institute of Culture, 15–34.

Bharati, Agehānanda (1976), *The Light at the Centre: Context and Pretext of Modern Mysticism*, London and The Hague: East–West Publications.

Biardeau, Madeleine (1959), 'Quelques réflexions sur l'apophatisme de Śaṅkara', *Indo-Iranian Journal*, **3**, 81–101.

Biardeau, Madeleine (1969), *La philosophie de Maṇḍana Miśra: vue à partir de la Brahmasiddhi*, Paris: École Française D'Extrême-Orient.

BonJour, Laurence (1992), 'Externalism/Internalism' in J. Dancy and E. Sosa (eds), *A Companion to Epistemology*, Oxford and Cambridge, MA: Blackwell, 132–36.

Brunton, Paul (1994), *A Search in Secret India*, York Beach, ME: Samuel Weiser.

Campbell, Joseph (1951), 'Appendix A: The Six Systems', in H. Zimmer (ed.), *Philosophies of India*, New York: Pantheon Books, 605–14.

Carman, John Braisted (1974), *The Theology of Rāmānuja: An Essay in Interreligious Understanding*, New Haven, CT and London: Yale University Press.

Carman, John Braisted (1993), 'The Dilemma of Diversity and the Boon of Understanding', Convocation Address delivered at the Harvard Divinity School (September 22), Cambridge, MA.

Carman, John and Narayanan, Vasudha (1989), *The Tamil Veda: Piḷḷan's Interpretation of the Tiruvāymoḻi*, London and Chicago, IL: University of Chicago Press.

Carter, John Ross and Palihawadana, Mahinda (1987), *The Dhammapada*, Oxford: Oxford University Press.

Cenkner, William (1983), *A Tradition of Teachers: Śaṅkara and the Jagadgurus Today*, Delhi: Motilal Banarsidass.

Chatterjee, Tara (1999), 'An Attempt to Understand *Svataḥ Prāmaṇyavāda* in Advaita Vedānta', *Journal of Indian Philosophy*, **19**, 229–48.

Chodron, Pema (1997), *When Things Fall Apart: Heart Advice for Difficult Times*, Boston, MA and London: Shambala.

Chodron, Pema (2001), *The Places that Scare You: A Guide to Fearlessness in Difficult Times*, Boston and London: Shambala.

Clooney, Francis X. (1992), 'Binding the Text: Vedānta as Philosophy and Commentary', in Timm Jeffrey R. (ed.), *Texts and Contexts: Traditional Hermeneutics in South Asia*, Albany, NY: State University of New York Press, 47–68.

Clooney, Francis X. (1993), *Theology After Vedānta: An Experiment in Comparative Theology*, Albany, NY: State University of New York Press.

Clooney, Francis X. (1995), 'The Emerging Field of Comparative Theology: A Bibliographical Review (1989–95)', *Theological Studies*, **56**, 521–50.

Clooney, Francis X. (1996), *Seeing Through Texts: Doing Theology Among the Śrīvaiṣṇavas of South India*, Albany, NY: State University of New York Press.

Clooney, Francis X. (1998), *Hindu Wisdom for All God's Children*, Maryknoll, NY: Orbis Books.

Clooney, Francis X. (2001), *Hindu God, Christian God: How Reason Helps Faith to Cross the Boundaries between Religions*, New York: Oxford University Press.

Cohen, S.S. (1993; 1st edn 1952), *Guru Ramana*, Tiruvannamalai: Sri Ramanasramam.

Cook, John W. (1988), 'Wittgenstein and Religious Belief', *Philosophy*, **63**, 427–52.

Coomaraswamy, Ananda (1988), *Buddha and the Gospel of Buddhism*, New York and Seacaucus, NJ: Citadel Press.

Cowell, E.B. and Gough, A.E. (trans. and ed.) (1989), *Sarva-Darśana-Saṅgraha of Mādhvācārya*, Delhi: Parimal Publications.

Cutler, Norman (1987), *Songs of Experience: The Poetics of Tamil Devotion*, Bloomington and Indianapolis, IN: University of Indiana Press.

Danielou, Alain (1955), *Yoga: The Method of Re-integration*, New York: University Books.

Dasgupta, Surendranath (1988), *A History of Indian Philosophy*, Delhi: Motilal Banarsidass. First published 1922, Cambridge: Cambridge University Press.

Datta, D.M. (1972), *The Six Ways of Knowing*, Calcutta: University of Calcutta.

de Smet, Richard (1953), 'The Theological Method of Śaṇkara', unpublished Ph.D. thesis, Pontifica Universitas Gregoriana.

de Smet, Richard (1954), 'Langage et connaissance chez Śaṇkara', *Revue Philosophique de Louvain*, **52**, 31–74.

de Smet, Richard (1961), 'The Logical Structure of "Tattvamasi" According to Sureśvara's *Naiṣkarmya Siddhi*', *Philosophical Quarterly*, **33**, 256–64.

Deutsch, Eliot (1969), *Advaita Vedānta: A Philosophical Reconstruction*, Honolulu: East–West Center Press.

Devaraja, N.K. (1962), *An Introduction to Śaṅkara's Theory of Knowledge*, Delhi: Motilal Banarsidass.

Dreyfus, Georges, 'Soteriology and Tibetan Scholastic Training', lecture delivered at the Divinity School of the University of Chicago, 31 January 1997.

Dumont, Louis (1970), 'A Fundamental Problem', in *Religion/Politics and History in India*, The Hague: Mouton.

Eck, Diana (1985), *Darśan: Seeing the Divine Image in India*, Chambersburg, PA: Anima.

Eliade, Mircea (1990), *Yoga: Immortality and Freedom*, trans. Willard R. Trask, Princeton, NJ: Princeton University Press.

Eliade, Mircea (1991), *Images and Symbols: Studies in Religious Symbolism*, trans. Philip Mairet, Princeton, NJ: Princeton University Press.

Evans, Donald (1988), 'Can Philosophers Limit What Mystics Can Do? A Critique of Steven Katz', *Religious Studies*, **25**, 53–60.

Fenton, John Y. (1981), 'Mystical Experience as a Bridge for Cross-cultural Philosophy of Religion: A Critique', *Journal of the American Academy of Religion*, **49**, 51–76.

Ferm, Vergilius (1971), 'Theology and Religious Experience', in J.S. Bixler, R.L. Calhoun and H.R. Neibuhr (eds), *The Nature of Religious Experience: Essays in Honor of Douglas Clyde Macintosh*, New York: Harper and Row. First published 1937, Freeport, NY: Books for Libraries Press.

Feuerstein, Georg (1989), *The Yoga-Sūtra of Patañjali: A New Translation and Commentary*, Rochester, VT: Inner Traditions International.

Fields, Rick (1992), *How the Swans Came to the Lake: A Narrative History of Buddhism in America*, Boston, MA and London: Shambala.

Flood, Gavin (1996), *An Introduction to Hinduism*, Cambridge: Cambridge University Press.

Forgie, J. William (1985), 'Hyper-Kantianism in Recent Discussions of Mystical Experience', *Religious Studies*, **21**, 205–18.

Forman, Robert K.C. (ed.) (1998), *The Innate Capacity: Mysticism, Psychology, and Philosophy*, Oxford: Oxford University Press.

Forsthoefel, Thomas A. (2001a), '*Review of Religious Experience, Justification, and History*, by Matthew C. Bagger', *Journal of Religion*, **81**, 152–54.

Forsthoefel, Thomas A. (2001b), 'The Sage of Pure Experience: The Appeal of Ramaṇa Maharṣi in the West,' *Hindu–Christian Studies Bulletin*, **14**, 31–6.

Fort, Andrew O. (1984), 'The Concept of Sākṣin in Advaita Vedānta', *Journal of Indian Philosophy*, **12**, pp. 277–90.

Fort, Andrew O. (1991), 'Knowing Brahman While Embodied: Śaṅkara on Jīvanmukti', *Journal of Indian Philosophy*, **19**, 369–89.

Fort, Andrew O. and Mumme, Patricia Y. (eds) (1996), *Living Liberation in Hindu Thought*, Albany, NY: State University of New York Press.

Fox, Douglas A. (1993), *Dispelling Illusion: Gauḍapāda's Alātaśānti*, Albany, NY: State University of New York Press.

Fredericks, James L. (1995), 'A Universal Religious Experience? Comparative Theology as an Alternative to a Theology of Religions', *Horizons*, **22**, 67–87.

Fumerton, Richard (1998), 'The Internalism/Externalism Controversy', *Philosophical Perspectives*, **2**, 443–59.

Gambhirananda, Swami (1989), *Eight Upaniṣads with the Commentary of Śaṅkara*, Calcutta: Advaita Ashrama.

Gambhirananda, Swami (1992a), 'Upaniṣadic Meditation', in S. Gambhirananda (trans.), *Chāndogya Upaniṣad*, Calcutta: Advaita Ashrama, xiii–xxxvii.

Gambhirananda, Swami (trans.) (1992b), *Chādogya Upaniṣad with the Commentary of Śaṇkarācarya*, Calcutta: Advaita Ashrama.

Ganguly, Adwaita (1995), *Vedanta Philosophy for the Unity of Mankind*, New Delhi: Vikas Publishing House.

Gettier, Edmund (1963), 'Is Justified True Belief Knowledge?', *Analysis*, **23**, 121–3.

Godman, David, (ed.) (1992), *Be As You Are: The Teachings of Ramana Maharshi*, New Delhi: Penguin India.

Gombrich, Richard (1984), 'Introduction: The Buddhist Way', in R. Gombrich and H. Bechert (eds), *The World of Buddhism*, New York: Thames and Hudson, 9–14.

Gombrich, Richard (1988), *Theravada Buddhism*, London and New York: Routledge.
Gonda, Jan (1963), *The Vision of the Vedic Poets*, The Hague: Mouton.
Grant, Sarah (1990), 'Foreword', in Abhisiktānanda, *Hindu–Christian Meeting Point*, Delhi: ISPCK, vii–ix.
Griffiths, Bede (1984), *Christ in India: Essays Towards a Hindu–Christian Dialogue*, Springfield, IL: Templegate.
Griffiths, Paul J. (1986), *On Being Mindless: Buddhist Meditation and the Mind–Body Problem*, La Salle, IL: Open Court.
Griffiths, Paul J. (1991), *Apology for Apologetics*, Maryknoll, NY: Orbis Books.
Griffiths, Paul J. (1994), *On Being Buddha: The Classical Doctrine of Buddhahood*, Albany, NY: State University of New York Press.
Grimes, John (1989), *A Concise Dictionary of Indian Philosophy*, Albany, NY: State University of New York Press.
Grimes, John (1990a), *The Seven Great Untenables*, Delhi: Motilal Banarsidass.
Grimes, John (1990b), 'Two Paradigms of Religious Language', *Studies in Religion/Sciences Religieuse*, **19**, 331–38.
Grimes, John (1992), 'Śaṅkara's Siren of Śruti', *Journal of Dharma*, **17**, 196–202.
Gupta, Bina (1991), *Perceiving in Advaita Vedānta: Epistemological Analysis and Interpretation*, Columbia, MO: Associated University Presses.
Gussner, Robert E. (1977), 'Śaṅkara's *Crest Jewel of Discrimination*: A Stylometric Approach to the Question of Authorship', *Journal of Indian Philosophy*, **4**, 265–78.
Hacker, Paul (1995), 'Śaṅkarācārya and Śaṅkarabhagavatpāda: Preliminary Remarks Concerning the Authorship Problem', in W. Halbfass (ed.), *Philology and Confrontation: Paul Hacker on Traditional and Modern Vedanta*, Albany, NY: State University of New York Press, 41–56.
Halbfass, Wilhelm (1983), *Studies in Kumārila and Śaṅkara*, Reinbeck: Verlag für Orientalistische Fachpublikationen.
Halbfass, Wilhelm (1990), *India and Europe: An Essay in Philosophical Understanding*, Delhi: Motilal Banarsidass.
Halbfass, Wilhelm (ed.) (1995), *Philology and Confrontration: Paul Hacker on Traditional and Modern Vedanta*, Albany, NY: State University of New York Press.
Hammer, Olav (2001), *Claiming Knowledge: Strategies of Epistemology from Theosophy to the New Age*, Leiden: Brill.
Hara, Minoru (1980), 'Hindu Concepts of Teacher, Sanskrit Guru and Ācārya', in M. Nagatomi (ed.), *Sanskrit and Indian Studies: Essays in Honour of Daniel H.H. Ingals*, Dordrecht: D. Reidel Publishing Co., 93–118.
Hardy, Friedhelm (1983), *Viraha-Bhakti: The Early History of Kṛṣṇa Devotion in South India*, Delhi: Oxford University Press.
Hawley, John Stratton and Juergensmeyer, Mark (1988), *Songs of the Saints of India*, New York and Oxford: Oxford University Press.

Hick, John (1966), *Faith and Knowledge*, Ithaca, NY: Cornell University Press.
Hick, John (1983), *The Philosophy of Religion*, Englewood Cliffs, NJ: Prentice Hall.
Hick, John (1989), *An Interpretation of Religion: Human Responses to the Transcendent*, New Haven, CT: Yale University Press.
Hiriyanna, Mysore (1957), *Indian Philosophical Studies*, Mysore: Kavyalaya Publishers.
Hiriyanna, Mysore (1972), *Indian Philosophical Studies*–II, Mysore: Kavyalaya Publishers.
Huxley, Aldous (1946), *The Perennial Philosophy*, London: Chatto and Windus.
Inden, Ronald (1990), *Imagining India*, Cambridge, MA and Oxford: Blackwell.
Indich, William (1995), *Consciousness in Advaita Vedānta*, Delhi: Motilal Banarsidass.
Ingalls, Daniel H.H. (1953), 'Śaṃkara on the Question: Whose is Avidya?', *Philosophy East and West*, **3**, 69–72.
James, William (1990), *The Varieties of Religious Experience*, New York: Vintage Books.
Jantzen, Grace M. (1995a), 'Review of *Mysticism and Language*, ed. Stephen T. Katz, *Religious Studies*, **31**, 133–36.
Jantzen, Grace M. (1995b), *Power, Gender, and Christian Mysticism*, Cambridge: Cambridge University Press.
Jayakaar, Pupal (1987), *J. Krishnamurti: A Biography*, Delhi: Penguin India.
Jung, C.G. (1988), 'Foreword: Śrī Ramana and His Message to Modern Man', in *The Spiritual Teaching of Ramana Maharshi*, Boston, MA and London: Shambala; originally published as the foreword in Heinrich Zimmer (1944).
Kant, Immanuel (1960), *Religion Within the Limits of Reason Alone*, trans. and ed. Theodore M. Green and Hoyt H. Hudson, New York: Harper and Row.
Karmarkar, Raghunath Damodar (trans. and ed.) (1973), *Gauḍapāda-Kārikā*, Poona: Bhandarkar Oriental Research Institute.
Katz, Steven T. (1978), 'Language, Epistemology, and Mysticism', in Steven T. Katz (ed.), *Mysticism and Philosophical Analysis*, London: Sheldon Press.
Katz, Steven T. (ed.) (1983), *Mysticism and Religious Traditions*, Oxford: Oxford University Press.
Katz, Steven T. (ed.) (2000), *Mysticism and Sacred Scripture*, New York: Oxford University Press.
Kaylor, R.D. and Venkatachari, K.K.A. (1981), *God Far, God Near: An Interpretation of the Thought of Nammalvar*, Bombay: Ananthacharya Indological Research Institute.
Keith, A.B. (1989), *The Religion and Philosophy of the Upanishads*, Vol. 2, Delhi: Motilal Banarsidass. First published 1925, Cambridge, MA: Harvard University Press.
King, Richard (1995), *Early Advaita Vedānta and Buddhism*, Albany, NY: State University of New York Press.

King, Sallie B. (1978), 'Concepts, Anti-Concepts and Religious Experience', *Religious Studies*, **14**, 445–58.

King, Sallie B. (1988), 'Two Epistemological Models for the Interpretation of Mysticism', *Journal of the American Academy of Religion*, **56**, 257–79.

Klostermaier, Klaus K. (1989), *A Survey of Hinduism*, Albany, NY: State University of New York Press.

Kolak, Daniel and Martin, Raymond (1993), *Self, Cosmos, God*, Fort Worth, TX: Harcourt Brace Jovanovich.

Kornfield, Jack (1995), *A Path with Heart*, New York: Bantam Books.

Kornfield, Jack (2000), *After the Ecstasy, the Laundry*, New York: Bantam Books.

Kripal, Jeffrey J. (1995), *Kālī's Child: The Mystical and the Erotic in the Life and Teachings of Ramakrishna*, Chicago, IL: University of Chicago Press.

Kristo, Jure (1980), 'Human Cognition and Mystical Knowledge: Joseph Maréchal's Analysis of Mystical Experience', *Mélanges de Science Réligieuse*, **37**, 53–73.

Kristo, Jure (1982), 'The Interpretation of Religious Experience: What Do Mystics Intend When They Talk about their Experiences?', *Journal of Religion*, **62**, 21–38.

Kriyananda [Donald Walters] (1973), *A Visit to Saints of India*, Nevada City, CA: Ananda Publications.

Lacombe, Oliver (1937), *L'absolu selon le Védânta: Les notions de Brahman et d'Atman dans les systèmes de Çankara et Râmânoudja*, Paris: Librairie Orientaliste Paul Geuthner.

Lester, Robert C. (1976), *Rāmānuja on the Yoga*, Adyar: The Adyar Library and Research Centre.

Lipner, Julius (1986), *The Face of Truth*, Albany, NY: State University of New York.

McGinn, Bernard (1995), *The Foundations of Mysticism: Origins to the Fifth Century*, New York: Crossroad.

Macquarrie, John (1992), 'The Logic of Religious and Theological Language', *Journal of Dharma*, **17**, 169–77.

Mādhavānanda, Swāmī (1992), *Vivekacūḍāmaṇi of Śrī Śaṅkarācārya*, Calcutta: Advaita Ashrama.

Mādhavānanda, Swāmī (trans.) (1993), *The Bṛhadāraṇyaka Upaniṣad with the Commentary of Śaṅkarācārya*, Calcutta: Advaita Ashrama.

Mahadevan, T.M.P. (trans. and ed.) (1972), *The Saṁbandha-Vārtika of Sureśvarācārya*, Madras: University of Madras.

Maharṣi, Ramaṇa (1987), *Śri Ramaṇa Nūṟṟiraṭṭu*, Tiruvannamalai: Sri Ramanasramam.

Maharṣi, Ramaṇa (1988), *Eka Śloki*, trans. C. Sudarsan, Bangalore: Ramana Maharshi Centre for Learning.

Maharṣi, Ramaṇa (1992), *Ulladu Narpadu: Forty Verses on Reality*, trans. S.S. Cohen, Tiruvannamalai: Sri Ramanasramam.

Maharṣi, Ramaṇa (1994), *Vicārasaṅgraham*, trans. T.M.P. Mahadevan, Tiruvannamalai: Sri Ramanasramam.

Maharṣi, Ramaṇa (1995a), *Who Am I (Nān Yār)?*, trans. T.M.P. Mahadevan, Tiruvannamalai: Sri Ramanasramam.

Maharṣi, Ramaṇa (1995b), *Upadeśa Sāram*, trans. A.R. Natarajan, Bangalore: Ramana Maharshi Centre for Learning.

Maharṣi, Ramaṇa (2000), *Talks with Ramana Maharshi* (first American edition), Carlsbad, CA: Inner Directions Foundation.

Marcaurelle, Roger (2000), *Freedom Through Inner Renunciation: Śaṅkara's Philosophy in a New Light*, Albany, NY: State University of New York Press.

Masson, J. Moussaieff and Masson, T.C. (1976), 'The Study of Mysticism: A Criticism of W.T. Stace', *Journal of Indian Philosophy*, **4**, 109–25.

Maximilien, Guy (1975a), *La démonstration du non-agir*, Paris: Institut de Civilisation Indienne.

Maximilien, Guy (1975b), 'Le langage et l'Ātman d'après USP 18', *Wiener Zeitschrift für die Kunde Süd- und Ostasiens und Archiv für Indische Philosophie*, **19**, 117–33.

Mayeda, Sengaku (1968), 'The Advaita Theory of Perception', *Wiener Zeitschrift für die Kunde Süd- und Ostasiens und Archiv für Indische Philosophie*, **12**, 221–39.

Mayeda, Sengaku (trans. and ed.) (1992), *A Thousand Teachings: The Upadeśasāhasrī of Śaṅkara*, Albany, NY: State University of New York Press.

Mayeda, Sengaku (1980), 'Śaṃkara and Sureśvara: Their Exegetical Method to Interpret the Great Sentence "*Tat Tvam Asi*"', *Adyar Library Bulletin*, **44–45**, 47–160.

Meeker, Kevin (1994), 'William Alston's Epistemology of Religious Experience: A "Reformed" Reformed Epistemology?', *Philosophy of Religion*, **35**, 89–110.

Merton, Thomas (1965), 'Review of *The Collected Works of Ramana Maharshi*', Arthur Osborne (ed.), *Collectanea Cisterciensia*, **27**, 79–80.

Merton, Thomas (1975), *The Asian Journal of Thomas Merton*, ed. Naomi Burton, Patrick Hart and James Laughlin, New York: New Directions.

Miller, Barbara Stoler (1986), *The Bhagavad Gītā: Krishna's Counsel in Time of War*, New York: Bantam.

Miller, Barbara Stoler (1995), *Yoga: Discipline of Freedom; The Yoga Sutra Attributed to Pantanjali*, Berkeley, CA: University of California Press.

Mudaliar, A. Devaraja (1989), *Day by Day with Bhagavan*, Tiruvannamalai: Sri Ramanasramam.

Muller-Ortega, Paul Eduardo (1989), *The Triadic Heart of Śiva: Kaula Tantricism of Abhinavgupta in the Non-Dual Shaivism of Kashmir*, Albany, NY: State University of New York Press.

Mumme, Patricia Y. (1988), *The Śrīvaiṣṇava Theological Dispute: Māṇavāḷamāmuni and Vedānta Deśika*, Madras: New Era.

Murty, Satchidananda (1959), *Revelation and Reason in Advaita Vedānta*, Waltair: Andhra University Press.

Narayanan, Vasudha (1994), *The Vernacular Veda: Revelation, Recitation, and Ritual*, Columbia, SC: University of South Carolina Press.

Natarajan, A.R. (trans.) (1983), *Selections from Ramana Maharshi*, London: Rider and Company.

Natarajan, A.R. (trans.) (1995), *Teachings of Ramana Maharshi: An Anthology*, Madras: Affiliated East–West Press.

Nelson, Lance (1996), 'Living Liberation in Śaṅkara and Classical Advaita: Sharing the Holy Waiting of God,' in Andrew O. Fort and Patricia Y. Mumme (eds), *Living Liberation in Hindu Thought*, Albany, NY: State University of New York Press, 17–62.

Olivelle, Patrick (1993), *The Āśrama System: The History and Hermeneutics of a Religious Institution*, Oxford: Oxford University Press.

Om, Sri Sadhu (1990), *The Path of Sri Ramana*, Tiruvannamalai: Sri Ramana Kshetra.

Osborne, Arthur, (ed.) (1989), *The Collected Works of Ramana Maharshi*, London: Rider and Company.

Osborne, Arthur (1954), *Ramana Maharshi and the Path of Self Knowledge*, London: Rider and Company.

Osborne, Arthur (ed.) (1993), *The Teachings of Sri Ramana Maharshi*, Tiruvannamalai: Sri Ramanasramam; reprint (1996), York Beach, ME: Samuel Weiser.

Otto, Rudolph (1923), *The Idea of the Holy*, trans. John Harvey, Oxford: Oxford University Press.

Penner, Hans (1983), 'The Mystical Illusion', in Steven T. Katz (ed.), *Mysticism and Religious Traditions*, Oxford: Oxford University Press, 89–116.

Peterson, Michael, Hasker, William, Reichenbach, Bruce and Basinger, David (1991), *Reason and Religious Belief: An Introduction to the Philosophy of Religion*, New York and Oxford: Oxford University Press.

Plantinga, Alvin (1993a), *Warrant and Proper Function*, New York and Oxford: Oxford University Press.

Plantinga, Alvin (1993b), *Warrant: The Current Debate*, New York and Oxford: Oxford University Press.

Plantinga, Alvin (2000), *Warranted Christian Belief*, New York and Oxford: Oxford University Press.

Pollock, John (1986), *Contemporary Theories of Knowledge*, Totowa, NJ: Rowman and Littlefield.

Potter, Karl (1991), *Presuppositions of India's Philosophies*, Delhi: Motilal Banarsidass.

Potter, Karl (ed.) (1981), *Advaita Vedānta up to Śaṃkara and His Pupils*, Delhi: Motilal Banarsidass.

Prabhavānanda, Swami and Isherwood, Christopher (1978), *Śaṅkara's Crest Jewel of Discrimination*, Hollywood, CA: Vedanta Society of California.

Prebish, Charles (1979), *American Buddhism*, North Scituate, MA: Duxbury Press.

Proudfoot, Wayne (1985), *Religious Experience*, Berkeley, CA: University of California Press.

Radhakrishnan, Sarvepalli (1957), 'General Introduction: History of Indian

Thought', in S. Radhakrishnan and Charles Moore (eds), *A Source Book of Indian Philosophy*, Princeton, NJ: Princeton University Press, xvii–xxxi.

Radhakrishnan, Sarvepalli (1976; 1st edn 1948), *The Bhagavadgītā*, New York: Harper and Row.

Radhakrishnan, Sarvepalli (1989; 1st edn 1923), *Indian Philosophy*, Vol. 2, New Delhi: Motilal Banarsidass.

Radhakrishnan, Sarvepalli (1992), *The Principal Upaniṣads*, Atlantic Highlands, NJ: Humanities Press International.

Raghavachar, S.S., (trans. and ed.) (1978), *Vedārtha-Saṅgraha of Śrī Rāmānujacārya*, Mysore: Sri Ramakrishna Ashrama.

Ramanujan, A.K. (1973), *Speaking of Śiva*, London: Penguin Books.

Ramanujan, A.K. (1993), *Hymns for the Drowning: Poems for Viṣṇu by Nammāḻvār*, New Delhi: Penguin Books.

Rambachand, Anantanand (1991), *Accomplishing the Accomplished: The Vedas as a Source of Valid Knowledge in Śaṅkara*, Honolulu: University of Hawaii Press, 1991.

Rambachand, Anantanand (1992), 'Where Words Can Set Free: The Liberating Potency of Vedic Words in the Hermeneutics of Śaṅkara', in Jeffrey R. Timm (ed.), *Texts in Contexts: Traditional Hermeneutics in South Asia*, Albany, NY: State University of New York Press, 33–46.

Rambachand, Anantanand (1994), 'Response to Professor Arvind Sharma', *Philosophy East and West*, **44**, 721–24.

Rawlinson, Andrew (1997), *The Book of Enlightened Masters: Western Teachers in Eastern Traditions*, La Salle, IL: Open Court.

Revathy, S. (trans.) (1994), *Mānamālā by Acyutakṛṣṇānandatīrtha with Rāmānanda's Commentary*, Adyar: The Adyar Library and Research Centre.

Russell, Bertrand (1921), *Mysticism, Logic, and Other Essays*, London: Longmans and Green.

Sādhu, Mouni (1957), *In Days of Great Peace*, London: Allen & Unwin.

Śaṅkara (1990), *Brahmasūtra with Śaṅkarabhāṣya*, Delhi: Motilal Banarsidass.

Sastri, D.M. (trans.) (1989), *The Maharshi's Way: Translation and Commentary on the Upadeśa Saram*, Tiruvannamalai: Sri Ramanasraman.

Sastri, S.S. Suryanarayana (trans. and ed.) (1948), *The Sāṅkhyakārikā of Īsvara Kṛṣṇa*, Madras: University of Madras.

Sastri, S.S. Suryanarayana (trans. and ed.) (1971), *Vedāntaparibhāṣa by Dharmarāja Adhvarin*, Adyar: The Adyar Library and Research Centre.

Sastri, S.S. and Ayyangar, T.R. (trans. and ed.) (1978), *Jīvanmuktiviveka of Vidyāraṇya*, Adyar: The Adyar Library and Research Centre.

Sawai, Yoshitsugu (1986), 'Śaṅkara's theory of Saṃnyāsa', *Journal of Indian Philosophy*, **14**, 371–87.

Schuon, Frithjof (1975), *De l'unité transcendante des religions*, trans. Peter Townsend, New York: Harper and Row.

Sharma, Arvind (1986), *The Hindu Gītā: Ancient and Classical Interpretations of the Bhagavadgītā*, La Salle, IL: Open Court.

Sharma, Arvind (1992), 'Is Anubhava a Pramāṇa According to Śaṅkara?', *Philosophy East and West*, **42**, 517–26.

Sharma, Arvind (1993a), *The Experiential Dimension of Advaita Vedanta*, Delhi: Motilal Banarsidass.

Sharma, Arvind (1993b), 'Review of *Accomplishing the Accomplished: The Vedas as a Source of Valid Knowledge in Śaṅkara*, by Anantanand Rambachand', *Philosophy East and West*, **43**, 736–37.

Sharma, Chandradhar (1991), *Critical Survey of Indian Philosophy*, Delhi: Motilal Banarsidass.

Sharpe, Eric J. (1985), *The Universal Gītā: Western Images of the Bhagavadgītā*, London: Gerald Duckworth.

Sinha, Debabrata (1983), *The Metaphysics of Experience in Advaita Vedānta*, Delhi: Motilal Banarsidass.

Skoog, Kim (1989), 'Śaṁkara on the Role of Śruti and Anubhava in Attaining Brahmajijñāna', *Philosophy East and West*, **39**, 67–74.

Smart, Ninian (1962), 'Mystical Experience', *Sophia*, **1**, 19–26.

Smart, Ninian (1964), *Doctrine and Argument in Indian Philosophy*, London: George Allen & Unwin.

Smart, Ninian (1965), 'Interpretation and Mystical Experience', *Religious Studies*, **1**, 75–87.

Smart, Ninian (1985), 'On Knowing What is Uncertain', Leroy S. Rouner (ed.), *Knowing Religiously*, Notre Dame: Notre Dame University Press, 76–86.

Smith, Huston (1958), *The Religions of Man*, New York: Harper and Row.

Smith, Huston (1987), 'Is there a Perennial Philosophy?', *Journal of the American Academy of Religion*, **55**, 553–66.

Stace, W.T. (1961), *Mysticism and Philosophy*, London: Macmillan.

Stoeber, Michael (1991), 'Constructivist Epistemologies of Mysticism: A Critique and a Revision', *Religious Studies*, **28**, 107–16.

Streng, Frederick (1976), 'Mystical Awareness, or How to be in the World but not of It', in Peter Slater (ed.), *Proceedings of the American Academy of Religion*, comp. Peter Slater, Atlanta, GA: American Academy of Religion.

Subrahmanyaśāstri, S. (ed.) (nd), *Upaniṣadbhāṣyam with the Commentaries of Ānandagiri and Others*, 3 vols, Varanasi: Mahesh Research Institute.

Subrahmanyaśāstri, S. (nd), *Upadeśasāhasrī with the Commentary of Ānandagiri*, Varanasi: Mahesh Research Institute.

Swain, Marshall (1988), 'Alston's Internalistic Externalism', *Philosophical Perspectives*, **2**, 461–73.

Swami, B.V. Narasimha (1993), *Self Realization: The Life and Teachings of Sri Ramana Maharshi*, Tiruvannamalai: Sri Ramanasramam.

Swarupananda, Swami (1993), *Srimad Bhagavad-Gita*, Calcutta: Advaita Ashrama.

Swinburne, Richard (1991), *The Existence of God*, Oxford: Oxford University Press.

Taber, John (1986), 'The Philosophical Evaluation of Religious Experience', *International Journal for the Philosophy of Religion*, **19**, 43–59.

Taber, John (1991), 'Review of *India and Europe: An Essay in Understanding*, by Wilhelm Halbfass', *Philosophy East and West*, **41**, 229–40.

Tennant, F.R. (1913), *The Aim and Scope of Philosophy of Religion*, London: SPCK.

Thibault, George, (trans.) (1988), *The Vedānta-Sūtras with the Commentary by Śaṅkarācārya*, Delhi: Motilal Banarsidass.

Turīyānanda, Swāmi (1992), *Vivekacūḍāmaṇi of Śrī Śaṅkarācārya*, Calcutta: Advaita Ashrama.

Underhill, Evelyn (1963), *Mysticism: A Study in the Nature and Development of Man's Spiritual Consciousness*, Cleveland, OH and New York: World.

van Boetzelaer, J.M. (1971), *Sureśvara's Taittirīyopaniṣad-Bhāṣyavārtikam*, Leiden: E.J. Brill.

van Buitenen, J.A.B. (1956), *Rāmānuja's Vedārthasaṃgraha: Introduction, Critical Edition and Annotated Translation*, Poona: Deccan College Postgraduate and Research Institute.

van Buitenen, J.A.B. (1968), *Rāmānuja on the Bhagavadgītā: A Condensed Rendering of His Gītābhāṣya with Copious Notes and an Introduction*, Delhi: Motilal Banarsidass.

van Buitenen, J.A.B. (1981), *The Bhagavadgītā in the Mahābhārata*, Chicago, IL and London: University of Chicago Press.

Venkatachari, K.K.A. (1978), *The Maṇipravāḷa Literature of the Śrīvaiṣṇava Ācāryas: 12th to 15th Century A.D.*, Bombay: Ananthacarya Research Institute.

Venkataramiah, D. (trans. and ed.) (1948), *The Pañcapādikā of Padmapāda*, Baroda: Oriental Institute.

Venkataramiah, Mungala S. (ed.) (1994), *Talks with Sri Ramana Maharshi*, Tiruvannamalai: Sri Ramanasramam.

Vidyābhuṣana, Satiśa Chandra (trans. and ed.) (1975), *The Nyāya Sūtras of Gotama*, New Delhi: Munshiram Manoharlal.

Virarāghavācārya, U.T. (ed.) (1989), *Śribhāṣya of Rāmānuja with the Commentary Śrutaprakāśikā of Sudarśana Sūri*, Madras: Sri Visishtadvaita Pracharini Sabha.

Wach, Joachim (1966; 1st edn 1958), *The Comparative Study of Religions*, New York and London: Columbia University Press.

Wainwright, William (1981), *Mysticism: A Study of its Nature, Cognitive Value, and Moral Implications*, Madison, WI: University of Wisconsin.

Warrier, A.G. Krishna (1981), *The Concept of Mukti in Advaita Vedānta*, Madras: Madras University.

Warrier, A.G. Krishna (trans. and ed.) (1993), *Śrīmad Bhagavad Gītā Bhāṣya of Sri Saṁkarācārya*, Madras: Ramakrishna Math.

Watts, Fraser and Williams, Mark (1988), *The Psychology of Religious Knowing*, Cambridge, Cambridge University Press.

Werner, Karel (1989), 'Mysticism as Doctrine and Experience', in K. Werner (ed.), *The Yogi and the Mystic*, London: Curzon.

Wilson, J.G. (1970), 'Sankara, Ramanuja, and the Function of Religious Language', *Religious Studies*, **6**, 57–68.

Winch, Peter (1977), 'Meaning and Religious Language', in Stuart C. Brown (ed.), *Reason and Religion*, Ithaca, NY: Cornell University Press, 193–221.

Wisdom Video (1997), *Abide as the Self: The Essential Teachings of Ramana Maharshi*, dir. B. Salzman, Los Angeles: Inner Directions Foundation.

Wittgenstein, Ludwig (nd), *Lectures and Conversations on Aesthetics, Psychology, and Religious Belief*, ed. Cyril Barrett, Berkeley and Los Angeles: University of California.

Wolters, Clifton (trans. and ed.) (1983; 1st edn 1961), *The Cloud of Unknowing and Other Works*, New York: Penguin.

Yandell, Keith (1993), *The Epistemology of Religious Experience*, Cambridge: Cambridge Universty Press.

Zaehner, R.C. (1961), *Mysticism Sacred and Profane*, New York: Oxford University Press.

Zaehner, R.C. (1969), *The Bhagavad-Gītā, with a commentary based on original sources*, Oxford: Clarendon Press.

Zaehner, R.C. (1976), *The Bhagavad-Gītā*, Oxford: Oxford University Press.

Zaehner, R.C. (1970), *Concordant Discord*, Oxford: Oxford University Press.

Zimmer, Heinrich (1944), *Der Weg zum Selbst: Lehre und Leben des indischen Heiligen Shri Ramana Maharshi aus Tiruvannamalai*, by C.G. Jung, Zurich: R. Verlag.

Zaehner, R.C. (1951), *Philosophies of India*, New York: Pantheon Books.

Index

adhikāra 62–5
Alagammal 153
Alston, A.J. 74
Alston, William 15, 24–5, 28–32, 37, 40, 65, 71, 74, 89, 95, 108, 113, 118, 160, 162, 176–7, 180
Anantānandagiri 76
Anselm, St 24
anubhava 35, 44–53, 69, 71, 81–5, 101–8, 122, 146, 160, 172
Aquinas, St Thomas 25, 29–30
Aristotle 25
Aruṇāchala hill 132–3
ascetic orders 67
āśrama system 151–2
Aurobindo, Śri 125
Ayyar, Sundaram 130

Babb, Lawrence 40
Bādarāyaṇa 36
Bader, Jonathan 38
Baillie, John 30
Balasubramanian, R. 74, 82, 86, 88–9, 92, 96–7
bathing in the Ganges 145
Berger, Peter 148
Bhagavad-Gītā 75
Bhāgavata Purāṇa 171
bhakti 12, 173–6
Bhāmatī school 100
Bharati, Agehānanda 126, 130
Bhāṣyakāra, the 170
Biardeau, Madeleine 37–8
Bonjour, Laurence 28
Bṛhadāraṇyaka Upaniṣad 120
Brahma Sūtra 32–3, 36, 41, 44, 63, 99
Brahmadatta 93–4
Brahman 22, 59–63, 80–83, 90–95, 103, 111–14, 139–40, 152
Brahmins and Brahmin ideology 39, 66, 68, 97–8, 121, 124, 130, 153, 154
Braithwaite, C.B. 2
breath control 140–42, 162
Brentano, Franz 15, 18
Brunton, Paul 127, 154
Buddha, the 42, 56, 116, 129, 131, 135
Buddhism 56, 162–6

Cantwell Smith, Wilfred 6
Carman, John 7, 172
caste 152–3
Chadwick, Major 154
chanting 97, 142
Chodron, Pema 165
Clooney, Francis 6, 35, 37, 45, 48, 127, 167, 172, 175
cognitivism and non-cognitivism 23–4, 37
Cohen, Andrew 127
Cohen, S.S. 154
Collins, Steven 116
commentary on Vedānta 37
constructivism 19, 124
Coomaraswamy, Ananda 56
Cowell, E.B. 21

Danielou, Alain 41
Dasgupta, Surendranath 98–9
Datta, D.M. 3
de Smet, Richard 77, 89
deontology 27
Descartes, René 27–9, 103
desire 96
Deutsch, Eliot 6, 44, 118
Devaraja, N.K. 46
Dharmarāja Adhvarin 46, 74
doxastic practices 29–32, 57, 61–2, 70, 78, 85, 90, 107, 116, 124, 157–62, 165, 170–73, 177–81
Dramiḍācārya 170
Dumont, Louis 8

Eck, Diana 40
Edwards, Jonathan 12–13
ego, the 103, 138, 151
Eliade, Mircea 140

epistemology 2–5, 20–21, 26–32, 113, 156–7, 161–7, 181
externalism *see* internalism and externalism

faith 144–5
Fenton, John 166
Ferm, Vergilius 10
Feuerstein, Georg 65
Fields, Rick 166
Flood, Gavin 125–6, 130
Forgie, J. William 19–20
foundationalism 28, 160

Ganguly, Adwaita 164
Gathier, Emile 136
Gauḍapāda 36, 54, 73, 79, 134
God, experiential awareness of 29–30
Godman, David 141
Gonda, Jan 40
Gough, A.E. 21
grace 142–4
Grant, Sarah 163
Griffiths, Bede 126–7
Griffiths, Paul 6
Grimes, John 163–4
gurus 65–9, 86, 142–7
Gussner, Robert 75

Hacker, Paul 39, 74–5
Halbfass, Wilhelm 6, 8, 40–48 *passim*, 81, 99–100, 128, 168
Hara, Minoru 68
Harding, Douglas 179
Hardy, Friedhelm 171
Harvard Center for the Study of World Religions 6
Harvey, Andrew 127
Hasker, William 68
Hemacandra 65
heresy 56
Hick, John 20, 27, 30
Hinduism 114, 124
Hiriyanna, Mysore 46, 95
Hirudayam, Ignatius 128
Huxley, Aldous 16, 19

immediacy 105–8
implication theory 94–5
Indich, William 44
ineffability 21–3
inferential reasoning 48
interiority 87
internalism and externalism 25–8, 32–3, 156–81
  in later Advaita 74–5, 78, 86–90, 97, 107–8, 111, 113–14, 122
  in Ramaṇa Maharṣi 124–8, 136–8, 153–5
  in Śaṅkara 35–42, 49, 56–8, 62, 66, 71
introspection 117, 123–4, 131, 135, 160–61, 179
intuition 91–2
Isherwood, Christopher 108, 121–2

James, William 6–7, 12–13, 52
Jantzen, Grace 22
Jeer, Nārāyaṇa 167
Jog, K.P. 78
al-Junaid 181
Jung, C.G. 126

Kaṇṇan 180–81
Kant, Immanuel 1, 13, 42
karma 95–7
Kaṭha Upaniṣad 21–2, 54, 118
Katz, Steven 16–23 *passim*, 30, 87, 124
Kaylor, R.D. 172
Keith, A.B. 43
Klostermaier, Klaus 8, 126, 128, 162
knowing beyond knowledge 160, 164, 181
knowledge
  as distinct from meditation 70
  gained from scripture 92
  theories of 20–21, 25–6
Kolak, Daniel 123
Kornfield, Jack 165
Krishnamurti, Jiddu 125
Krīyānanda 163
Kumārila Bhaṭṭa 102, 117

Lacombe, Olivier 129
Le Saux, Henri 126–7
Lester, Robert 52
liberation, culture of
  in later Advaita 77, 84–9, 94, 97–8, 118–22
  in Ramaṇa Maharṣi 129, 138–5
  in Śaṅkara 56–71
Locke, John 12

Macquarrie, John 174
Mahadevan, T.M.P. 78, 83, 130

Maharaj, Nisargadatta 126
Maharṣi, Ramaṇa 33, 53, 55, 57, 73, 76, 87, 98, 114, 122, 124–5, 129, 138, 142–3, 160–70, 179
Maṇḍana 10, 60, 76–7
Māṇḍūkya Upaniṣad 19, 120
Martin, Raymond 123
Maximilien, Guy 91–3, 95
Mayeda, Sengaku 39
meditation 70, 93, 139, 149, 174
Meeker, Kevin 26
memory 175–9
mental functioning 53–6
Merton, Thomas 7, 31, 108, 126
metaphysics 2–5, 14, 32, 113–14, 163, 170, 181
Mill, James 11
Mīmāṃsā 59, 81, 96
mind, the 53–6
Mishra, Ramamurthy 166
Mudaliar, A. Devaraja 144, 152–3
Muṇḍaka Upaniṣad 44, 54, 108–9
mundane experience 49–52, 80–84, 102, 107, 117, 178
Murty, Satchidananda 45
mysticism 22–3, 29–31, 176

Nakamura, Hajime 39
Nālāyira Tiviya Pirapantam 171
Nammāḻvār 167, 172, 180–81
Nārāyaṇa 169, 175
Narayanan, Vasudha 171–2
Newton, Isaac 12
Nome, Master 127
Nyāya Sūtra 5, 21

Osborne, Arthur 142–3, 145, 153–5
Otto, Rudolph 13
overpervasion 47

Padmapāda 73–4, 80–81, 89, 98–108, 117–18, 123, 134, 164
Palaniswami 153
Pañcapādikā, the 98–9
Parliament of the World's Religions (1993) 6–7, 17, 164
Patañjali 64
Penner, Hans 16
perception
  filtering of 81
  sensory and *mystical* 29–31
perspectivalism 154
Peterson, Michael 14–15, 68
phenomenological analysis 52
Phillips, D.Z. 2
Plantinga, Alvin 15, 24–9, 37, 53, 157, 162
Pollock, John 162
Poonja, H.W.L. 179
Potter, Karl 6, 45–6, 56, 82, 92, 95, 99
Prabhākara 102, 104
Prabhavānanda, Swami 108
Prakāśātman 79, 99
preaching 143
Prebish, Charles 166
Proudfoot, Wayne 14, 30, 174

Radhakrishnan, Sarvepalli 11, 45, 57, 123, 129, 167
Raghavachar, S.S. 169
Ramakrishna 124–5, 154
Ramakrishna Mission 75, 166
Rāmānuja 32–3, 37, 40, 49, 60, 80, 92, 120, 155, 167–78 *passim*
Rambachand, Anantanand 35, 45, 48, 87
reflection theory 74
reliabilism 28–9, 157
Revathy, S. 21
revelation 9, 91
ritual 69–70, 96–7
Russell, Bertrand 23

Sadānanda 95
Sadhu, Mouni 126, 154
Śaṅkara 4–5, 9, 32–107 *passim*, 112–14, 117, 121, 123, 133–4, 142, 152–5, 161–70 *passim*, 179
Sanskrit 171
Sarvajñatman 95
Śāstri, Gaṇapati 132, 137, 153
Sastri, S.S. Suryanarayana 4, 21
saving knowledge 174
Sawai, Yoshitsugu 97–8
Schuon, Frithjof 16–17, 19
Self, the 41, 81–91, 95, 101–7, 111–12, 117–18, 133–8, 146, 151–4, 166, 179
shamanism 165–6
Sharma, Arvind 11–12, 45–7, 57
Shinto 165
Shoun Hino 78
Sinha, Debabrata 42
Śivānanda 166
Skoog, Kim 45

Smart, Ninian 17–18, 52, 180
Smith, Adam 12
Smith, Huston 16–17, 19
social implications 161–7
spiritual perception 29
Śrīvaiṣṇavism 171–2, 177–9
śruti 48, 78, 89–95, 106–7, 120, 145–6, 149, 164, 167–71
Stace, Walter 16, 30
superimposition 62–3, 74, 99, 101, 105
Sureśvara 60–61, 73–102, 107, 117, 123, 134, 142, 161, 168
Swami, B.V. Narasimha 130

Taber, John 41
Taittirīya Upaniṣad 22, 89, 113, 120
Tanka 170–71
teacher-student relationship 67–9
Tennant, F.R. 2
Teresa, St 181
testimony 158–9
Tillich, Paul 174

Underhill, Evelyn 16
universalism 114–15, 119–24, 128–9, 138, 153–5, 162–6, 171, 177, 179
Upadeśasāhasrī, the 38–9, 66–7, 75

Vācaspati Misra 79
van Boetzelaer, J.M. 74, 81, 89, 91
van Buitenen, J.A.B. 167–8
Vedanta Society 108
Venkatachari, K.K.A. 172
Venketaramiah, D. 104–6, 138, 143, 146, 154
veridicality 21
Vidyāraṇya 95, 98
Viśiṣṭādvaita 32–3, 36, 167–8, 177–9
Vivārana school 80, 99–100
Vivekacūḍāmaṇi, the 73–6, 108–22, 133–4, 140, 144–50
Vivekānanda, Swami 154

Wach, Joachim 30
Wainwright, William 30
warrant-conferring processes 26–8, 86, 156
Warrier, A.G. Krishna 50
Watts, Fraser 24, 30
Werner, Karel 52
Williams, Mark 24, 30
Wittgenstein, Ludwig 23–4
women, attitudes to 153

Yamuna 173
Yandell, Keith 21–2
yoga 54, 64–5, 110, 139–41, 175

Zaehner, R.C. 7, 14, 16–17
Zimmer, Heinrich 126

For Product Safety Concerns and Information please contact our EU
representative GPSR@taylorandfrancis.com
Taylor & Francis Verlag GmbH, Kaufingerstraße 24, 80331 München, Germany

www.ingramcontent.com/pod-product-compliance
Lightning Source LLC
Chambersburg PA
CBHW052114300426
44116CB00010B/1661
* 9 7 8 1 1 3 8 7 2 1 4 9 4 *